VOTES FOR COLLEGE WOMEN

Votes for College Women

*Alumni, Students, and the
Woman Suffrage Campaign*

Kelly L. Marino

NEW YORK UNIVERSITY PRESS
New York

NEW YORK UNIVERSITY PRESS
New York www.nyupress.org

Please contact the Library of Congress for Cataloging-in-Publication data.

ISBN: 9781479825196 (hardback)
ISBN: 9781479825240 (library ebook)
ISBN: 9781479825219 (consumer ebook)

This book is printed on acid-free paper, and its binding materials are chosen for strength and durability. We strive to use environmentally responsible suppliers and materials to the greatest extent possible in publishing our books.

Manufactured in the United States of America

10 9 8 7 6 5 4 3 2 1

Also available as an ebook

For my family and friends

CONTENTS

Introduction

In 1917, the leaders of the College Equal Suffrage League (CESL), an organization in the United States dedicated to recruiting university students and alumni to the women's rights movement, announced that attitudes toward woman suffrage among highly educated Americans had evolved and that this shift in sentiment made continued activism unnecessary. Leaders explained that a "revolution in educated opinion" had taken place.[1] When the first branch of the CESL formed in 1900, the group faced many obstacles, including apathy and opposition, to organizing among college-educated Americans. One league representative recalled, "Suffrage could scarcely be mentioned" to most academic audiences.[2] By the 1910s, opinion and support vastly differed. Prominent reformers such as Florence Kelley delighted in the development, telling students at a campus lecture in 1908, "Suddenly, during the past two years, there has swept over the country in universities, colleges and schools a wave of lively interest in women's enfranchisement and its probable results."[3] Other suffrage leaders such as Ethel Puffer Howes recalled that by 1914, when she had taken office as executive secretary of the CESL, the primary group at the forefront of undergraduate mobilization, "the situation" in academia had been "transformed" and attitudes had "changed" to favor the issue of women's voting rights.[4]

In 1917, branches of the CESL existed at "all the leading women's colleges," except for Smith, as well as several coeducational institutions.[5] Campus suffrage clubs formed in many states, from West Virginia and Tennessee to Nebraska and South Dakota. Supporters included the female administrators of prominent educational institutions such as Bryn Mawr, Mount Holyoke, and Oberlin colleges and the University of Wisconsin.[6] By 1917, the CESL had five thousand registered members across more than fifty alumni leagues and college chapters.[7] Leaders argued that the group had met its stated goal, given that "practically all the members" of the faculties and even "most" of the students were "already suffragists."[8]

This shift in sentiment toward the organized women's rights movement among university students and alumni in the United States during the early twentieth century was a significant development. This study explores how and why the woman-suffrage issue transformed from being unpopular to being popular among college-educated Americans—a shift I attribute to the work of the CESL (an affiliate of the National American Woman Suffrage Association, or NAWSA—the most prominent woman-suffrage organization in the United States). The book examines the effects these changes in attitudes had on the women's rights cause and higher education. I argue that the CESL's recruitment of students and alumni to the campaign was central to the passage of the Nineteenth Amendment because of the respectability that they added to the movement. The move to campaign on campus set important trends in female political activism that shaped the women's rights movement for generations and even today.

College-educated Americans became valuable allies in the women's rights campaign in the early twentieth century because they helped to remake the movement's image in a more professionalized light. They added what CESL leader Maud Wood Park termed "intellectual prestige" to the suffrage movement.[9] Students and alumni used their academic training and educational experiences to raise the standard of women's rights protests by creating new presentations and political propaganda based on the Progressive Era passion for research, evidence, and statistics. Often dismissed in contemporary studies, the educational organization of suffragists in groups such as the CESL was essential for advancing the equal-franchise campaign. If the suffragists had not worked so diligently to teach Americans about the "votes for women" movement, the headline-generating demonstrations that followed, such as the tactics of the National Woman's Party (NWP), might not have garnered the same results.

Much scholarship emphasizes the significance of the attention-generating tactics of twentieth-century suffragists, such as the NWP's hunger strikes, picketing, and jail time. The women's liberation movement of the 1960s and 1970s shaped the perspective of scholars such that they have emphasized the more radical methods of the woman-suffrage movement.[10] As a result, most studies downplay the less sensational educational activism utilized by the NAWSA and its affiliates, such as the CESL. The organizing of groups such as the CESL provided the public and national leaders with important context for radical protests and other militant campaigns. Their activism made the work of others seem less irrational, marginal, and untimely. The CESL's campaigns deserve more attention in the suffrage historiography and the scholarship on women's history, educational history, and social and political campaigns.

Of all the transitions in Progressive Era society, perhaps the advances in higher education for women after the Civil War were some of the most decisive. These overlooked factors helped to win converts to the suffragists' cause and add validity to activists' arguments that women deserved an equal role in society. Women could now say that they were intellectually equal to men and equally as literate, if not more so. In early America, some opportunities for women's education had developed because of popular ideologies, such as "Republican Motherhood," which encouraged female citizens' literacy to build more stable families and a stronger nation. As historian Linda Kerber has written, civically informed and politically aware mothers could arguably teach their sons to be "sensible republicans." Educational opportunities in colonial America, however, were not as sweeping or as extensive as in later periods, such as the post–Civil War era, which bolstered activists' claims for suffrage at the turn of the twentieth century. Despite there also being advances in the antebellum years, some Americans still perceived "highly educated women" as potentially dangerous to society, established gender norms, and the custom of "separate spheres."[11] Most colleges and universities did not open to women until the mid- to late nineteenth century, and when they did, they eventually fueled new support for the equal-franchise campaign and cultivated key audiences and stages on campuses upon which the modern women's rights movement could tread.

In addition to demonstrating the significance of college women to the movement, this study challenges traditional arguments about suffrage chronology. Influenced by the late-twentieth-century feminist movement, scholarship from the 1960s and 1970s forward has centered on the post-1917 period in suffrage history and the last few years of the campaign because of the media attention generated by the New York State victory and the actions of the NWP in Washington, DC. The period between 1896 and 1910, when the CESL formed, scholars too often dismiss as "the doldrums" of the woman-suffrage movement because no new states passed equal-franchise legislation and federal progress on the issue slowed. Investigating the activism of the CESL provides under-explored evidence to counter this interpretation.[12] As the historian Sara Hunter Graham argues, rather than producing a lull in the campaign for the ballot, the years from 1896 to 1910 represented a period of "re-naissance." During this time, suffragists carried out important internal work to professionalize their organizing, and changes in the larger society created the cultural circumstances that allowed woman suffrage to be successful.[13] As stated above, once women's collegiate institutions flourished, they created the intellectual conditions that contributed to suffrage victory. Groups such as the CESL emerged to generate support among students and alumni and harness this new potential constituency. College-educated Americans improved the image of the suffrage movement by making it more professional and respectable, and in doing so, furthered the broader goals of the NAWSA.[14]

This book reconsiders the political engagement of early college and university women during the Gilded Age and Progressive Era to argue that they were much more involved in politics and government than has traditionally been suggested. Scholars have possibly overlooked the influence that the increased number of women in higher education had on shaping the movement for women's voting rights because the number of female students attending colleges and universities during the Progressive Era remained low compared with the late twentieth century (but high and increasingly relevant compared with decades prior). In 1870, only 0.7 percent of college-aged women aged eighteen to twenty-one years enrolled in institutions of higher learning. By 1910, this figure had increased to 3.8 percent and continued to increase at a time when going to college remained a rarity for most Americans. Grade school education was not even compulsory across most of the United States. However, by 1910, female students made up 39.6 percent of all pupils at colleges and universities across the country—nearing close to half within a decade.[15]

Many scholars erroneously maintain that the initial generations of female university students expressed an overall lack of interest in suffrage and other outside causes, particularly those causes related to government. Some studies suggest that, during the nineteenth century, the first undergraduate women were serious students who focused on academics and improving educational opportunities for their gender by showing that they belonged on campus alongside men. Too busy with their studies, they supposedly avoided the contentious equal-franchise campaign while students on campus. Scholars depict second- and third-generation university women as uninvolved in suffrage activism, frivolous and self-centered, and more focused on finding upper-class men at school for marriage. If women of either generation engaged in altruistic endeavors, they were a minority of exceptional women who engaged in charity work or social reform. This work often occurred after graduation rather than as a central objective while in college. Some college women participated in social reform on campuses before 1900, using their schooling to improve society through, for example, settlement house work, temperance societies, and charity associations. Scholars suggest that their involvement in organized political campaigns remained rare.[16] Many studies present most female students as more focused on "the pursuit of happiness," recreation, and dating than on larger issues, such as fighting for political rights.[17]

Major works on the history of women in higher education advance the perspective that the suffrage movement did not make quick or expansive inroads on campus, making a revisionist perspective needed. The scholar Barbara Solomon, for example, has contended that most institutions of higher learning "were not potent breeding grounds" for the equal-franchise campaign and that student activism garnered little popularity until after 1915.[18] Lynn Gordon has argued that once the CESL formed, some students showed interest in suffrage activism but that opposition remained strong in most colleges and universities.[19] Helen Lefkowitz Horowitz's scholarship stresses that organizing for the vote gained the backing of some college women and most of the all-female "Seven Sisters" schools.[20] However, early campus campaigning for woman suffrage was much more viable, diverse, and widespread.

Scholars overlook this activism because few studies of collegiate feminism explore colleges outside these traditional northeastern schools. Scholars miss the story of suffrage on campuses because it occurred at the grassroots level and among students on school grounds rather than in the national political arena or among mainstream organizations. Rather than making national headlines, the evidence of activism is not always well organized or accessible and must be retrieved from documents such as institutional records, club minutes, yearbooks, and college newspapers. I suggest that moving beyond the locations and colleges traditionally connected to the women's rights movement in the North-east, such as the "Seven Sisters," and considering southern and western universities, coeducational public schools, and historically Black institu-tions, as well as the students and alumni from such institutions who sup-ported the campaign, causes a different picture of activism to form. The story of suffrage on campus becomes one of a much more prevalent and popular equal-franchise movement among college-educated Americans and on campuses than earlier historians suggest.

This study further challenges the popular depiction of suffragists and the suffrage movement as typically spearheaded by middle-aged or older women. In the early twentieth century, the CESL and its branches helped to introduce generational change to the women's movement. His-torian Anne Boylan writes that upper- and middle-class married women past their childbearing years fueled nineteenth-century activism. Older women who had fulfilled their duties as wives and mothers held ex-ecutive positions in the club and reform movements. Leaders relegated young and single women to subordinate roles, perhaps to preserve their public reputations and protect them from any controversies that could influence their marriageability.[21] The CESL brought young activists, par-ticularly college students between the ages of eighteen and twenty-one, as well as recent university graduates in their twenties and thirties, to the forefront of women's rights organizing in large numbers and in a nationwide fashion for the first time. The league was the first organiza-tion to undertake this type of initiative in a sweeping and organized way.

The ages of female college students changed over time. Although first-generation college women varied in age, from the very young to the very old, by the time second- and third-generation female students entered universities, the gap in age "narrowed"—most college women whom suffragists encountered were of the traditional eighteen to twenty-one age range.[22] This youth mobilization represented a new departure in the organized women's movement in the twentieth century. Younger women would continue to play important leadership roles in later eras, particu-larly in the 1960s and 1970s, with the younger generation moving the women's rights campaign forward in significant ways.

In addition to considering age and the suffrage movement, this study explores class and race. Recent scholars have shown that although

White suffrage leaders won greater endorsement among others of a similar profile in the early twentieth century—namely, the White and the elite—they eventually formed coalitions with self-supporting and working women of their own race, thereby recognizing women's growing presence in the labor force. The tactics of the NAWSA and affiliated groups such as the CESL sometimes deterred potential support from and discriminated against immigrants and Black women.

The parameters of NAWSA leader Carrie Chapman Catt's "Society Plan," which attracted more elite White women to the movement, and other NAWSA methods limited the scope of the association's and the CESL's campaigns to mainly White neighborhoods and arenas. These tactics rarely did much in Black city districts and educational institutions, and fueled tensions with African American supporters. In the southern states, suffragists often upheld racist and nativist arguments. Northerners and westerners worried about losing their support. Equal-franchise activists had to be cautious because some people claimed that granting the vote to all women would threaten White supremacy, which many people still upheld, if not politically then socially.[23] Historians note that to maintain southern suffragists' support, NAWSA leaders, desperate to bring a new legislative victory, even if it came at a cost, would intentionally keep cross-racial alliances to a minimum. Even in the North, nativist, imperialist, and anti-radical perspectives also limited campaigns. Some White women argued that they deserved the vote because they belonged to the superior and more civilized race. They suggested that their sex and race suited them for a greater public role because they could use their "moral superiority" to uplift any inferior peoples. In a time when eugenics was popular among Progressives, emphasizing their racial, cultural, and innate gender-based privilege allowed White women to assert their right to lead the country alongside "elite" White men and stressed their differences from minorities.[24]

Many national women's rights organizations, such as the NAWSA and the CESL, blocked a membership inclusive of African Americans. I bolster the claims made by other recent historians that Black men and women were still leaders in equal-franchise activism but pushed their campaign forward through other avenues, such as the club movement, social-reform organizations, and African American suffrage groups.[25] Grassroots branches of the National Association of Colored Women (later known as the National Association of Colored Women's Clubs), in particular, encouraged Black men and women and, as I show, Black alumni and college students to take a position on the woman-suffrage issue, among the other topics. Other groups, such as the NAACP, supported the cause as part of its agenda, although it was not founded until the final decade of the suffrage movement. I explore how Black student and faculty organizations also started movements to support women's right to vote on campuses. On campuses, Black debate clubs took up the issue, and African American sororities engaged in suffrage mobilization. Several scholarly works mention Black sorority women's participation in the NAWSA's parade in 1913; however, most studies do not provide much detail beyond this event.[26]

The CESL was smaller and generated less attention than some other national associations, such as the NAWSA and the NWP; however, the group moved the women's rights cause forward in significant ways. The college league launched several trends in political organization that shaped the activism of major groups such as the NAWSA and its successor, the League of Women Voters (LWV). But the college league also shaped the work of other social and political movements as well as altered higher education. The organization's work resonated beyond its lifespan.

Early accounts of the woman-suffrage movement note the perceptions that the equal-franchise organizing was a disappointment because female citizens did not cast ballots in large numbers or form an expected strong voting bloc after 1920. For example, the scholar Kristi Andersen discusses extensively the origins of the myth that woman suffrage was a "failure."[27] Over the past thirty years, however, Andersen and other scholars have countered this interpretation by pointing out the other many important influences the Nineteenth Amendment had on American politics, especially at the grassroots level. According to some historians, for example, woman suffrage increased voter registration, spurred changes to political rules and traditions, altered party practices, and created new jobs in government for female employees. Over the past thirty years, some scholars have moved from emphasizing the macro to emphasizing the micro influences of woman suffrage to illustrate a broader impact.[28] This study considers the college and university environment. I explore how these trends resonated on a grassroots level on campuses to shape collegiate politics and government in similar ways, as the organization of campus life mimicked aspects of the larger society.

This work further contributes to an early suggestion by historian Ellen Carol DuBois that receives relatively little scholarly attention, namely, the argument that historians must look beyond politics to recognize the full consequences of the equal-franchise movement for modern society. DuBois writes that winning women's enfranchisement, for example, raised awareness about female subordination and sex discrimination in the larger society.[29] By examining women's rights campaigns in academic institutions, I reveal another significant social and cultural effect of the equal-franchise movement on twentieth-century American life, which was its role in shaping higher education. Scholar Jana Nidiffer, for one, contends that CESL members were not just at the forefront of women's activism but were "pioneers of student activism" in general.[30] Nidiffer writes that the CESL was innovative because it became one of the first major adult political groups to go to campuses and recruit both male and female university students.[31] I argue that the CESL also helped to popularize civic and citizenship education, important to the academic curriculum at all levels even today.

Suffragists' activism created change that reformed academic practices and culture in ways that affected all people, regardless of age, race, class, or gender. Students debated the woman-suffrage issue in college lecture halls, cafeterias, gymnasiums, and theaters, and played an important role in sparking new discussions in the nation's classrooms about racism, classism, sexism, gender inequality, and female subordination. Suffragists staged early classes on the history of women, promoted improved civics training and Americanization efforts, influenced teaching styles, tools, and opportunities, and generated new topics for student extracurriculars, debates, essays, theses, and publications. Learning about difficult issues such as equity, White supremacy, nativism, patriarchy, and woman suffrage, rights, and history became a more common college pastime and laid the groundwork for future programs in areas such as gender and sexuality studies. The CESL's campaigns challenged rules related to ageism and policies barring political activists and events from school grounds. Debates about equal franchise entangled with other causes, such as battles for institutional equality and free speech, that, headed by various sympathetic clubs and organizations, had been going on for years. The collegiate suffrage movement transformed what it meant to be a citizen within the space and community of the campus.

Many studies of student social and political movements on campuses have, in general, emphasized activism in the 1930s and 1960s and downplayed campaigns preceding these two periods. The scholar Philip Altbach writes, for example, "Student activism during the entire 1900–1930 period had little impact on society at large. There were few, if any, major student demonstrations or campaigns directed at national issues and locally oriented protests were not usually effective."[32] In recent years, however, scholarship on social and political movements, such as Jacquelyn Dowd Hall's work on civil rights organizing, has encouraged a reperiodization of movements and campaigns, often pushing the trajectory backward.[33] Using Hall's framework, I call attention to a "long" organized women's rights movement on college campuses that dates back to the turn of the twentieth century.

Studies place the origins of women's rights activism at colleges and universities in the later twentieth century, especially in the 1960s and 1970s. Scholars attribute college activism for women's rights during the late twentieth century to the influence of the rise of the modern civil rights movement, second-wave feminism, and anti–Vietnam War activism. These connections mostly ignore prior women's rights campaigns on campuses generations before and the important precedents that earlier activists set. Even Linda Eisenmann's earlier work on how competing gender ideologies influenced women's activism for equality in higher education focuses on the period from 1945 to 1965. Most works follow Gordon and discuss suffrage activism on campus only in passing when commenting on well-known and headline-making controversies, such as tension over students forming an equal-franchise club at Vassar College, and not much change has occurred in modern scholarship.[34] Once again, I shift the attention to the earlier era of women's rights protests on school grounds. I emphasize a longer history of college-educated activism to support movements for gender equality by examining the CESL and its organizing.

This work focuses on the CESL's activism in and around the following five major locations: Boston, where the first alumni league formed; New York, where the second branch emerged; the San Francisco Bay Area, where the most successful western section developed; New

Orleans, where the CESL found the most southern support; and Washington, DC, where representatives contributed to federal amendment work. During the early twentieth century, these urban centers harbored some of the oldest and most prominent institutions of higher learning for women in their respective regions. They were ideal places for CESL campaigns and locations where the group often gained the strongest footing in each region. To explore campus activism in these areas, I correspondingly examine student organizing at Harvard University and Radcliffe College, Columbia University and Barnard College, the University of California–Berkeley, and Tulane University and Newcomb College. The CESL voted to target their activism at these schools in particular and generated the most success there. I additionally explore activism on all-Black campuses such as Lincoln University, Howard University, and the Tuskegee Institute. At the other institutions under study, administrators often did not admit Black students, and especially Black women, but they were still involved in the campaign in each location. This study considers African American activism in each of the five locations focused on in the project.

The book relies on various primary sources to uncover student and alumni activism in these five locations before and after 1920. Sources include collections in university archives, public libraries, and historical societies documenting college-educated Americans' activities in local suffrage and antisuffrage organizations. I explore campus activism using institutional records, club minutes, yearbooks, school newspapers, and university magazines from both Black and White colleges. Papers on state suffrage and antisuffrage groups, the collections of major CESL leaders such as Maud Wood Park, and local newspapers from across the nation reveal insights into alumni campaigns. A third set of primary sources, including the records of umbrella organizations such as the NAWSA and the NWP, publications such as *The Suffragist*, and widely circulated periodicals such as the *New York Times* and the *Washington Post*, shed light on college-educated participation in federal amendment work.

As chapters 1 and 2 illustrate, the CESL aided the grassroots movement for the ballot in American cities by forming new coalitions to bolster state activism. CESL members (initially college alumni) used their college-educated and self-supporting backgrounds strategically to appeal to diverse Americans at different moments and locations. On the one hand, CESL activists cultivated support by emphasizing their university training and experience when organizing among their upper- and middle-class colleagues and peers. They depicted themselves as a new group of young professionals and authorities on the women's rights issue. They raised the standards and quality of suffrage arguments and publications using their knowledge and training. However, suffragists took a different approach while speaking to working-class audiences and looking to form other alliances. In these situations, members of the CESL emphasized their shared experiences, such as struggles in the occupational realm, to mobilize new support.[35] The CESL succeeded at coalition building with the labor movement in places such as New York and California, where their activism contributed to pre-1920 state victories.

Chapter 3 shows how on campuses, suffragists used educational activism as a central political tool to advance women's rights within a collegiate environment hostile to an organized women's movement on campuses. Representatives from groups such as the CESL, who faced difficult audiences on school grounds, connected their activities to the existing academic culture. This strategy allowed women to promote equal franchise covertly, without engaging in direct, sensational, or violent demonstrations against the administration or established gender norms (such demonstrations were more common off campus). College suffragists framed the woman-suffrage question as an issue of improper or inadequate education to better align their campaigns with the purposes of universities. The CESL developed college clubs that sponsored events such as lectures, debates, polls, and essay and art contests to entice students to become involved in women's rights. Through the CESL's efforts, suffragists turned colleges into crucial new training grounds for the next generation of activists and began to open the doors to future political campaigns. The CESL's activities politicized many young women, inspiring them to become involved in activism against other inequalities, both inside and outside of colleges and universities.

Organizing for suffrage on campuses, however, was not easy. Chapter 4 examines the opposition that activists faced, including the many challenges suffragists encountered in college spaces and in creating new arenas for campaigns. In colleges, just as suffragists worked hard to promote changes to established gender norms, antisuffragists and their supporters fought aggressively to maintain them. Opponents of women's right to vote found receptive audiences at institutions of higher education among the older generation of administrators and faculty. Most administrators did not support women's rights activism at first. Indeed, they feared that their association with the suffrage movement would threaten their schools' future by influencing the credibility of their institutions.[36] Undergraduates who avoided advocacy for the vote shared this negative sentiment bolstering Victorian gender ideology. They believed that their involvement might tarnish their reputations, affect their employment, or influence their attractiveness to a potential spouse. Opponents capitalized on the anxieties of the academic community to increase support for their cause. They staged campaigns that emphasized how woman suffrage meant to corrupt the youth and undermine the goals of higher education. Although antisuffragists were unsuccessful in preventing female voting rights, their work placed pro-suffrage supporters on the defensive, which strengthened the equal-franchise movement by encouraging campaigners to enhance their tactics and arguments. Opponents' activism did not stop women from becoming involved in politics. Their campaigns spurred a new, conservative political organization among female college students that also influenced campus cultures and the women's rights movement in the years that followed.

By the 1910s, through the activities of groups such as the CESL, attitudes toward woman-suffrage organization among college-educated Americans had improved, and eventual success seemed more plausible. Women's rights activists effectively mobilized thousands of students and alumni in the service of their cause, and many of these individuals became important leaders in national and federal amendment work. Chapter 5 explores the work of the National College Equal Suffrage League, the alumni league in Washington, DC, and select college chapters. These groups positioned university women at the forefront of the campaign for the Nineteenth Amendment and helped make them the new face of the movement. In placing college and university students and alumni front and center in the campaign, activists challenged many of antisuffragists' most fundamental arguments about the disinterest of the modern generation, particularly the modern generation of women.

When the Nineteenth Amendment passed in 1920, national women's associations, civil rights groups, and women's rights organizations did not abandon student and alumni campaigns for gender equality. Groups such as the League of Women Voters, the National Woman's Party, the National Association for the Advancement of Colored People, and the National Association of Colored Women's Clubs, as it was then known, continued to advance the methods of the CESL and the vision of Maud Wood Park in many ways. These groups urged students and alumni to take a greater interest in politics and public life and become educated, registered voters (and, specifically for women, civic and public leaders, advocates of gender equality, and equal partners) within their communities. In doing so, these organizations continued some of the work of the CESL and the NAWSA into the twentieth century, both on and off campus, to encourage the younger generation to become engaged in politics and government. Their worked laid the groundwork for educated women in American leadership today.

1

Adding "Intellectual Prestige"

On February 14, 1900, Maud Wood Park, a twenty-nine-year-old Massachusetts teacher, Radcliffe graduate, and state organizer, attended her first National American Woman Suffrage Association (NAWSA) convention in Washington, DC. The year marked Susan B. Anthony's eightieth birthday celebration and retirement as NAWSA president. The program included many heartfelt reminiscences about the aging leader and tales of past battles fought by activists in campaigns for women's right to vote. Passing-the-torch celebrations included a display honoring the retiring suffragist, with eighty children carrying roses to commemorate each year of Anthony's life.[1] According to Park, one of the most significant moments occurred when Anthony stepped down and introduced NAWSA's new president, former western school superintendent, writer, and public speaker Carrie Chapman Catt, symbolizing the leadership's transition from one generation to the next.

Earlier in the program, Anthony explained her reasons for stepping down when she told an emotional audience, "I am not retiring now because I feel unable, mentally or physically, to do the necessary work, but because I wish to see the organization in the hands of those who are to have its management in the future."[2] She tried to lighten the mood, continuing, "I want to see you all at work, while I am alive, so I can scold if you do not do it well."[3] Reflecting on the gathering, Park commented in her writings that learning more about the pioneer's devotion imprinted on her the deep significance of the women's rights cause.[4] "I promised myself when Miss Anthony made her speech of resignation that I would try to make more women see the things as I had seen"—particularly, the dedication and perseverance of the older generation of activists, which Park evoked as motivation for her organizing all throughout the campaign.[5] Stunned by the aging audience at the convention and the lack of many other women like herself—vibrant, fashionable, and educated—she argued that greater numbers of younger women, particularly those who benefited from the work of earlier activists like the graduates and students of the nation's colleges and universities, should support the suffrage movement in the new era. They should repay early activists for fighting against gender discrimination and creating more opportunities for women in the public realm.

After the convention, Park returned to Massachusetts, inspired to recruit more supporters for the woman-suffrage campaign. She discussed plans to further the movement by launching a new group called the College Equal Suffrage League (CESL) with her former Radcliffe colleague and fellow teacher, Inez Haynes Irwin (formerly known as Inez Haynes Gillmore).[6] In 1900, the CESL's first alumni league formed in Boston, with a charter membership of twenty-five supporters aiming to gain greater backing among the state's college and university graduates.[7] Not long after, alumni leagues developed in other places across the United States like New York, bolstering grassroots suffrage activism. In the seventeen years that they were active, between 1900 and 1917, the alumni leagues of the CESL contributed to local women's rights movements through coalition-building initiatives meant to attract the country's professionals—and later, ordinary workers—to the equal-franchise cause. These cross-class alliances were particularly effective in places with vibrant organized labor movements such as New York. Alumni leagues recruited supporters using their status as "college educated" and their experience as "self-supporting" to appeal to Americans with different backgrounds living in major cities. Through these tactics, the organization promoted cross-class unity in the women's rights movement at the state level and contributed to NAWSA's larger efforts to present a strong pro-suffrage front to the nation's politicians. College-educated Americans' contributions to grassroots activism were central to local and state success. These supporters not only helped to expand the movement's support base but also added key credibility.

Examining the campaigns of the CESL alumni leagues reveals a more complex image of grassroots suffrage activism, one that considers the state and local contributions of many groups to the efforts of suffragists at the national level beyond traditional large-scale statewide organizations affiliated with the NAWSA. Studying the CESL's activism during the first and second decades of the twentieth century reveals more about how members, like others in the larger NAWSA, used this time to work to broaden their support base. They expanded their associations and improved the equal-franchise movement's image at the beginning of the modern era despite limitations such as racism and ethnic prejudice, which continued to prevent the movement from ever being as effective as it could have been. Much of this work was internal and did not always make newspaper headlines.

However, changing class relations and public protests fueled state suffrage victories in the early twentieth century, as these tactics contributed to the larger cultural and industrial changes taking place, allowing the suffrage movement to reach a modern audience. College-educated Americans' contributions to grassroots activism were more central to local and state suffrage success than has typically been argued.[8] In areas like New York, where upper- and middle-class professionals allied with other workers in greater numbers and took to the streets to promote women's right to vote, suffragists achieved victory more quickly than in places where a strong, united front did not develop.[9]

The campaign for women's rights in the United States before 1900 was slow moving and full of setbacks. Women had been pushing for greater equality in a patriarchal society for generations with only small victories and little significant legislative change. Organized national agitation for woman suffrage in the United States did not occur until the late nineteenth century, when women involved themselves in a broader cross-racial struggle to expand the electorate beyond prominent White men, who traditionally held the greatest power. A major factor in the development of an organized women's movement was female involvement in abolition. During the antebellum period, several women's rights conventions occurred, such as the famous 1848 Seneca Falls Convention, where activists formulated a plan, creating the Declaration of Sentiments and publicly announcing women's chief goals for advancement. Significant mobilization, however, did not come until the late nineteenth century.

In 1866, supporters of women's rights and African American rights united to work toward political equality through an organization called the American Equal Rights Association (AERA). Many former abolitionists and leading suffragists participated in the group, including Frederick Douglass, Susan B. Anthony, Elizabeth Cady Stanton, and Lucy Stone. The union between these two distinct factions of supporters,

however, proved tumultuous, and members argued over the organization's chief goals.[10] AERA members debated whether Black men should
have the vote before women, specifically White women, or the other way
around.

During the association's early years, avid supporters of African American rights vied with woman suffragists for control. The prominent Black
reformer Frederick Douglass became one of the most outspoken leaders
who fought to prioritize activism that would support the advancement
of his race. At a tension-filled AERA meeting in 1869, Douglass told
an audience, "I must say that I do not see how anyone can pretend that
there is the same urgency in giving the ballot to woman as to the Negro.
With us, the matter is a question of life and death."[11] Like other fervent
advocates of African American equality, he stressed to listeners that the
dire social, economic, and political conditions that Blacks faced in the
United States should make ensuring voting rights for African Americans the primary concern: "When women, because they are women, are
hunted down through the cities of New York and New Orleans; when
they are dragged from their houses and hung upon lamp-posts; when
their children are torn from their arms, and their brains dashed out
upon the pavement; when they are objects of insult and outrage at every
turn; when they are in danger of having their homes burnt down over
their heads; when their children are not allowed to enter schools," Douglass dramatically concluded, "then they will have an urgency to obtain
the ballot equal to our own."[12] These remarks resonated with many other
supporters of racial equality who, inspired by recent political victories
after the Civil War, viewed the period as a unique window through
which to push greater rights for African Americans.

Many well-known advocates of woman suffrage assisted in the struggle for Black rights; however, by the mid-1800s, they became increasingly discontented with the unrelenting discrimination that members of
the female sex still encountered. They lacked the patience to prioritize
former abolitionists' aims or to wait any longer for change for American
women.[13] Issues of women's education and intellectual fitness for politics became central to the discriminatory debates that arose at the center of the conflict. Numerous activists vehemently argued that educated
women, especially White women, deserved the ballot more than those
whom they viewed as the lower classes. Susan B. Anthony responded

to Douglass at the AERA convention by stating firmly, "The old anti-slavery schools say women must stand back and wait until the Negroes shall be recognized. But we say if you will not give the whole loaf of suffrage to the entire people, give it to the most intelligent. . . . Let the question of woman be brought up first."[14] Anthony's colleague, Elizabeth Cady Stanton, refrained from following up on Douglass's statement at the AERA meeting; however, she had made her stance clear many times prior to that. Two years before, she had argued to an audience that if American women were looking for any type of political change, then enfranchising Black men alone would not create it. Allowing larger numbers of male citizens greater political power would only lead to the same governmental policies and procedures.[15]

Going further, Stanton, like Anthony, emphasized her opinion that educated White women were more qualified to participate in civic life than most Black men. Stanton questioned, "Would Horace Greeley, Wendell Phillips, Gerrit Smith, or Theodore Tilton be willing to stand aside and trust their individual interests, and the whole welfare of the nation, to the lowest strata of manhood?"[16] She stressed, "If not, why ask educated women, who love their country, who feel that their enfranchisement is of vital importance . . . why ask them to stand aside while two million ignorant men are ushered into the halls of legislation?"[17] Suffrage leaders such as Anthony and Stanton pushed others in their activist circles to adopt their perspective by placing their full support behind the issue of women's right to vote. Many suffragists believed that women's advancement in education and their increasing intellectual equity were strong arguments for their advancement in political life.

The two emerging woman-suffrage leaders found a key ally initially in the fellow women's rights supporter and former abolitionist Lucy Stone. In 1869, Stone spoke after Anthony at the AERA gathering, announcing her support for female political equality as taking priority over Black citizenship rights. She commented that, while both the female sex and the African American race had faced their own "ocean of wrongs," she believed that women's entrance into politics would best support "the safety of the government" by helping to foster "restoration and harmony" in contemporary society.[18] In the aftermath of the Civil War, many advocates of female advancement in the public sphere stressed that women in politics could have a positive influence on the nation by helping to bring Americans back together. Stone advanced this viewpoint, telling listeners, "I believe that the influence of woman will save the country before every other power."[19] Her declaration served as a surprising announcement considering her background as such a devoted supporter of African American rights.

Irreconcilable differences in AERA tore the organization apart when most members voted to endorse the Fifteenth Amendment as proposed, which stood to grant Black men the right to vote and leave out women.[20] Following the disagreement, those activists eager to focus on winning female political rights started their own national organizations. Anthony and Stanton formed the National Woman Suffrage Association (NWSA) in 1869. NWSA rejected the Fifteenth Amendment's passage if it continued to exclude members of the female sex, and the group pushed instead for federal legislation to extend suffrage to women.[21] Lucy Stone and her husband, Henry Blackwell, disagreed with this approach, and they created a second organization, the American Woman Suffrage Association (AWSA), that same year. AWSA differed from NWSA in that it supported the Fifteenth Amendment despite Stone's earlier comments and advocated state-by-state organizing for female enfranchisement. The group viewed this method as the best way to avoid distracting from the national struggle for Black rights occurring at the same time.[22]

The two associations competed for publicity, support, and campaigners until the 1880s, when a new generation of activists, including Alice Stone Blackwell, Stone's daughter, stepped up to convince leaders to bring the groups together.[23] In 1888, Blackwell met with Anthony to begin negotiations for a merger, and these talks continued for two years until leaders reached an agreement.[24] Finally, in 1890, the organizations combined to form the NAWSA, which incorporated both parties' techniques to use state and national campaigns in the fight for women's political rights. NAWSA developed a vast network of diverse branches and auxiliaries to carry out this work during the period that followed. However, while in the late nineteenth century NAWSA was more open to Black members, the organization became more exclusionary and desperate to get the support of White men over time, leading to more prejudiced positions.

* * *

At the turn of the twentieth century, teachers Maud Wood Park and Inez Haynes Irwin hoped to lead the woman-suffrage campaign among college-educated Americans through their association, the CESL (which eventually became a NAWSA affiliate in 1908).[25] The CESL's first work began among alumni in cities before eventually moving to campuses and finally developing a national umbrella body that contributed to federal amendment work and oversaw grassroots activism. Their campaigns would support the vision of NAWSA president Carrie Chapman Catt, who hoped to see the suffragists create a viable professional female political party to fight for the interests of women.

Both supporters' backgrounds and early educational encounters influenced their participation in the movement. Park's parents, James and Mary, resided in Massachusetts at the time of her birth in 1871. Her father worked for the Boston police and at a detective agency that he had started in the city. His prior service as a scout for union general and future president Ulysses S. Grant during the Civil War fueled his local success. Although Irwin, like Park, grew up in Massachusetts, she was born in Rio de Janeiro in 1873. American entrepreneurs, her parents moved to Brazil from the United States to seek wealth through participation in the nation's prosperous coffee industry; however, her family returned to Boston after this endeavor proved unsuccessful. Irwin's father, Gideon, took up several occupations throughout his lifetime, from actor and politician to writer and prison reformer, while her mother, Emma, spent her younger years working in Lowell Mills. Irwin often bragged about her parents' ancestry. She noted that her father originated from northeastern agriculturalists who came to America as early as the 1600s, while her mother descended from *Mayflower* voyagers who helped to found one of the earliest successful European settlements in the nation. The two women's families earned respect in their local communities through generations of hard work. They passed along resourcefulness, creativity, perseverance, and diligence to their children, qualities that proved valuable to the two girls' future as suffrage campaigners.[26]

Both Park and Irwin developed an interest in women's rights early in life. The subject caught Park's attention while she was a student at St. Agnes boarding school in Albany, New York. The headmistress called the senior class together for a meeting before graduation. She told the girls, "Conduct yourselves and your homes according to your husband's wishes. Remember that he is the head and ruler of the household."[27] Park recalled that "something" inside of her "rose up in rebellion" upon hearing this comment, and it occurred to her to start "to question a social order which relegated women to a subservient position."[28] Her discontent only increased in the years that followed despite the conservative training and values promoted by the grade school. St. Agnes School was associated with the Episcopal Cathedral and Right Reverend William Croswell Doane of Albany, New York. Bishop Doane gained a reputation as one of the most aggressive college-educated opponents of women's political equality in the country.[29]

Irwin's childhood experiences fostered a similar sense of "horror" in her when she considered the plight of the average woman.[30] She feared falling victim to the dullness of repeated childbearing, household chores, and constant relegation to the domestic realm. Her anxieties amplified as she watched her mother attempt to raise seventeen children, seven from her husband's first marriage and ten from her own.[31] Simple tasks such as preparing a meal took strenuous effort and endless hours of preparation. Irwin once reflected on these memories, stating frankly,

> The mid-day Sunday dinner seemed in some curious way to symbolize everything that I hated and dreaded. . . . The plethoric meal—the huge roast, the blood pouring out of it as the man of the house carved; the many vegetables, all steaming; the heavy pudding. And when the meal was finished—the table a shambles that positively made me shudder—the smooth replete retreat of the men to their cushioned chairs, their Sunday papers, their vacuous nap, while the women removed all vestiges of the horror. Sunday-noon dinners! They set a scar upon my soul. I still shudder when I think of them.[32]

Repelled by what many Americans at the time would have perceived as women's customary duties, from a young age Irwin envisioned a different future, which extended beyond the customs and confines of the private sphere. These unique family dynamics drove her to contemplate women's status frequently as a young person, and she took an aggressive stand in support of suffrage when asked by a teacher to submit a write-up on the issue at Bowdoin Grammar School in Boston.[33]

Park's and Irwin's nontraditional paths to university also shaped their involvement in political activism for women's rights. Both women took several years off to teach in Massachusetts before pursuing college training. Park obtained her first jobs in Bedford and Chelsea high schools, where she saved her income for college, while Irwin took a position in the Boston Public Schools before she arranged for university.[34] At the time when the two women started their careers, female educators faced many injustices, like unequal pay. Men who worked in Massachusetts as early education teachers typically earned between seventeen hundred and thirty-two hundred dollars per year, while institutions paid women only six hundred to twelve hundred dollars. Most secondary schools correspondingly offered male teachers between seventeen hundred and four thousand dollars and female educators only one to two thousand dollars.[35] Women instructors made so little compared to their male colleagues that the Massachusetts Board of Education declared it "humiliating" when the organization reported their wages together in 1893.[36]

Park and Irwin enrolled in Radcliffe College as nontraditional students at twenty-four years old in part because they hoped that university credentials might offer them the training and opportunities that they needed to improve their futures. The two women's terms overlapped as Park entered university in 1895, and Irwin started shortly thereafter, in 1897.[37] These experiences helped to awaken their political consciousness, which developed further during their time in college. Park's and Irwin's three-year stints in college drew them into grassroots suffrage activism directly and spurred their friendship in the late nineteenth century.[38]

Park's initial experiences with active suffrage campaigning came in 1898 when one of the institution's founders, Stella Scott Gilman, held a tea at her home that was open to students from the senior class.[39] Gilman invited a representative from the Massachusetts Association Opposed to the Further Extension of Suffrage to Women to discuss her cause (the antisuffrage organization was among the most formidable challengers to pro-suffrage advocates in the state). The representative passed around a paper to sign, according to Park, "as if it were a mere formality" rather than a statement of support for her organization.[40] While Park avoided the presentation, what she heard from her classmates intrigued her. She recalled, "A group of my friends held an indignation meeting afterward, complaining that something had been 'put over' on the girls who were there, and that in common justice the other side of the question should have been represented."[41] She united with Irwin, a fellow suffrage supporter on campus, to rectify the situation and hear both perspectives.

Under the auspices of the Emanuel Club, they planned a debate on women's right to vote.[42] The young women secured Alice Blackwell, the nationally known suffrage organizer, as a speaker at the event, which turned into a discussion of women's political equality when neither Park nor Irwin succeeded in finding Blackwell an opponent. Park recalled that this meeting with Blackwell influenced her life immensely and instilled in her a sense of "duty" to participate in the women's rights cause after graduation.[43] She described it later as "the link" which "bound" her "to suffrage work for more than twenty years" and pushed her toward activism.[44]

Blackwell remained in contact with the two Radcliffe students after the meeting. Seeing the promise in Park, she encouraged her to join the state campaign and groomed her to lead the College Committee of the Massachusetts Woman Suffrage Association (MWSA), created in the 1890s. The committee was pioneering in its efforts to reach university students and faculty in an organized fashion, beginning the tradition of women's rights agitation in the academy by sending suffrage speakers and distributing literature to campuses. Upon the urging of Blackwell and other leaders, the organization officially appointed Park as chairperson of the committee in 1898.[45] The valuable experiences and time that she spent leading the small and short-lived group contributed to her later interest in mobilizing college-educated Americans on a larger scale alongside her friend Inez Haynes Irwin.

The two up-and-coming organizers confronted a grave situation when they moved to enter their new organization, the CESL, into a campaign for women's political rights in Massachusetts and across the country in the early 1900s. As many scholars comment, by the turn of the twentieth century, the suffrage campaign's visibility and urgency were fading. Founding suffragists who had spearheaded the nineteenth-century movement stepped down because of factors such as declining health, age, apathy, or distraction. The deaths of prominent suffragists, including Lucy Stone in 1893, Elizabeth Cady Stanton in 1902, and Susan B. Anthony in 1906, meant that the campaign entered the new century

Figure 1.1. Maud Wood Park in her Radcliffe cap and gown. Photo courtesy of the Schlesinger Library, Harvard Radcliffe Institute.

without its most respected leaders.[46] Progress stalled as the number of experienced organizers dwindled.

Although four states granted women's right to vote before 1900, grassroots victories dried up by the late nineteenth century. From 1896 onward, no additional states passed woman-suffrage legislation until 1910.[47] Suffragists were not capturing the headlines and made no noticeable progress at the federal level, and according to many scholars, the movement appeared outwardly to have reached a standstill.[48] Reshaping the campaign from the inside would be an urgent priority in the new era of women leaders such as Park, Irwin, and Catt.

Under Catt's direction, NAWSA suffragists experimented and reconfigured their organizations and movement for the modern era and

Figure 1.2. Inez Haynes Irwin as a Radcliffe student.
Photo courtesy of the Schlesinger Library, Harvard
Radcliffe Institute.

new political culture. By the early 1900s, Park and Irwin's move to bring greater numbers of college-educated recruits into the campaign for women's right to vote bolstered the actions of other rising leaders who also planned to execute innovative strategies to garner endorsement for full female suffrage across the country. In 1893, NAWSA leader Catt tested an idea called the "Society Plan," a move to organize wealthy elites in support of the Colorado state campaign, and in 1904, as president, she took steps to implement this tactic on a national level, inspired by its successful grassroots outcomes. As scholar Carolyn Summers Vacca notes, Catt hoped to gather more upper-class support and thus funding for NAWSA's campaigns. She aimed to project a professionalized public image that reached the upper classes especially and aspired for NAWSA to become a political entity that made up for the major party's lack of consideration for women's issues.[49]

State organizers such as Harriot Stanton Blatch and Maud Younger also began efforts to rally working-class women to the equal-franchise movement in New York and California in the early twentieth century, hoping to broaden the group's support base. The two organizations that they developed, the Equality League of Self-Supporting Women (1907) and the San Francisco Wage Earners' Suffrage League (1908), attracted laborers throughout their respective locations, as women started to see the value in working across class lines and to understand that changing times would mean that more women would be stepping into public vocations.[50] Not only NAWSA but other forces inspired their work as well, such as growing international women's rights campaigns and the US labor movement. Suffragists made their campaign more egalitarian when they incorporated men's leagues into the crusade and formed closer alliances with prominent organizers such as Max Eastman and influential male Progressives.[51] This mobilization was not always easy, and differences in race, class, ethnicity, gender, region, and political styles created irreconcilable conflicts in some instances. The moves to organize diverse Americans, however, did push the movement forward in the twentieth century and further into public consciousness.[52]

Park and Irwin's CESL fitted with this work. Organizing college-educated Americans could be another critical strategy to rejuvenate the cause, one that would also fall in line with Catt and NAWSA's larger efforts to increase the number of well-educated and well-connected men and women involved in the movement and legitimize the organization in the eyes of the public and the upper classes. The Boston alumni league started initial efforts to attract new college-educated professionals to local women's rights activism in cities in 1900. Because of the perceived opposition within higher education, the CESL targeted university graduates working near campuses as lawyers, doctors, educators, social reformers, and scientists. Inspired by Catt's tactics, cofounder Maud Wood Park advertised the CESL as differing from nineteenth-century women's rights groups, infamous because of some members' controversial behavior, such as allegedly promoting spinsterhood, defying conventional womanly decorum, and advocating aggressive or unlawful challenges to disenfranchisement. The stories of Susan B. Anthony illegally voting in 1872 in Rochester, New York, and Victoria Woodhull, a controversial free-love advocate, stockbroker, and female presidential political candidate, who became associated with the campaign, are just two of the most notorious examples that fueled negative perceptions.

The college league's leaders asserted, however, that, unlike these women, the CESL represented a "new order" of well-dressed, articulate, and intellectually advanced organizers poised to carry the movement forward.[53] Park described the average CESL member as "a dainty feminine creature with the prettiest of manners and clothes and a vast store of logical argument on the tip of her tongue."[54] Park wrote that the CESL aspired to add "intellectual prestige" to the image of the contemporary suffragist and align with the larger respected culture of progressive reform.[55] Irwin, similarly, commented that university-educated supporters would bring "something special to the movement." College-educated women would be "brilliant—fluent, concise, logical, unafraid."[56] They would be women that upper-class male voters and politicians could not ignore as intellectual and socioeconomic equals. Their presence and that of other elite women in the movement would, in historian Lauren C. Santangelo's words, "pique journalists' curiosity."[57] The two women's long-time ally from the larger MWSA, Alice Blackwell, wrote about the CESL, "A pleasant fact is that most of the officers of the new League are remarkable not only for brains but for beauty, and beauty of a distinctly feminine type. There is not a mannish-looking woman among them."[58] Members of the CESL represented NAWSA's new ideal for the new century, so much so that the national association would eventually recognize the group as an official affiliate and encourage the development of a CESL national body.

* * *

To generate the early support of peers—other upper- and middle-class professionals with college degrees—Boston activists, such as Park and Irwin, first used their academic skills to distinguish themselves, speak with expertise on women's rights, and preserve a feminine image. CESL representatives presented the group as a dignified, engaged, and civically enlightened organization concerned with uncovering the facts behind the suffrage debate. In the beginning, the Boston alumni league did not

Figure 1.3. Maud Wood Park as she would have appeared during her years as a leader in the suffrage movement. Photo courtesy of the Schlesinger Library, Harvard Radcliffe Institute.

take part in public or headline-making demonstrations for female voting rights, as some suffragists had done in prior eras. Instead, members mostly remained in the background, working independently and using their intellectual training to conduct research and surveys that promoted the cause, especially among the upper classes. As one publication commented, "A very important part of the work of the League would seem to be the collection, publication, and dissemination of accurate and statistical information and arguments on the subject of equal suffrage which are calculated to convince college women and men."[59] The suffrage newspaper, the *Woman's Journal*, supported by NAWSA members and local allies of Park, aided the league's early work by publicizing their efforts, especially in Massachusetts.[60]

Figure 1.4. Inez Haynes Irwin in her adult years as
a writer and suffragist. Photo courtesy of the
Schlesinger Library, Harvard Radcliffe Institute.

Park and Irwin used their knowledge and scholarly training to collect, assess, and present to others of their class data that countered
popular arguments against woman suffrage. The group became like
a "think tank" for the movement that replaced the older suffrage arguments and literature with new persuasive points and materials that
tapped into the culture of the Progressive Era. Their work focused on
quantifiable facts and figures that challenged nineteenth-century pseu-
doscience about women's inferiority and unsuitability for the franchise.
The CESL's evidence—relayed in books, articles, pamphlets, and other
publications, and later taken to the public in newspapers and speeches—
was vital campaign material to win over politicians, lawyers, scientists,

eugenicists, and other college-educated Americans skeptical about how enfranchising women might affect the country and still clinging to sexist Victorian gender ideology.[61]

The Boston league investigated popular antisuffrage claims, such as the common argument that giving women the vote would be harmful to the nation because doing so would increase the foreign, uneducated, and criminal influence on politics. Park and Irwin instructed league members to gather data indicating that including more female citizens in civic life would uplift the electorate because most Progressive Era women had a better education and would be more upstanding as citizens than men. Citing Commissioner of Education reports from 1880 to 1900, Boston suffragists wrote that illiteracy among women was much lower than it was among men.[62] Among Americans aged ten to twenty-one, there were 117,362 more illiterate men than women in Massachusetts, and these would be the future voters. More women graduated from high schools and colleges nationwide. From 1889 to 1900, the number of women who graduated from colleges increased a shocking 159.1 percent, while that of men graduates increased by only 60.6 percent. The group shared information from a 1902 Massachusetts report stating that in the previous year there were 18,690 more girls than boys who graduated from high schools.[63]

These trends held strong since industrialization and the growth of the capitalist economy had ushered more men out of college and into occupations, creating more opportunities for women to advance their education. CESL members highlighted in their publications that if the government continued to refuse women the right to vote, the "nearly illiterate minority," primarily comprised of men, would be "governing the more educated majority," mostly made up of women.[64]

Playing on notions of ethnic superiority, the CESL generated research showing that granting women suffrage would involve more native-born and "respectable" Americans in government, an argument compelling among Americans concerned about immigration trends at the time. In 1902 and 1903, the group circulated reports stating that because women made up only 28 percent of the immigrant population, if women were given the ballot, the number of native-born enfranchised women would outweigh the number of foreigners by about three to one.[65] Nationwide, woman suffrage stood to enfranchise more native-born female citizens than it did foreigners since the number of American women was 32,467,041 while the number of foreigners totaled only 10,341,276 between 1902 and 1903.[66]

Many women were leaving the domestic sphere and had become a vital component of academic classes, the workforce, and the professions in several urban areas. For them to extend their contributions to the political realm was the next logical step. In the United States, the census of 1900 showed that between three and four million women engaged in wage-earning occupations outside of domestic service. Suffragists argued that they needed the vote to protect their interests. Data showed that women worked in all but two areas of the 155 occupations listed in the census: sailors and soldiers, and telephone and telegraph linemen. The report stated that there were 503,574 women working in trade and transportation, 980,025 in agriculture, and 1,315,354 in manufacturing and mechanical pursuits.[67] Activists maintained that White working women would make up the majority of new voters and that having the vote would be crucial to improving their conditions. These prejudiced arguments appealed to men who did not want to extend the immigrant influence, particularly to nontraditional new groups, and increase their power. They appealed to Progressives who hoped to bolster notions of their superiority by enfranchising those Americans who would support their visions for the future, wherein they were in leadership.

The league drew attention to women's morality, good character, and vaunted behavior to dispute charges by opponents that extending suffrage would negatively influence the electorate by increasing unqualified and delinquent votes. The CESL emphasized that throughout the country, the female sex constituted the minority of alcoholics, gamblers, thieves, and other criminals. According to the Boston CESL's reports, it was a testament to women's good nature and character that in Massachusetts and New York, only 8 percent of all prisoners in 1905 were women. In states that granted woman suffrage before 1900, there was only about one woman for every 252 men in jail.[68] The Boston league tried to convince readers that including female voters would help instead of hinder civic life, using enlightened and statistically backed claims that emphasized women's superiority and fitness for the franchise rather than basing their arguments on ideology, opinion, or religious doctrine, as in prior periods.

The Boston CESL also collected new findings on electoral trends, political developments, and social changes in suffrage states that had passed grassroots legislation to enfranchise women to support the argument that if enfranchised, female voters would use their new rights and make positive contributions. In the early twentieth century, women were already successfully casting ballots in Wyoming (1869), Colorado (1893), Utah (1896), and Idaho (1896) and helping to positively shape politics.[69] With their research, the CESL challenged opponents who suggested that women were not making use of the ballot. For example, the CESL issued a resolution to counter Dr. Woodrow Wilson's (then a professor and administrator at Princeton University) claim that "where women have the ballot very few of them vote." They highlighted publicly released statistics stating that 80 percent of Colorado women registered and approximately 72 percent voted in elections. In Wyoming, 90 percent of women typically voted. They noted that the chief justice of Idaho and all the justices of the state supreme court had signed a document attesting that women made up a large percentage of voters in their state.[70] Female electors endorsed measures popular among male Progressive politicians, such as campaigns to curb prostitution, alcoholism, gambling, and child abuse. Women voters backed laws to strengthen American health through a pure food act, stricter sanitation policies, and new mandates for public recreation, among other issues, often supported by liberal male politicians.[71] By listing the constructive changes that women voters helped to enact in suffrage states, the CESL demonstrated to other Americans that women would not be negligent or uninvolved electors.

The CESL convinced others that not enfranchising women was behind the times by publishing colored maps and lists with dates of countries that supported the franchise for women outside the United States. By the early twentieth century, the league had reported full suffrage for women in Australia since 1884, New Zealand since 1893, Finland since 1906, and Norway since 1907. Women had had municipal suffrage in England and Wales since 1869, Scotland since 1881, and Ireland since 1898, and in provinces in Canada, Sweden, Denmark, and Iceland various franchise laws passed before 1910. They kept track of these milestones, and the CESL used these statistics to show that woman suffrage was inevitable. Americans looked behind the times at a moment when the government worked to develop the country's image and place in the international community. "It is no longer a question of whether or not women shall vote, but of whether American women shall be the last of civilized women to receive the franchise," the organization wrote to play on the emotions of political leaders who were hoping to continue building a reputation of US cosmopolitanism and exceptionalism.[72]

In addition to challenging their opponents' arguments, the Boston CESL's literature sometimes summarized all the most convincing suffrage arguments popular at the current moment that would be most persuasive to college-educated audiences. One flyer noted, for example, that twentieth-century college women should "Desire the Ballot" for several key reasons. First, it is "mere justice" because the government taxed women, and therefore they deserve representation, just like men. Second, as upstanding citizens, most women should not be classified by the government with minors, aliens, imbeciles, and criminals. Disenfranchisement was "unfair." The realities of the industrial world forced women out of the home, and they needed the ballot for "protection." Finally, women were better qualified than men to legislate for certain civic reforms given their unique dispositions and experiences. Suffragists ended by directly calling out their opponents: "The political boss, the brewer, the saloon keeper, the employer of child labor, the white slaver all fear the granting of the vote to women" because the moral woman voter would challenge their corruption. But ultimately, they asserted, women voters would help to uplift society.[73] Boston activists also sometimes wrote that women should have the ballot because women's indirect political influence was not enough. It was "slow," "uncertain," "humiliating," and lacked "dignity." "A woman who is vitally interested in the enactment of a law . . . should not have to wheedle legislators; she should be able to approach them as one of the electorate to whom they are responsible."[74] Men did not adequately represent women with their votes.[75]

The CESL dramatized their arguments and research in pageants and plays to teach the public about the cause of women's rights. Irwin and her first husband, Rufus Gillmore, both worked as writers and authored plays performed for the benefit of the organization. For example, in 1900, the CESL produced Gillmore's play *The Weathervane of Love*, described as "a pretty love-drama" with Irwin in the cast. That same year, Park was in a play called *The Judgement of Minerva*, written by Florence

Howe Hall.[76] The play included a band of suffragists approaching the Greek God Zeus, asking him to consider their cause, and facing a group of protesting antisuffragists. In 1902, Irwin helped arrange the productions of *The Land of Heart's Desire* and *Nance Oldfield*. She acted in and planned with Park a play called *The Ladies' Battle* in 1904. In 1905, there was *Monsegneur* and then, in 1906, *Mirandolina*.[77]

Many of the plays were love stories, dramas with comedic elements that pulled the suffrage issue into the plot in a clever way. They theatrically compelled people to understand the plight of women and why they might want or need the ballot. Participants might walk away with a suffrage button, pamphlet, or flyer. Their ticket fees subsidized the CESL's other activism, literature, and publications. The plays drew viewers to the campaign. Productions continued to be advertised in the *Boston Globe* until both women, Park and Irwin, became involved in new initiatives with the league and NAWSA. The performances were especially popular in urban areas during the early twentieth century, as workers sought inexpensive entertainment on the weekends, and the upper classes still enjoyed the theater as a fashionable pastime.

* * *

By 1904, Park and Irwin began to execute other new plans to expand their small Massachusetts organization beyond the state's borders. With their help, for over two years, the Boston women affiliated with the CESL worked with interested campaigners in the Northeast to establish a second branch, the Collegiate Equal Suffrage League of New York.[78] New York in many ways had similarities to Boston, given its growing options for women's higher education, robust public school system, cosmopolitan urban setting, and prominent scholarly institutions such as libraries and government agencies, all of which provided activists with potential allies, theaters, and resources.[79] By the time their work concluded, in 1906, the CESL listed over 250 members in the Boston organization, and the New York group seemed poised to flourish into potentially even larger membership.[80] At first, the New York alumni league furthered the research conducted in Massachusetts before becoming leaders active in working with self-supporting women and allies of the labor movement. They helped to unite the cause of woman suffrage with other local campaigns going on in the city and nationwide in urban areas.[81] One of the

New York association's initial endeavors involved directing a 1906 study of female voting patterns in the suffrage state of Colorado, where state voting rights for women had passed early.

Helen L. Sumner, an economist who lived in Colorado at the time, headed the CESL efforts in the West under the direction of colleagues from New York. Sumner had ties to New England, where she had attended college at Wellesley in Massachusetts (later returning home for graduate training at the University of Wisconsin–Madison). Like many NAWSA activists, she held deep concerns about the conditions that women and children faced in the modern industrializing world. She hoped that the female vote would make a positive difference. With a team of assistants, Sumner spent two years exploring how woman suffrage influenced society politically, economically, and socially. CESL representatives created a list of questions and collected survey data from nearly twelve hundred people to gauge the changes caused by female voting rights in Colorado. They studied newspapers, state, county, and city records, census data, Bureau of Labor reports, political conventions, and voter registration books. Suffragists published and circulated their findings in 1909.

While the findings, overall, did not show that female voters had a major impact on the conditions in Colorado, there was evidence that, since women had begun voting in the state in 1893, some positive outcomes had occurred. One review summarized the report's conclusions: "A few new employments have opened to women and their salaries in most public positions has been made equal to those of men doing the same work." Colorado labor laws were mostly "good," "especially for the protection of women and children." Overall, Sumner commented that woman suffrage seemed to have "tended to cultivate intelligent public spirit." The responsibilities of full citizenship helped to "enlarge" women's interest in government and "develop their [political] ability." The reviewer noted that the conclusions of the publication, however, showed that outcomes were much more "neutral" than expected.[82]

The league hoped that sharing the results would advance the suffrage cause among other women of similar academic standing in a powerful manner and challenge the arguments of their opponents. The document did not make a persuasive case for strong change, but it did show that female voters had not hindered the state or local government in any significant way. Many antisuffragists would later capitalize on the short-comings of this research in their campaigns to challenge the CESL and NAWSA, much to the two groups' discontent.[83]

The New York CESL also began to become a part of the larger state suffrage scene, particularly in the city. Santangelo writes that, in the early twentieth century, the Colony Club became a hub for elite women involved in the movement. Membership included hundreds of upper-class New Yorkers, including notables such as Anne Morgan, Jeannette Gilder, and Ethel Barrymore. The organization formed in 1903, and among recreational resources such as a pool and a ballroom, it offered an array of programs, including educational lectures in the evenings on topics of popular interest for members, such as child labor and educational reform. Recognizing that this space was a potential stage and source of support for their campaign, members of the CESL made connections with local leaders. In 1907, they used their network to plan a benefit at the group's Madison Avenue clubhouse to support "suffrage research."[84] The CESL and other state suffragists realized that working with the club would be an effective avenue to reach New York's most powerful and influential women.

* * *

By 1909 and 1910, however, the national suffrage movement was transforming, and the CESL was ready, like many others, to try other new things. The league moved beyond investigating woman suffrage to engaging in more public demonstrations in urban spaces and reaching diverse audiences, like other suffrage groups in the United States and internationally. In 1909, NAWSA had relocated its headquarters to New York City, and the new urban realities influenced the leaders' campaign ideology.[85] Inspired by Progressive Era politics and social and political campaigns, NAWSA activists realized the value of publicity-generating protest to appeal to various groups of Americans. For NAWSA, these tactics included producing plays but also using new technology, such as early motion pictures, and organizing booths at community events, fairs, and festivals where the suffrage issue reached people of different backgrounds. Their activism included putting up posters and displays in cities and shop windows to take advantage of mass media and consumerism. Their campaigns included creating suffrage parades and lobbying politicians more aggressively in government spaces. Suffragists gave out-door or open-air speeches on busy public street corners or at popular locations such as parks and beaches—methods that bought people face to face with the issue in direct and unavoidable ways. The goal was to bring the cause to the public and eventually make it an inescapable polit-ical issue at the center rather than the fringes of government.

The CESL responded to these trends by shifting their activism from rallying the elite and working in the background to being on the front lines of efforts to form cross-class alliances with women workers. Par-ticipating in public activism together would present a unified image of support for suffrage to politicians and show that all women in the United States wanted the ballot.[86] Park and Irwin recognized their unique po-sition given their training and constituency. The CESL could use their education to add credibility to suffragists' claims among the upper classes, as they had done in the past, while also—given the number of self-supporting professionals in their organization—using their shared occupational experience to connect with ordinary workers. The New York CESL was among the first of the local suffrage groups to take the suffrage message to lower-class laborers throughout the city and aim to form new alliances. As Santangelo writes, "Gotham provided an ideal laboratory for this cross-class experiment: it claimed the most 'female breadwinners' of any city in the nation." While there were slum areas and areas of privilege in New York, the urban environment made it so these women intermingled much more in their daily lives than others of dif-ferent backgrounds in more rural areas.[87] Thus, the upper classes found it harder to shut out the realities of the working classes, and vice versa, as both sides of life remained vividly and publicly displayed to one another on a regular basis.

During the winter of 1909, the New York alumni league created a special committee with the Equality League of Self-Supporting Women (ELSSW), a group formed in Manhattan to campaign for suffrage among working women of all classes (later known as the Women's Po-litical Union or WPU). The organization hoped to advance this commit-tee. By that year, the ELSSW had approximately twenty-two thousand members. Santangelo comments that membership included women from many occupations, "ranging from doctors and lawyers to shirt makers."[88] Suffragists chose ELSSW founder Harriot Stanton Blatch, a

Vassar College graduate, to head the joint activism of the CESL and the ELSSW. Blatch likely endorsed the union of the two groups because it fell in line with her vision for the ELSSW's future. According to historian Ellen Carol DuBois, Blatch intended that the ELSSW would connect "industrial workers, not with 'club women,' but with educated, professional workers." Blatch alleged that the alliance between these groups would be a powerful force in leading the women's rights campaign and making it relevant and compelling to modern audiences.[89]

Blatch, daughter of nineteenth-century NAWSA leader Elizabeth Cady Stanton, strongly believed that recruiting women of all economic backgrounds and ethnicities to create a powerful contingent to pressure politicians to support women's right to vote was a winning strategy for the future. She advocated taking the cause to the streets to raise awareness among local residents and to confront opponents directly. Blatch's approach drew on the methods used by others, including the British suffragettes in the United Kingdom, who, fueled by the leadership of women such as Emmeline Pankhurst, were bolder in their public demonstrations for women's voting rights. Pankhurst advocated daring challenges to gender-based discrimination in Europe based on mimicking male methods of creating political change, including waging war. In the fall of 1909, Pankhurst accepted an invitation to speak in New York at Carnegie Hall under the auspices of the ELSSW, with many CESL members in attendance. Although controversial, she often spoke to American audiences because so many responded with curiosity about the headlines that they read in the newspaper regarding suffragette violence for the vote in Europe. Pankhurst told working women, college women, and other state suffragists, "You have heard much of our methods. . . . It may be violent but where did men get anything but by violence? Where would this republic be if your fathers had not thrown the tea into Boston harbor?"[90] Pankhurst went on to comment that the difference between the American and British suffrage movements was that in America, activists had not succeeded yet in making suffrage a political issue. Catt had long suggested the same. Pankhurst further argued that to be successful, activists should "study the things the men have done and profit by their mistakes."[91] In her view, studying methods of warfare could provide instruction in how to win the vote. Suffragists needed to become a visible, recognized force in government. This goal was an ambition that

Catt and Park, who would go on to be a key lobbyist for NAWSA in later years, also believed in achieving, even if they were critical of Pankhurst's radical methods.

In New York, the CESL credited Pankhurst with encouraging the league to rethink its campaign and begin different initiatives. CESL president Jessie Ashley commented that Pankhurst, upon coming to New York, set a "revolutionary pace" and stirred "growing resentment and deep protest," especially among members of the college league.[92] Activists hoped to do more to vocalize their discontent with women's inequality to the nation's leading men. At one CESL meeting in the summer of 1910, for example, the speaker even suggested that the women protest disenfranchisement by pledging not to sing "My Country, 'Tis of Thee, Sweet Land of Liberty" until women won the vote. She argued that until the government enfranchised women, Americans, particularly politicians, were hypocrites.[93]

At Pankhurst's urging, Jessie Ashley, along with CESL allies Harriet Burton Laidlaw, a wealthy New York English teacher, and Caroline Lexow, a Barnard College graduate devoted to suffrage and a secretary for Blatch, committed to stepping up their challenges to discrimination. Not long after, the group planned to travel to Washington to present a resolution to the State Department to see what it could do about American suffragist Alice Paul's detainment in the United Kingdom at the Holloway Prison. Activists saw detainment for her involvement in suffrage activism overseas as an unjust strike against one of their own and an overt example of the government's sexism. Paul, a recent Swarthmore College graduate, made a name for herself in American and UK suffrage circles, and the government charged her with throwing stones at the window of a public building, shattering the glass during the banquet for the lord mayor of London. Viewing the young Swarthmore alum as one of their own, the CESL argued that the State Department was not doing enough to free Paul because she was a woman. The league argued that all parties responsible for her detainment should treat her as a political prisoner and not a "mere ordinary criminal."[94]

The group also proposed sending a special committee to England to study the suffragette movement firsthand overseas and report back on the facts to dispel the fictions reported in the US media about the women's movement in the United Kingdom. Blatch led this committee of five women, setting sail in January 1910, and the CESL planned a reception upon Paul's return to the United States in honor of her struggle.[95] The CESL's mission was to support Paul and publicly challenge the federal government's inaction with respect to her release. Their plans to send representatives to Washington, DC, in protest, and even abroad to collect information, represented a bolder style of activism and an overt challenge to female inequality.

The previous December, Blatch and the committee had also initiated a new movement that challenged antisuffrage sentiment among state politicians from a cross-class vantage point. One of the most notable activities occurred that spring in May 1910, when the CESL and the ELSSW sent representatives to a mass meeting in Union Square to urge the legislature to consider the voting-rights question more seriously.[96] The event involved an immense procession, including automobiles, nearly twelve hundred marchers, and two hundred CESL members in caps and gowns—some of whom delivered pro-suffrage speeches. This event culminated in the presentation of a joint resolution for woman suffrage to the New York state government that insisted that leaders not sideline the cause any longer. The CESL declared to politicians at the event, "This meeting, representing every political division and every class of women in the State of New York, protests against the tyrannical action of the Judiciary Committees and calls upon those who cherish their freedom to defeat at the polls the false representatives who withhold from the voters an opportunity to vote upon the greatest political question ever before the citizens of the State of New York."[97] By promoting a theme of unity among all women, Blatch and the committee pressed the local government not only to acknowledge the widespread support for female voting rights but also to act immediately.

Jessie Ashley, the New York CESL president at the time, was talented at debates and not afraid to aggressively lobby for her perspective, much like Blatch. Ashley, a native New Yorker, came from a wealthy elite background but did not follow customary conventions of her gender or class. Her father gained economic and social status as an executive in the railroad industry, which afforded her a private school education and the ability to pursue a law degree at New York University, where her brother was the dean. Ashley was passionate about studying the law as it relates to gender. Wanting to put her education to use after graduation, she, along with female friends, had opened their private practice in 1905 on Fifth Avenue. Intellectually sharp and not afraid to address an audience, she taught courses at NYU, supported the Socialist Party, and, in addition to suffrage, became involved in the contentious labor and birth-control movements. Radical feminist and labor advocate Emma Goldman later wrote in her memoir that Ashley was a "valiant rebel."[98]

Ashley publicly affirmed the bolder college league tactics following the expansive 1910 Union Square suffrage demonstration. She told the press that the CESL would seek working-class alliances and take campaigns into the public sphere alongside other city suffragists. She viewed winning the endorsement of working women as necessary for success: "Nothing revolutionary can be accomplished without the working people and the working people can't be reached in parlors or college halls. The people can be reached by going to them in the streets, and if you take a just cause to the people, the people will stand by you. The suffrage will be given to women through the vote of the workingman."[99] Using such arguments, Ashley and her New York allies set precedents in the college league's campaigns by asserting that the CESL could no longer be as exclusive or demure as before if it wanted to initiate actual change. This rhetoric helped to lay the groundwork for the activism of other alumni branches. Ashley reframed the CESL as an evolving and progressive group that recognized the significance of female solidarity, self-sufficiency, and activism across class lines. She remarked, "The Collegiate League is made up of young, energetic women, who can speak and write and work, and they will not respond to any organization that puts their dignity before efficiency, that is blind to present day conditions. They know beyond a doubt that true democracy is at hand, and they will not tolerate a timid halting policy in their organizations."[100] According to Ashley and members of the New York league, cross-class coalitions and public protests seemed to represent the best avenue for suffrage work moving forward.

By this juncture, many members of NAWSA would agree that organizing among women workers was an important initiative. Some state-led campaigns to reach workers were stronger than others, depending on the local culture and setting. The New York movement was known for achieving more diversity over time—as there was a suffrage body in the city that represented almost every party imaginable. Forming alliances and engaging different recruits happened more quickly and easily there than in other places like Massachusetts. There the antisuffrage stronghold and those fearful of the effects of voting women on their lifestyle and culture created tougher hurdles. The New York CESL and ELSSW were unique groups in that most other grassroots suffrage organizations were small and did not always attract a large membership, and subsequently a lot of publicity, whereas these groups did.

In 1911, the CESL staged many demonstrations in New York alongside its new working-class allies, further connecting the suffrage and labor causes and generating attention for woman suffrage. In the spring, the league was one of the most visible groups that helped protest industrial disasters after the Triangle Shirtwaist Factory fire, which killed 146 garment workers. On Saturday, March 25, 1911, a fire had developed on the upper floors of the New York shirtwaist factory, one of the largest and most popular producers of women's attire in the country. The firefighters who showed up faced dismay and horror when they found that their ladders were not tall enough to reach the top of the multistory building where the crisis broke out. The lack of adequate fire safety measures and accessible fire escapes trapped the workers, mostly young immigrant women. Their employers had locked exit doors, fearing theft or unauthorized breaks. These measures left the women in many cases to burn alive or jump to their deaths, in some cases even impaling themselves on the fence below. The scene of the women screaming, jumping in desperation, lying in mangled positions on the pavement, and the burned interior of the building traumatized all who witnessed it or went to identify the charred corpses. There were survivors. However, the event marked one of the worst and most widely publicized industrial disasters in New York history. The fire signaled that sweeping changes to safety precautions and workers' rights, particularly working women's rights, needed to take place. Suffragists viewed the protest as a crucial opportunity to advocate for "votes for women" as one answer to remedy similar unjust and hazardous situations.[101]

The CESL planned a mass meeting at the Cooper Union to call attention to how woman suffrage could improve fire safety. A banner on the platform read, "Votes for women! Nov. 26—Twenty-five women killed in Newark factory fire. March 25—One hundred and thirty women killed in Triangle fire. The women could not, the voters would not, alter these conditions. We demand for all women the right to protect themselves."[102] Ashley blasted electoral laws and claimed that they handicapped female workers. Existing suffrage legislation denied women the power to challenge poor labor practices and politicians the ability to respond adequately to incidents like fires.[103] Female enfranchisement could ensure that the city officials upheld or improved existing employment protocols, investigated unsafe working environments, and punished corporate violations. Woman suffrage would give female laborers a voice with which to demand redress for tragedies that occurred because of locked doors, overcrowding, and a lack of emergency exits. Ashley and other members called on state legislators to appoint a commission, at least half composed of women, to draft a new fire safety bill.[104] The bold actions by college-educated supporters demonstrated their commitment to a unified campaign with women workers and highlighted to their peers and the public the many reasons why modern women needed the same political rights as men.

That spring, the CESL of New York participated in another major initiative affirming its new alliance with women workers and pressing politicians for the vote when they joined a large parade through the city streets with around three thousand suffragists. Marchers processed from Fifty-Seventh Street to Union Square and ended with a rally to an estimated audience of ten thousand people. Three representatives— one from the WPU, one from the CESL, and one from the Woman Suffrage Party—headed the procession under a large banner, which read, "Forward out of error, Leave behind the night: Forward through the darkness, Forward into light." The banner underscored their campaign's progressive nature and the united pledge of all state suffragists to better the lives of women by securing the ballot.[105] Behind the CESL sign, suffragists in caps and gowns appeared down the line. Members of the Women's Trade Union League marched forward with a banner reading "Women Need Votes to End Sweat Shops," and Triangle Shirtwaist Factory fire survivors carried "crimson banners draped in black" to honor their fallen colleagues.[106] Blatch's WPU sprinkled representatives throughout the procession. The Triangle survivors' presence during the march was a poignant reminder to Americans about the deep significance of granting women the right to vote and the cost of not doing so in the contemporary and industrializing world.

* * *

More was at stake than White women's rights, however. In Progressive Era cities like New York, many Black women workers also filled domestic and other low-paying positions involving hazardous and unequal labor conditions. After the Civil War, African Americans migrated via the railroads from the South to the North, where they faced challenging urban environments. Competing for jobs and housing with immigrants from other locations, Blacks often found life in the North just as tough as it had been in the South. Discrimination existed everywhere. Harlem developed a growing African American community because it was one of the only locations where property owners would rent to Black tenants. A thriving African American subculture developed.[107] Many Blacks participated politically and socially in city life. Instead of inviting the African American women to join the mainstream suffragists' ranks, NAWSA and many White women's organizations remained exclusionary. NAWSA admitted some African American members in the Victorian era. By the early twentieth century, however, sometimes old arguments resurfaced about White women's superiority and their right to receive the franchise first because of their alleged special morality and more civilized nature. As White activists became more desperate and fearful of losing southern support, some campaigners became increasingly nativist and racist in their approach to advancing the movement in the twentieth century.

Like most NAWSA branches, the CESL's alumni leagues remained exclusively White. Historians have written extensively on NAWSA's racism. They highlight how it limited the movement and tarnished the legacies of the organizations' proponents.[108] Founded by NAWSA members Park and Irwin, the CESL followed the umbrella organization's lead regarding race relations.[109] Scholar Barbara Berenson writes, "The 'unwritten and largely unspoken NAWSA policy on black suffragists was to ignore them, and if pressed, refuse their allegiance and aid.'"[110] The alumni leagues had no official policies excluding African Americans (nor did Park or Irwin make any public statements about these measures). However, they sent few members into Black neighborhoods, city wards, or institutions, sending a message to others.[111] It is possible that some of these women's discrimination was not conscious. They may not have even considered the voting rights of African Americans as an important issue. Activists operated from a schema in which racism and prejudice existed as politically sanctioned, institutionalized, and deeply entrenched cultural and political realities.[112]

Although NAWSA and the CESL neglected Black suffragists, African American college alumni were active in the women's rights movement. The groups that they mobilized through, the methods they used, and their campaign platforms differed from those of White activists.[113] Many upper-class and college-educated Black female suffragists allied with popular reform organizations headed by African Americans, groups such as the National Association of Colored Women (NACW) and, later, the National Association for the Advancement of Colored People (which did not develop until 1909). They promoted woman suffrage at the grassroots level alongside other causes important to the African American community: the campaign to protect Black male citizenship, the movement to improve educational and medical access, the activism against segregation, and the antilynching crusade.

The NACW formed in 1896 from the merger of two smaller organizations dedicated to bettering the Black community: the National Federation of Afro-American Women (1895) and the National League of Colored Women (1896). Mary Church Terrell, an educator and activist from Memphis, became the NACW's first president, and branches of her organization developed nationwide.[114] The NACW was the respectable and logical choice for many politically and socially engaged Black women. The group was expansive, with a growing network of grassroots affiliates to attract local members. The NACW, like NAWSA, was interested in using educational activism to promote its agenda. The NAACP was also interested in public demonstrations and legal challenges to inequality.

Terrell, while campaigning for distinct issues and confronting distinct challenges, was in some ways like Park and Irwin. Well educated, from a prominent background, and articulate, Terrell skillfully inserted herself into the political scene. A graduate of the progressive Oberlin College, she was an upwardly mobile African American from Tennessee whose father, after becoming free, became a

Figure 1.5. Mary Church Terrell, a leader in social and
political causes to advance Black women's rights.
Photo courtesy of the Library of Congress, Prints and
Photographs Division, photograph by Harris & Ewing.

wealthy businessperson, a Black millionaire. Her mother succeeded as
a beauty salon owner. After gaining a bachelor's and master's degree,
Terrell taught at Wilberforce College (later known as Wilberforce University) before moving to Washington, DC, to teach high school and
participate in civil rights and women's rights activism. She shared with
Park and Irwin the economic means and intellectual ability for a life
dedicated not only to supporting herself but to becoming involved in reform work like suffrage activism. All three were part of a new generation
of educated and intellectual female citizens discontent with traditions
and hoping to gain greater equality with men.

As many scholars note, with an agenda of seeking racial progress by initiating philanthropic, educational, social, and political change, NACW members like Terrell and others often attracted African American female alumni hoping to do more than make a public contribution alongside motherhood and housekeeping.[115] Historian Deborah Gray White comments that Black clubwomen like the NACW members believed that the keys to uplifting the race were social service and self-help work.[116] Woman suffrage was one of the major goals that they wanted to achieve. Instead of protesting for the ballot in controversial ways, like the New Yorkers who marched down prominent public streets blocking traffic in parades, they took a different approach. Scholar Jean Gould Bryant writes that representatives often tempered their campaigns, using socially acceptable tactics to conform to mainstream White "middle-class values" and "behavior patterns." This approach was a strategy for African American advancement in the existing racist society, in some ways not unlike much of the initial activism used by the Boston CESL to get the support of the upper classes: holding meetings, publishing literature, and researching statistics and collecting evidence to make their arguments more persuasive.[117]

Black college-educated women joined well-regarded NACW affiliates in the North, East, and eventually the South and the West, when the CESL and other White suffrage organizations made little effort to reach out. For example, Boston's Black alumni joined organizations such as the Woman's Era Club to promote equal suffrage and other popular reforms. African American activist Josephine St. Pierre Ruffin founded the club in 1893 to "help to make the world better." A well-educated Black woman whose husband was the first African American graduate of Harvard Law School, Ruffin was unusual among Black suffragists in that she did some early work with the MWSA that she drew upon when creating her own club and helped produce a newspaper, the *Woman's Era*, to promote equality in voting and civil rights in her state. The goal of the paper was to create a medium through which women, particularly "educated and refined" Black women, could voice their opinions on current society and politics.[118] Like Park and Irwin, Ruffin realized the benefits of recruiting upper-class Black women to the campaign as well as their working-class counterparts. She also supported rights for all regardless of race and, despite discrimination, sometimes worked with White women.[119]

College-educated African Americans in New York could choose from an assortment of NACW groups, as historian Rosalyn Terborg-Penn identifies. These groups included the popular Women's Loyal Union, led by Victoria Earle Matthews, a Georgia native and respected social worker. After doing only a short stint in public school, she educated herself while working as a domestic servant by reading books in her employer's library. She eventually became a journalist for multiple papers and an advocate of the vote.[120]

Though they were rarer, interested African American alumni could find all-Black suffrage associations to join in certain states. In New York City, educator Sarah J. Garnet created the Equal Suffrage League in Brooklyn in 1902 to rally endorsement for the vote, and the league held its meetings at her home and the local YMCA, drawing middle-class Black men and women in the local area to its events to learn about the campaign.[121] Two Black sections of state suffrage parties (presumably connected to NAWSA through its New York affiliates) took off in the 1910s in Manhattan and Harlem, which drew the local African American community into the suffrage movement and helped to generate support among voters for state suffrage legislation.[122] Some White suffragists spoke to Black audiences, and vice versa. The organizations' activities all helped in NAWSA's larger efforts to make the movement more visible to politicians and voters.

Similar patterns occurred in other regions outside the Northeast. In the South, Black woman-suffrage organizations were fewer than in other, more progressive regions, but college-educated Black women did participate in many similar social and political reform groups that supported woman suffrage and affiliated with the NACW. For example, in 1894, Sylvanie F. Williams, a local principal and teacher, created the Phyllis Wheatley Club of New Orleans, named in honor of the famous Black female poet, and other regional civic associations. Under her direction, in addition to promoting suffrage, the organization pushed forward various causes to benefit educated and professional Black women, including opening a training sanitarium and hospital for Black nurses and a day care and kindergarten for Black working mothers.[123] Her work inspired others across the state.[124] In the West, in areas such as Woodland and Oakland, suffrage organizations developed that endured into the twentieth century. By 1910, for example, Black citizens in the San Francisco Bay

Area could participate in many small pro-suffrage associations, such as the Colored American Equal Suffrage League, led by Myra V. Simmons, who worked as a domestic servant and a newspaper salesperson to fund her education. She organized suffrage meetings and rallies, picketed on Election Day, and assisted with civic education work.[125]

Perhaps the most well-known of all the African American woman-suffrage groups in the country was the Alpha Suffrage Club in Chicago, Illinois, created in 1913 with the help of the well-known journalist and organizer Ida B. Wells. Wells made a name for herself as a sociologist and writer who campaigned against the horrors of lynching in the United States. Although she never completed her college degree, she attended Rust College in Mississippi for a period when she was young and later took courses at other institutions in Tennessee. Historians have acknowledged that the Alpha Suffrage Club she helped to organize promoted not only woman suffrage but also Black political leadership and education in the city.[126] Wells gained a reputation for her direction and public challenges to White suffragists' racism, for which she generated publicity on the national stage.

Going to Black churches remained possibly the most effective strategy for mobilizing support in all locations and was taken up by all activists at different moments in the campaign.[127] American society was becoming more secular overall. However, church membership and attendance remained important prerequisites for respectability and status in Black communities, where behavior and actions helped determine one's social standing and reputation sometimes even more so than wealth. Church attendance among African Americans remained high during the period, even as it declined among the public nationwide. African American churches were places where Blacks could gather and discuss important social and political topics without the harassment from Whites that existed in other locations. African American organizers, including Myra Simmons and Naomi Anderson in the San Francisco Bay Area and Annie Lewis in Harlem, planned meetings in local churches to reach the upper crust of Black society.[128] They pressed congregation members and pastors to become allies in the woman-suffrage campaign, using their influence to recruit in their localities, especially among those who had the time, financial resources, and intellect to contribute—the college-educated population.[129]

Unusual as it was, even in the few cases of cross-racial activism among NAWSA suffragists in the twentieth century, campaigners often went to local churches, recognizing the advantages of this public space as a stage from which to reach a diverse audience. In New York, White suffragist and wealthy socialite Alva Belmont addressed the Negro Women's Business League at New York's Mount Olivet Baptist Church in 1910, for example, hoping to attract new members to her controversial cross-racial suffrage organization. She staged one of the first major suffrage gatherings in the city at the church, bringing together Black urban professionals, among others, to hear her comments about the vote. More than one hundred citizens attended and joined Belmont's Political Equality League.[130] African American men and women represented a large potential and untapped group that could have furthered the CESL's activism had the organization and NAWSA been more inclusive concerning race relations. However, segregation in the movement remained the norm rather than the exception in the twentieth century. Discrimination slowed the advancement of the campaign not just for the CESL but also for other predominantly White suffrage groups nationwide.

* * *

By the 1910s, however, not all was lost. Few new states passed woman-suffrage legislation in the early twentieth century. But some special-interest groups, such as the college league, made a name for themselves, gained respect among NAWSA leaders, and expanded their number of grassroots branches. Particularly in the Northeast, the CESL continued to grow. The group eventually moved beyond Boston and New York City. Park, Irwin, and fellow suffrage leaders focused on possible new locations for alumni branches.

From its founding, the CESL worked diligently to emerge as a central force in advancing state organizing for woman suffrage. The group's branches collaborated with other grassroots associations to generate greater endorsement and form cross-class unions to further the campaign. In northern urban centers, like Boston and New York, where the CESL first developed branches, alumni sections started a research-based and fact-finding mission to challenge the opposition by debunking popular arguments against extending the ballot, using their intellectual training and college education to uplift the movement's central claims and literature. This work legitimized these perspectives to the scholarly and learned public. There, the group's local activism improved the suffrage movement's image among the upper classes at the state level, professionalizing the woman-suffrage campaign and fueling Catt's "Society Plan" to attract more "elites" to the women's rights cause. The CESL's activism gained its leaders like Park favor within NAWSA. The Boston suffragists clustered around many elite colleges and universities were especially effective at executing these tactics.

As the organization spread and time passed, influenced by other sources, such as the labor movement and the work of varied social and political reformers, the CESL's campaigns developed into a much broader effort to unite university graduates, often "self-supporting" women and lower-class laborers, in a joint grassroots movement for the vote. The success of this cross-class campaign varied by local conditions and was particularly effective early on in New York. There activists used their shared experience in the workforce as a tool to form unions that presented a stronger and more united pro-suffrage front to the nation's politicians. Although labor activists' and wage earners' contributions to the suffrage movement receive some attention by scholars, the work of their college league allies and the two groups' cooperative campaigns receive less consideration. This work helped to make suffrage a relevant cause for which women were united. The CESL's alumni leagues played an important role in bringing self-supporting women of different backgrounds into grassroots suffrage organizing in the early twentieth century and in doing so bolstered the state activism for woman suffrage headed by NAWSA's various local affiliates.

2

Successes in the West, Struggles in the South,
and Widespread Effects

The death of her first husband, the architect Charles Park, in 1904, sad-
dened CESL cofounder Maud Wood Park, but unlike many women of
her age and background, she was also left momentarily free, with the
time and resources necessary to dedicate her life more fully to activism and exploration. She would not marry again until 1908, when she
secretly wed Robert Hunter, an actor and theatrical agent. The couple
had a "modern" arrangement whereby they lived apart most of the time
and pursued their own interests.[1] Park took interest in the experiences
of women of different classes, locations, and nationalities. In addition
to becoming a leader in multiple suffrage organizations besides the
CESL, including the Massachusetts Woman Suffrage Association and
the Boston Equal Suffrage Association for Good Government, she took
up settlement work, lived in tenement houses, and traveled extensively,
advising from afar the college league and other groups of which she was
a part.

Massachusetts suffrage allies helped to pay for her to spend a year
living in a San Francisco settlement. Not long after, they assisted with
funds for a two-year stint referred to as Park's "trip around the world"
with her friend, Mabel Willard. The goal was not only to give Park a
break from work in Massachusetts but also to allow her the opportunity
to research the conditions of women outside the Northeast. Few American women knew much about woman-suffrage legislation beyond the
United States or how it related to, for example, the female experience in
Asian countries. Her findings could strengthen the NAWSA's campaign
in her home state and elsewhere. Park would be an eyewitness who
could offer new evidence to support women's right to vote. The research
and travel would increase her profile in national and international suffrage circles.[2] She would not return to full-time work in Massachusetts
until around 1910.[3]

Though few CESL suffragists traversed the barriers of race, the league over time did attempt to overcome regional divides at the suggestion of Park, Irwin (who went to California for a period with her first husband and knew the local scene), and others who supported new campaigns in the West and the South.[4] CESL members from Massachusetts and New York traveled across the country by the second decade of their campaign to expand the group's influence in places that showed support for NAWSA and had large bodies of college-educated women. CESL branches existed in fifteen states by 1908, and activists aspired to continue to increase these numbers.[5] Park had made connections with college-educated women from the local area while in California doing settlement work, which helped her to organize alumni leagues.

In early 1908, in the San Francisco Bay Area, Park established the Northern California league (one of a couple of branches in the state), which took off in the early 1910s. She won support by announcing again that the organization would not be comprised of the "shrieking sisters" of past stereotypes. The alumni league became not only one of the most active local suffrage groups but also, as Park recalled, central to the state's pre-1920 victory.[6] The local league, headed by president Charlotte Anita Whitney at the time of the successful 1911 referendum, included more than one thousand active members and had progressive alliances with women workers, similar to what New York suffragists had achieved and would expand upon.[7] Later reflecting on the history of the CESL, although she mentioned no other specific state or local branch, in the final line of a document that Park wrote about the history of the CESL, she typed, "In San Francisco the league that I started came to be a vital factor in the winning campaign for a state constitutional amendment," lauding the work in Northern California and underscoring its important contributions.[8] The California organization was one of the CESL's greatest points of pride and achievement.

California suffragists pioneered the practice of using arguments about municipal housekeeping, civic altruism, and gender essentialism in nuanced ways to gain the ballot. They set examples for other female social and political activists on how to use Victorian rhetoric in new ways to argue for women's place in politics and how to associate suffrage with progressive reform. The winning California state suffrage coalition and its publicity machine provided a model for others throughout the United

States. Historian Gayle Gullett comments that their tactics made them relevant to urban politics in gendered ways that emphasized how women would fill a much-needed space that men could not. The CESL's California suffragists contributed to the state suffrage campaign by adopting this rhetoric to mobilize constituencies, especially teachers in the state, who had been slow to join the local suffrage movement. The CESL did not find the same support in the South. However, the California activities drove new work in places such as Massachusetts and New York by raising morale and creating a winning model to follow. Despite the influence of the California suffrage movement, the emphasis on the New York State story in the last decade of grassroots activism for the vote overshadows the story of the California woman-suffrage victory and of its activists, even today.[9]

Exploring the CESL's California campaign for women's voting rights among alumni until its conclusion in 1911 and following similar state work shaped by its campaigns until 1917, when most grassroots organizations transitioned to the federal amendment, provides new insight into suffrage history. Considering suffrage from this vantage point makes it more apparent that the transitions in suffrage arguments, identified in some studies as permeating the campaign by 1900, were much less clear-cut at the local level. In terms of state and local activism, examining the work of the CESL offers another example of how activists used what scholar Aileen Kraditor first termed "justice" claims and "expediency" reasoning throughout the movement. The argument from "justice" promoted woman suffrage on the basis of women's equal humanity with men, while the argument from "expediency" affirmed the benefits of extending women's domestic caretaking and other distinct attributes into politics. Throughout their organizing, activists often changed their pleas based on the audience and the local social and political culture. As historian Lauren C. Santangelo notes, activists' reasons for supporting the vote were often very diverse.[10] This diversity made it difficult to pin down one line of argument that predominated over another. Suffragists adjusted their arguments to persuade different audiences in different times and places.

As the campaign progressed, instead of expediency claims becoming more dominant in the women's rights movement, as traditionally proposed in scholarship, the CESL used both arguments side by side.

If one predominated over the other in the final few years of grassroots movements, among CESL activists, traditional justice reasoning seemed more common. This trend was especially evident in the northeastern cities with important ties to the country's founding and heritage and as the United States became more formally involved in World War I.[11] Perhaps, as women's education improved, ideas about gender roles changed, and US engagement in military conflict seemed imminent leading up to 1917, the arguments about how women's difference and moral superiority suited them for the franchise no longer swayed the alumni of colleges and universities. They had a more egalitarian view of the sexes and women's place in the modernizing world. Activists often promoted suffrage because they argued that women were intellectually equal to men and already contributing to society in the same ways.

* * *

Leading up to woman-suffrage legislation passing in California in early October 1911, five other western states had voted to enfranchise women, namely, Wyoming, Utah, Colorado, Idaho, and Washington. These victories set trends in the region that left suffragists hopeful. The West was swifter in giving rights and opportunities to women than other areas because of the different environment in which communities emerged and families developed. Western society required women to take a greater role outside the domestic sphere earlier on for survival in more difficult and less developed surroundings. Historians downplay the importance of other western victories in comparison to the work in California, emphasizing its significance in the region despite their lack of attention to the state in larger narratives. Gullett writes, "These lightly populated states commanded few electoral votes in presidential elections. Thus, women voters in Wyoming, Utah, Colorado, Idaho, and Washington had little influence in national elections." Suffragists realized that a California victory would be different because of the state's vast size. It represented a main focal point for suffragists.[12] Victory in California would be a major push forward for their campaign in the new era.

State activists came close several times to legislative victory but lost by a small margin. In 1893, the California legislature passed a bill that would recognize women's right to vote, but the governor vetoed it. In

1896, the issue made it onto the ballot as California Amendment 6 but failed to gain enough support. Gullett comments that after this loss, the movement struggled for a period. State suffrage groups lost many members until clubwomen took over leadership in the suffrage campaign. They helped to increase the respectability of the movement and worked with male reformers who also saw political corruption as an obstacle to their ambitions of creating a better world. The new suffrage leaders believed that winning woman suffrage could extend their greater goal of fostering "home protection."[13] Suffragists won further key political allies, not just among women but also among men, when they linked their movement to Progressivism in the twentieth century. They contributed to the "good government" movement in which suffrage was one of many desirable reforms designed to improve and "clean-up" California.[14]

By the time the CESL entered the state movement in 1908, California suffragists had transformed their campaign several times. The CESL contributed to the current iteration by becoming leaders in the effort to promote new rhetoric, where activists took older Victorian ideology that supported voting and revised it to fit the modernizing culture in California. The local CESL used two chief lines of reasoning that were popular among mainstream activists and extended them to recruit others of their class and background. One argument was that not granting women the ballot was unjust and went against the country's democratic ideals. An extension of that argument was that denying women the right to vote was especially unfair. It prevented women from having a voice in public issues over which female influence and expertise had always extended, specifically matters affecting the family, children, and the female sex.[15] Political participation in these realms would be a natural extension of women's existing family responsibilities.[16] Women, they argued, were more naturally suited than men to take up these causes because of their unique disposition and experiences.

These arguments showed up repeatedly in CESL presentations and events leading up to the 1911 state referendum. CESL activists saw the unfairness of political inequality and highlighted it in frank terms that called into question American values. At other times, they fell in line with the popular rhetoric of the mainstream suffrage movement in California during that period, one steeped in arguments that lauded women's differences and how these suited them to participate in public life, especially in terms of their political voice. In these cases, they emphasized, like other California women, that since women were "moral, altruistic, and civic minded" in ways that most men supposedly were not, they deserved the vote.[17] In the words of Gullett, suffragists of the day positioned themselves as "moral guardians," "city mothers," and "public servants" to fit within the culture of progressive reform.[18] They hoped to work with male progressives to build a new "civic area"—a political and public landscape in California in which men and women would work together for the long-standing but often obscure goal of the "public good."[19] Activists hoped that together, they could make California more "moral," "humane," and "harmonious."[20] They positioned women as key partners in this campaign. Activists argued that women were not trying to change society—such change was already taking place because of industrial capitalism. They were reacting to the changes and now needed the vote to be able to take care of their families in the modern world.[21]

Reflecting these arguments, Dr. Adelaide Brown, for example, the Northern California CESL vice president, wrote a lengthy article to the press in which she used both claims to support the vote. Her article began, "Equal suffrage, with a full recognition of duty to the state and an opportunity to share in the work of the state, is a matter of justice to the women of California." Drawing on democratic ideals, she questioned whether the public wanted to uphold them in the state. In California, "American freedom means political freedom for men only?" she posed. Should "taxation without representation" be as much a reality now for women who held property as it was in 1776? "Is this a true democracy?" she queried.[22]

In Brown's piece, titled "Mothers with Franchise Right Will Develop Better Citizens," she also appealed to women in California by using arguments about women's caretaking and mothering propensities and connecting them to the current realities of urban life. For example, she stated to her female readers that the "mental, moral, and physical welfare of the child is our inalienable right as women to be concerned about." She continued, "The normal center for woman's activities is the home, but its walls have spread over her town, her city and her state." The rise of industrialization and capitalism had naturally pushed women's concerns beyond the domestic sphere, thereby justifying their extended influence. "With the evolution of the home, the evolution of the great industries has gone side by side," Brown wrote. To take care of their families, modern women had to seek outside the home goods and services that they or loved ones had previously produced domestically. This change in production and women's extended influence as consumers in the modern economy naturally extended their sphere of influence. Brown commented, "She is no longer concerned with the condition of the well on her premises or the corn in her backyard, but depends on her municipality for the water and milk, etc., and therefore for the health of her family."[23]

Brown further argued that women deserved the vote, particularly on issues that directly involved their maternal role. "The public school takes her child for five hours a day. Has she not a right to co-operate on all the new lines in which popular education is extending? Is the mother not vitally interested in playgrounds, in popular lectures, in juvenile courts, in censorship of nickelodeons and the myriad of matters which concern her child in a large city?"[24] Brown went on to argue that men and women had "equal interest and pride in being American citizens" and that women, if given the ballot, as "partakers in the new democracy," would then have the political power to help improve their homes, the public schools, and the next generation of children.[25]

Other speakers similarly advanced these arguments. When Lida Munson Hume, a teacher and Oakland clubwoman, addressed the CESL, she argued that the era of women's confinement to the domestic sphere was "past" and that "there would be no return." A woman's "sphere now extends outside the home, and she is concerned with everything in municipal housekeeping." She argued that modern women were rightfully interested in "municipal improvements, parks, playgrounds, pure milk, streets, censoring picture shows and delinquent children." Their interest in these areas "has not perverted woman's nature," but the modern woman is "simply an enlarged edition of the old-fashioned mother, and the responsibility of modern municipal housekeeping is being gradually turned over to her by the men."[26] At another CESL meeting, May Treat Morrison, a wealthy philanthropist, told the audience that women had entered into "the commercial, industrial and professional life of the world," so that they "may now enter into the political life of the state for its civic betterment."[27] Londa Stebbins Fletcher, giving an open-air speech, stated, "They say a woman's place is in the home; that is true, but under modern conditions the home does not stop at the threshold of the house. The whole city is the home of the city resident." Fletcher thus underscored the theme that women's domestic role should be rightfully, and had been already, moving beyond the traditional realm of the household.[28]

* * *

Like others across the country, the California campaign was changing not just ideologically but also demographically in the early twentieth century. Before 1911, White middle- and upper-class women, who were often social reformers and temperance advocates, predominantly promoted the cause in the state. But in 1911, the campaign shifted to include more women of different ethnicities and classes. Activism entered the cities and rural areas more publicly and aggressively.[29] These measures proved crucial to victory, as did the state's changing political leadership, which in turn created new allies and recruits for woman suffrage. Political leadership increasingly transferred to the more progressive Republican Party that now recognized the women's voices and had the power to do something. Men and the wives of men of this party were now suffragists themselves. These changing factors made the college-educated women of the CESL valuable new allies in the movement and made their campaign welcome among other state suffrage organizations. The rural vote would carry the state suffrage victory in California; however, the activism of urban suffragists in groups such as the CESL helped to create new political alliances with men who would seek women's electoral support in the future and to develop political interest among the state's women. These alliances did not completely fade after the suffrage campaign ended.

Charlotte Anita Whitney, the local CESL president, was a chief advocate of the new state suffrage rhetoric and methods in California. A San Francisco native, she had graduated from Wellesley College in 1889 and worked as a teacher in Massachusetts and at the College Settlement House in New York City, where she became interested in improving conditions in the slums. A progressive reformer herself, she planned to pursue a career in social work upon returning home, and by 1911, the CESL elected her as leader and NAWSA as its vice president. Accounts described Whitney as an "indefatigable" worker, "a young woman of the finest femininity" with "much personal magnetism" and "great executive ability." She saw the value of suffrage for women and of building allies with campaigners who supported other reforms and political changes popular at that moment among the current dominant party. When speaking of the campaign, Whitney once argued inspirationally that for it to be a success, every worker "must believe in equal suffrage as a great, world-wide movement—an essential part of a moral and spiritual awakening; believe in it so firmly that faith begets courage and enthusiasm; and never forget that because it is a great educational movement, the foundation of work must be laid with all sincerity and truth."[30] These altruistic and idealistic claims reflected the culture of community betterment and uplift supported by many during the period connected with progressive reform.

Whitney embraced Park's vision for the CESL and a new suffrage group that was, in Park's words, "smartly gowned, softly spoken and intellectually advanced."[31] Women of the CESL such as Whitney saw suffrage as an "absolute necessity," given the current realities that the new generations faced. It was a quickly transitioning world full of vice and corruption to stamp out. They hoped to put the issue forward in a rational, poised, and broad-minded way that appealed to those in power.[32] Under her direction, the CESL became a leader among state suffrage bodies, perhaps because the league's women represented and embodied the ideal California campaigner at that time.

Like other alumni leagues, the CESL of Northern California was interested in how to best reach women with reputable public positions outside the home, such as social reformers and other professionals. The rhetoric described above worked especially well with these groups, given their politics and the educational and cultural schema within which they operated. But what set the Northern California CESL apart from many other suffrage organizations in California also hoping to reach the middle and upper classes was the special attention they placed on rallying teachers (a traditionally hard-to-reach group). They recognized that teachers would create a positive image for their state organization among the educated public, perhaps more than many others.

Most teachers had attended college, or at least normal school, by the early 1900s and thus could connect with CESL's activists because of their shared training. The league's members realized that although teachers were difficult to convert, earning their educated backing could be a powerful source of endorsement that would make the suffrage cause seem less controversial to politicians and the public and help introduce the issue into scholarly circles.[33] Teachers had essential community contacts in all classes and generations. Thus, as Whitney contended, educators' position could strongly influence local and future voters.[34] The California league put many resources into their recruitment.

Scholars such as Jackie Blount comment that although some public as well as private school teachers had become central supporters of woman suffrage in California by this point, much opposition remained in the profession.[35] Female teachers often were disillusioned with the inequalities that they faced on a day-to-day basis but reluctant to get involved in the suffrage campaign because of misconceptions and fears of retaliation by employers.[36] Historian Rosalind Rosenberg argues that dissatisfied teachers often set off to work for greater voting rights in their school systems if they engaged with the issue at all. They avoided participating in state and national suffrage campaigns.[37] Starting in the western states, movements and laws that would allow women school suffrage emerged in the late nineteenth century in response to the broader women's rights campaign and spread nationwide in the twentieth century. Other NAWSA groups attempted to recruit educators to the movement, albeit with limited success, in the nineteenth and early twentieth centuries. By 1910, local municipalities granted female teachers the right to the institutional franchise in twenty-four states.[38]

Some state suffragists supported these endeavors, backing initiatives to create institutional change and occasionally working to recruit participants to the broader movement. But organizers sustained few widespread mobilization efforts overall in local schools. Grassroots initiatives often were short lived and inconsistent and faded quickly as campaigners gave up in frustration. Either the administration barred teachers from contributing or more enticing activities that would propel them into larger-scale activism attracted their attention. Describing the difficulty in organizing educators, one CESL member wrote in 1911 that "among the teachers," activists frequently found "the inertia of the 'lay' suffragist," or those interested in the cause but whose "affairs made it impossible" for them to be "officially active in campaign work."[39]

In early spring 1911, the CESL in Northern California started a new canvas of public schools to try to gain support. They hoped that this

time would be different, given the changing politics and the new referendum campaign. Their engagement with educators would be more dili-
gent and comprehensive. From June to August, throughout the summer,
the CESL used various tactics to confront educators with their cause
and bring it into their consciousness in unavoidable ways. To take the
issue into the schools, the CESL announced that it would sponsor special essay contests on woman suffrage for schoolchildren in northern
counties of California. The league offered a total of 138 prizes, with the
largest monetary awards going to winners from San Francisco. They invited high school students to read essays at their meetings about why
women should vote.[40] The CESL's leaders went on to announce that they
planned to hold gatherings in the Palace Hotel in San Francisco during
the National Educational Association's convention there, to raise attention to their campaign and make opportunities for involvement more
accessible.[41] The group mailed cards that asked various questions, such
as whether teachers would join a suffrage organization or, if they did not
want to commit, whether they would still promote the women's rights
cause in other ways in their communities. Hoping to connect activists and teachers in a new amicable alliance, Whitney even offered the
CESL's headquarters as a meeting place for interested parties to discuss
the issue.[42] Dora Israel, the CESL's chair of teacher activism, by late summer, requested the consent of the relevant Boards of Education to hold
CESL assemblies at five institutions for a week during lunch hours when
schools, including local grammar and high schools, were back in session.[43] Activists addressed meetings of the local teachers' associations.[44]

Through these initiatives, some teachers who supported woman
suffrage came to view voting rights at the state and national level as a
new possible tool to help them achieve legislation that would support
greater occupational autonomy in an oppressive environment. Jackie
Blount points out that before the feminization of the teaching profession, many instructors, who were mostly male, had relatively unbridled
freedom in the classroom. By the late nineteenth century, however, as
more women entered academic occupations, there was anxiety among
men about the loss of their institutional control. Thus, men, often in
administrative positions, enforced new rules and stricter structures to
reassert their authority. By the twentieth century, female teachers had
been converted to the movement through many arguments, including

the persuasive stance that women's involvement in activism and reform, including the suffrage movement, could not only better society but also lead to changes that would help lift these restrictions and usher educated women into leadership positions in the schools.[45] Winning woman suffrage would benefit teachers in terms of their workplace conditions and their jobs.

Fannie McLean, the head of the English Department at Berkeley High School, became a prominent convert and CESL member who spoke to educators in practical terms. Her parents were well-off migrants from Connecticut. Her father, a graduate of Yale University, worked in insurance and real estate. McLean graduated from the University of California–Berkeley before becoming a local teacher at a one-room schoolhouse with forty students. She became a devoted speaker and organizer for the CESL, inspired by the group's message and known for rallying others with statements such as, "If we can teach voters, why can't we vote?" She felt that arguments against female participation in government that were based on how women's differences created unsuitability and intellectual inferiority were a farce. Excluding women from the electorate was a waste of intelligent citizens' potential.[46] She advocated woman suffrage to others in her profession by emphasizing the links between female voting rights and academic improvement.[47] McLean claimed frankly that woman suffrage would allow more female teachers to perform better in the classroom. She stated, "There are in the schools of California more than 10,000 teachers, of whom 85 percent are women. The teaching of civics is obligatory."[48] However, by not giving women political experience, lawmakers were affecting female educators' ability to do their jobs. McLean asked, "Is it fair to expect a woman, without the last sign of civic responsibility, the ballot, to possess such comprehending and practical knowledge of public affairs and machinery as future voters and office holders? Is such a teacher in a dignified position? How can she teach the fundamental principles of a democracy . . . when she herself has no vote?"[49]

The country's leaders asked female educators to present the nation in a democratic light and to celebrate popular American ideals in the classroom. However, at work, in public, and at home, women experienced injustice, inequality, discrimination, and a lack of representation. Some female teachers, such as McLean, contended that this inequality undermined their authority and their ability to uphold American ideals.

During the summer of 1911, the CESL further became a topic of conversation among teachers in the state because of the organization's successful recruitment of Margaret Haley as a touring guest speaker. Haley caused a buzz in educational circles and had become quite well known for her bold actions in Chicago in challenging corrupt companies. She was the daughter of a union activist and at sixteen years of age had become a teacher in the city's public school system. John Dewey's progressive politics and perceptions on education inspired her. Haley viewed unionization as the best method to improve schools and hoped that they would become increasingly democratic and less tyrannical. She "criticized the 'factoryizing' of education that turned the classroom teacher into an 'automaton.'"[50] She believed that through unionization, classroom teachers, rather than administrators and other authorities, would have a better shot at extending their influence and gaining a viable voice.

Unionization would contribute to professionalizing the field of teaching, she argued.[51] Her work led her to found the Chicago Teachers' Federation in 1898 and, most notably, successfully campaign to "win back taxes from corporations [who had failed to pay their share because of corrupt practices] and raise teachers' pay" using the new money generated. She encouraged the National Education Association to become more like a union instead of a special-interest group and to step up campaigns for higher salaries, tenure and pensions, smaller classes, and respect for its members among other professionals, which were issues popular among teachers.[52] These initiatives and the bold strategies that she used to pursue them, coupled with her victories in the courts, which helped funnel more money into the schools in Chicago and away from wealthy and corrupt local companies, made her a source of inspiration nationwide. As the *San Francisco Call* wrote when the CESL announced her involvement with their campaign, "Requests are already coming in from all over California, for the people of the state are eager to hear the teacher who cleaned up graft in the tax collector's office in Chicago."[53] Haley joined CESL members on a speaking tour of towns from Truckee to San Francisco. She attracted not only suffragists but also curious educators and those interested in the organized labor movement, inspired by her activism.[54]

* * *

By 1911, the CESL of Northern California, like the New York league, started to broaden the group's support by forming coalitions with ordinary workers in factories and companies outside of the more professional class. Gullett comments that as more women entered the workforce, suffragists started to believe that they were deserving of the vote, and their participation in the public sphere via labor justified their claim to the ballot.[55] They also came to see suffrage as something that could benefit all women "as a group," as Gullett wrote, and thus middle-class women needed working-class allies.[56] College women in California, as in other areas, were sensitive to the needs of women workers because they viewed themselves as women workers as well. As Gullett suggests, "They were influenced by the rising number of women attending college and the growing number of women who were entering the paid labor force."[57] All of this made cross-class campaigns seem more compelling.

Rather than surprising storeowners, interrupting workflow, or showing up at factory gates to make contentious pleas, the CESL maintained the respectable and orderly campaigns that the group, and the larger state movement, was known for. The league maintained a positive community image that was appealing to progressive politicians. That summer, the league joined forces with different local suffrage organizations mobilizing working women, such as the Wage Earners' Suffrage League (WESL), founded in 1908 in part by the efforts of labor activist Maud Younger. Younger, a popular suffragist and labor reformer from San Francisco, pioneered methods for suffrage activism among working women and had made a name for herself nationally a few years previously.

State suffragists had tried working with organized labor before in California, but they faced conflict. Lower-class women were suspicious of, instead of welcoming to, the middle- and upper-class activists. Gullett noted that in 1908, for example, Minna O'Donnell, a member of the women's auxiliary of the typographical union and then president of the Wage Earner's Suffrage League, spoke before the California suffrage convention and argued that she felt, based on current attitudes, that an alliance between suffragists and working women seemed "out of the question." The two groups had very different motivations for wanting the ballot. Working women desired it to better their own conditions and their own lives, while upper-class women wished for the ballot to help improve the lives of others and were out of touch with the realities that the working class faced, namely, what it really meant to be "wage earning."[58] Gullett wrote that women who represented trade unions also complained at the same convention that the upper-class women did not really care about their needs but "merely wished to gain their added strength of members."[59] By 1909, however, attitudes were beginning to change, and more campaigners put the ultimate goal of winning the vote above their own differences—recognizing the power that this could give any woman to change her circumstances.[60] In 1909, suffragists presented, as Gullett notes, a "united front" to the state legislature, and that front became even stronger in 1911.[61]

* * *

Maud Younger was a particularly talented and popular ally of mainstream suffragists and helped the CESL to generate support among women workers. Her father, a local dentist during her childhood, had raised Younger and her siblings after her mother died when she was twelve. Her mother left her a large inheritance that allowed her to pursue her education and social and political interests. In 1901, she moved to New York, where she worked in the College Settlement and as a waitress and a labor and suffrage activist. Eventually returning to California, she took what she had learned from the Northeast with her and became involved in union activity in the Sunshine State, eventually becoming a suffrage leader. Working with and studying women's conditions from the viewpoint of different socioeconomic classes, she seemed to be an effective intermediary for both sides. She became a friend of CESL cofounder Inez Haynes Irwin. After state suffrage passed in 1911 in California, she pushed especially hard to entitle women to an eight-hour workday and for other labor causes.[62]

Younger's organization and the local CESL planned mutual events and campaign tactics, like those of New Yorkers, to strengthen their ties. Notably, in early June, the CESL and the Wage Earner's League held a combined gathering at the MacDonough Theater and distributed pamphlets that relayed the pro-suffrage arguments of women workers and college-educated Americans. Speakers representing both groups shared the platform to demonstrate the bridging of the class divide to the audience, media, and members. Placards highlighting that "teachers, writers, taxpayers, social workers, mothers and business women" all wanted to vote were positioned in key locations.[63] At the event, CESL president Charlotte Anita Whitney told audiences that suffrage for women was "part of the onward rush of progress and enlightenment" and that the suffragists aimed to see that "every voter has been presented" in some way with a reason for supporting state legislation for woman suffrage.[64] Suffragists who represented those "connected with the universities" and "the schools" sat together with "those engaged in domestic and commercial life" in a public showing of solidarity, as activists had done in New York.[65]

In the summer, league members also obtained permission from business owners to present suffrage lectures to employees during down time and breaks, just as they had with teachers.[66] The press reported on the successful after-hours gatherings, which included nighttime meetings at factories and corporations such as the American Biscuit Company, where the league aided interested female workers in forming a suffrage club. Not long after, the press declared that the girls from the company were "not going to be kept out of the fight" and proudly displayed the "votes for women" buttons supplied.[67]

Mass media and new trends in consumerism shaped the new western organizing in California. Activists learned how to creatively use public spaces to promote their campaign in eye-catching ways to all classes but did not fuel demonstrations as fiery or contentious as those sometimes occurring in New York.[68] Activism in California was more innovative, creative, and artistic. Scholar Jessica Sewell noted that the league produced diverse literature in five languages—Italian, French, German, Portuguese, and Chinese—to reach the lower classes in the San Francisco Bay Area, sent propaganda to foreign language papers, and ventured into immigrant neighborhoods to attract new supporters for woman suffrage among people who might not normally have taken an interest in the college league's cause.[69] Santangelo writes that activists recognized that their gender, race, and class often made them outsiders in the streets in such urban locations, but they used that outsider status to their advantage to draw attention to their cause.[70] At other times, they found allies who could reach audiences as intermediaries between the two worlds given their background and training. The CESL recruited, for example, Ettore Patrizi, the editor of *L'Italia*, to help with work in the Italian quarter and give speeches in a foreign language.[71] Their scope was especially comprehensive, and this was in part because activists were increasingly diverse in background and in the skill sets that they had to offer the movement. Turn-of-the-century California not only had Europeans but also Asians, Latinos, and Hispanics to consider. These groups were in different ratios than in other areas. It also had a different climate that allowed for outdoor activism twelve months a year and for methods not always possible in the Northeast.

To appeal to workers, bosses, and consumers in California, the CESL especially used window displays in stores in heavily trafficked areas of cities to counter negative depictions of suffragists as masculine, out of date, and undignified and to raise support.[72] In August, the college league secured the right to construct exhibits in over fifty shops in the San Francisco Bay Area—window shopping was a popular hobby in the sunny city—dressing windows in a bright yellow, "the official suffrage color." Yellow had appeared everywhere by late summer: "Yellow fabrics of all sorts" appeared in dry goods shops and other downtown areas, and on Fillmore Street, Shreve's jewelry house had a display of yellow gems.[73] Suffragists used symbols, colors, and imagery to advance the campaign. Sewell commented that one popular suffrage poster that the CESL presented in its displays showed a feminine woman dressed in "Indian draperies" in front of the "Golden Gate," with a "setting sun" that appeared to form a "halo" around her head.[74] As Sewell noted, the poster portrayed the college league's campaign as relevant, youthful, welcoming, and womanly—a staple message that reinforced the idea that women could participate in public life and yet not lose their femininity.[75]

Equal voting rights or the possession of intellect did not make a woman less of a woman, and to show this, the suffragists used their feminine skills of decoration and adornment to beautify the public spaces of California. By the fall, the *San Francisco Call* commented that permission had been "secured by the CESL for the decorating of the streets with suffrage banners and flags," and that "pieces of bunting reminding the voters that the amendment election is to be held October 10 will be

Figure 2.1. The popular "Golden Gate" suffrage poster used widely throughout California. Photo courtesy of Schlesinger Library, Harvard Radcliffe Institute.

Figure 2.2. Front of a yellow CESL suffrage banner. Photo courtesy of Harvard University Archives and the Schlesinger Library, Harvard Radcliffe Institute.

Figure 2.3. Back of a yellow CESL suffrage banner. Photo courtesy of Harvard University Archives and the Schlesinger Library, Harvard Radcliffe Institute.

hung."[76] California activists were lauded by NAWSA suffragists for their use of media, decorations, and publicity and their production of leaflets, flyers, and other propaganda to support their cause. Their disseminations were diverse, artistic, public, and prolific. This activism made an impact on campaigners from other areas.

In addition to this work, the CESL of Northern California joined the Central Campaign Committee, a coalition of diverse state suffrage organizations that included the Wage Earners Suffrage League, to address activism among male voters and politicians leading up to the suffrage referendum in the fall of 1911.[77] During the early fall, to celebrate the CESL's participation in the new alliance, the college league and its working-class allies built an elegant float for the San Francisco Labor Day parade that highlighted how the ballot would benefit modern women. The display included figures of female employees labeling fruit cans, operating ribbon counters, using typewriters, and wearing nursing uniforms and university caps and gowns. As historian Rebecca Mead describes it, to dramatize their point, diverse suffragists surrounded the float with signs stating, "These women need the vote."[78] The exhibit made a powerful statement to voters about the common motivations of female citizens who promoted woman suffrage to improve their futures and their working conditions. As Santangelo also argues, suffragists' participation in staging these types of city demonstrations helped to normalize women's place in the streets and the public sphere.[79]

In the fall, the CESL sent a new round of letters to government leaders in which they asserted that, "as college women," they were making "a direct appeal to the college men" for the vote.[80] They began an automobile open-air speech campaign, conducted for several weeks in September and October, which included a diverse crew of speakers who worked from the CESL's touring car. Parking in key public spaces, activists appealed to various audiences, from the educated crowd to the working class. The *San Francisco Call* commented that "the talks were along common sense suffrage lines." One speaker told wage earners, for example, "The working girl must go to her toll in the streetcars hanging on to the strap. Shall she have no voice in how the city shall regulate that car line?" She continued, "The wife of the working man shares his hardships with him, meets his problems with him. Shall she not join her vote with his in their mutual effort to better conditions?"[81] Most notably, suffrage events and activities concluded with a large rally in San Francisco, fireworks, and a band concert opened to the public and all supporters of their campaign that electoral season.[82]

On voting day, October 10, 1911, the league participated in poll watching with other city supporters, whereby volunteers stood at the "100-foot line," the closest that government officials would let activists come, to advocate their cause (California Proposition 4, Senate Constitutional Amendment No. 8) to male electors on the day that ballots were cast.[83] Requests went out by the CESL for four thousand female volunteers to stand at the polls on October 10. Over one hundred students from the University of California–Berkeley participated under the direction of the CESL alone. Participants were to hand out campaign literature near election booths and work as "watchers" during the vote count to ensure just methods once the polls closed. The volunteers worked in shifts, and organizers gave them cards to hand to voters. The methods endorsed by the CESL mimicked and expanded upon what suffragists had done in Washington State during the earlier successful western campaign for the ballot.[84] Their presence put subtle pressure on all involved. Their activism illustrates how suffragists learned and borrowed from each other. Members of the CESL argued that the reason why the suffrage legislation had typically failed in different states was political corruption, namely, "wholesale frauds in the election booths, bought votes and tyranny on the part of the men of the state."[85] Activists hoped the presence of impeccably groomed and intelligent women at the polls would dissuade the men involved from these types of nefarious activities and that their continued presence at these events would help to assert their place in the electorate. Santangelo writes that suffragists' strategies at the polls also helped to "pull back the 'veil' from the voting booth" and allow the women to get up close and personal with the political process.[86]

At first, the news from the polls seemed bleak. In the urban area of San Francisco Bay, voters defeated woman-suffrage legislation (62 percent against versus 38 percent for), and in Los Angeles, it had only passed by a small number of votes, despite strong support among progressive men and women. Believing that they had failed, some activists allegedly began contemplating another campaign. But much to their surprise, when "late reports" from rural areas, where opposition was much less organized and well funded than in cities, started to come in, the vote began to switch in their favor. Counting and collecting the results took several days. Woman suffrage passed in California by only 3,587 votes, with a final total being 125,037 to 121,450. According to scholars, victory in California was particularly important because it meant that the number of women who could vote in the United States would double.

The city of San Francisco would become "the most populous city in the world in which women could vote."[87]

Although the legislation passed by only a small margin in the end, the continued pressure from all California suffragists resulted in the celebrated state legislation granting women the ballot in 1911. This was a nationally venerated moment for suffragists, as California was a large and politically influential area. In San Francisco, women had carved out a clear space for themselves in the public sphere and had convinced many of their sex to take an interest in political issues. In the aftermath, the local CESL reorganized to become the California Civic League to register female citizens to vote and educate them about the process. The grassroots group helped set a precedent for the later work of the League of Women Voters after 1920.[88] Statewide, suffragists celebrated, and in addition to engaging in citizenship-education work, some activists left California to help with campaigns in other states that seemed close to victory or supported the federal amendment work of the larger NAWSA.

Although their state suffrage campaign had concluded, other women and men who supported the cause stayed active via different groups and channels to ensure that the government equally incorporated women into the state's political scene. For example, as Gullett writes, "Although California women won the right to vote in 1911, male lawyers and judges successfully contended that this did not grant women the right to serve on juries." This was just one way that the government continued to politically exclude women. Women had to work for that goal until 1917, and it took time for them to gain other political positions.[89]

The success of state suffrage legislation in California, however, raised morale and reinvigorated the CESL's campaigns in other areas. After hearing of the victory, Massachusetts suffragists staged a victory party in Faneuil Hall, at which Park supposedly stated, "I'm just standing on my head with joy!"[90] The victory reminded college-educated suffragists of the power inherent in presenting a united front among women of different backgrounds and the effectiveness of mass media. The new CESL alumni league campaigns nationwide continued to focus on ways to broaden the organization's support among the targeted classes of both White professionals and White workers. Alice Stone Blackwell, one of Park's early role models and mentors and then editor of the *Woman's*

Journal, a key suffrage paper, commented publicly on the victory, saying that California was "the greatest single advance that the suffrage movement in America has yet made."[91]

* * *

Although the college league found quick success in northern and western cities, members struggled to gain backing as they moved south. Early alumni branches emerged in Louisville, Kentucky, and New Orleans, Louisiana, but they fizzled out quickly.[92] In New Orleans, Park had difficulty getting an alumni branch off the ground. After her visit in 1909, local suffragists planned to meet in the city, but little came of it.[93] Scholar Joan Marie Johnson comments that Ann Hero, a Louisiana native, Vassar graduate, and chemistry professor from Newcomb College, was chosen as the New Orleans leader (possibly because of her connections to university students and alumni and her experience as head of the local Southern Association of College Women).[94] Despite these credentials, no political propaganda from the city's league or mention of the group's activism was recorded in prominent community newspapers or in the CESL or NAWSA records. Around the same time, Park laid the groundwork for another alumni league in Louisville. No information appeared concerning the organization's activities in records or publications, other than a mention of its formation. Outside New Orleans and Louisville, the CESL and the NAWSA referenced no other viable southern alumni league development.[95] Although creating a viable and long-lasting CESL alumni league did not prove to be an effective tactic for the organization, the group did help inspire student activism for women's right to vote on some southern campuses, such as Tulane University and Newcomb College, which contributed to campus campaigns for the vote and helped to support federal amendment activism after 1917.

Many factors could explain the CESL's trouble in the South, including differences in how the women's movement came about in the region. As scholars such as Anne Firor Scott argue, in many southern states, the trajectory of woman-suffrage activism diverged from that in the North and the West, as southern women were slower to campaign for full voting rights, given the heavily patriarchal society.[96] The post–Civil War influx into southern states of northern White women and upper-class southerners with a northern education was a central force that powered local movements for woman suffrage during the late nineteenth century. These migrants introduced new ideas about gender roles and responsibilities. Though a few southern suffrage associations emerged in the 1880s, scholars have claimed that the woman-suffrage movement did not become popular in the region until the 1910s. Many grassroots groups developed during the period to support women's right to vote nationally, as victory seemed inevitable.[97]

Because southern women had a plethora of domestic options for participating in the campaign by the 1910s, northern CESL organizers who hoped to establish new branches of their associations in the South faced obstacles in communities often unwelcoming to the outsiders. In the final decade of the woman-suffrage campaign, southern White women in New Orleans, for example, could belong to many groups headed by Louisiana women, which they preferred to groups headed by northern CESL activists. The city had several well-established social and civic reform organizations that endorsed woman suffrage, including the Era Club (sometimes written as ERA Club, referring to Equal Rights Association or Equal Rights for All).[98]

The Era Club attracted many prominent, wealthy, socially engaged, and well-educated women in New Orleans, the heart of Louisiana. The organization's roots trace back to 1892, when Caroline E. Merrick, an elite clubwoman and social reformer, had helped to form a group called the Portia Club in the city, which became an early affiliate of NAWSA. The goal was to prove to political men that women were civically astute and engaged and ready for the responsibility of the ballot. Wanting to focus on more than just suffrage legislation, other activists, including the sisters Kate and Jean Gordon, created the Era Club to focus on advancing not only the suffrage amendment but also progressive reform, particularly city improvements. In 1896, faculty from Newcomb College became involved with the group. The Gordon sisters remained influential leaders of the Era Club during the suffrage campaign and well known in national suffrage circles. They gave several presentations promoting women's right to vote to audiences at Tulane University and Newcomb College. They also helped to organize debates and competitions for students. They even became involved with a campaign to have women accepted to the Tulane University School of Medicine. However, over time, they had ideological conflicts with NAWSA leaders who focused on the federal amendment, which was unpopular among many southern suffragists interested in preserving states' rights and White supremacy.

Gordon did not believe in extending voting rights to African Americans and was overtly racist in her declarations about and advocacy for local voting restrictions based on race. "I feel that if the franchise comes to women of the South through the state and that we can continue the present restrictions, there will be no trouble for the negro women, but if by any chance the national amendment does carry, I think there will be trouble for them."[99] She went on to argue that if woman suffrage was initiated by a national amendment, the heightened racial prejudice that would result from the passage of woman-suffrage legislation would undermine the positive effects. Her comments foreshadowed an increase in southern racial tension.

Multiple branches of state suffrage associations affiliated with the NAWSA emerged in the 1910s, offering southern women other options. Members of the Portia and Era Clubs had helped to form the Louisiana Woman Suffrage Association in the late 1800s.[100] The region's women backed the Southern States Woman Suffrage Conference (SSWSC), a group dedicated to state over federal suffrage for women and critical of NAWSA; Kate Gordon swung attention toward this group over time.[101] Still other women chose adversarial groups such as the Woman Suffrage Party of Louisiana, which believed in a federal amendment and thereby presented a challenge to Gordon and others.[102] Because of these organizations' local power and leadership in New Orleans and the South, they drew backing away from outsider groups such as the CESL. Local campaigners were skeptical of outsiders because of long-standing regional divides that continued after the Civil War and irrepressible differences in culture that did not die. All aspects of life, including in social and political movements, reflected these divides.

* * *

Despite difficulty gaining southern support, the CESL of Boston had announced that the organization as a whole had grown nationally, expanding nationwide to twenty-four alumni leagues (and twenty-five college chapters) by around 1910, with additional branches emerging all the time.[103] Boston suffragists noted that the climate was changing in Massachusetts, in particular, creating new opportunity for the campaign. While opposition remained strong among antisuffrage organizers, many Massachusetts male politicians, including most state Democrats and about half of Republicans, were starting to support the campaign.[104] By 1913, the Massachusetts branch of the CESL also had over 450 members, in part because of the leadership of women like Park. Even when she was not contributing to the CESL, she helped the state movement in other ways, such as by creating "street corner amateur nights," whereby women new to giving public suffrage lectures could practice their skills on Boston streetcorners with their colleagues.[105]

Refocused on ways to increase membership in the Northeast, where the group found the most receptive audiences, beginning in 1914, the Boston CESL recommitted to carrying out new research and coalition-building work with groups of working women whom the activists had been slow to reach in past periods. By that time, the college league worked more closely with the Massachusetts Woman Suffrage Association (MWSA; also an affiliate of NAWSA), which had modernized and expanded its campaign to include more laborers (especially among Jewish, Irish, and Italian immigrants), connect with new trends in using mass media, and tap into progressive reform, although not as successfully as in California and New York because of the staunch opposition. State activists became well known for using outdoor tactics, such as hot air balloon and wagon platforms and trolley and automobile tours, to reach broad audiences in urban areas and make headlines for their activism.[106]

Impressed with the college league's campaigns, the MWSA officially appointed CESL members, who had risen over the past few years to become respected experts in the grassroots movement, to lead the MWSA's local presswork in the new era and become the mouthpiece of the more public movement.[107] The CESL handled many tasks for the MWSA, including monitoring local newspapers for writings on suffrage, producing pieces for publication, and managing literature and sales at headquarters.[108] The league also managed a poster prize contest, a candy table at the Bay State Suffrage Festival, and refreshments at a suffrage performance called the "Ballet of Sylvia," and provided workers for the Boston Suffrage Shop on Tremont Street.[109] They used these events to gain publicity and distribute printed media. Often, the state's flock of young suffrage newsies, who sold the *Woman's Journal* and were sometimes college students who took this job for the larger MWSA, aided their activism.[110]

The Boston branch gathered new data on attitudes toward woman suffrage among college-educated Americans to help the MWSA and scope out new areas for activism. The CESL wanted to discover why more college women and men had not joined their group in 1914 and to assess areas for future campaigns. In late spring, league members canvassed six thousand Massachusetts college women unaffiliated with their association by sending out leaflets promoting woman suffrage, announcements about meetings, and postcards with the following questions: "Are you in favor of Equal Suffrage? Are you indifferent? Are you opposed? Are you willing to join the College League?" To the CESL's surprise, more than half of the responses reflected support for or interest in their organization, signaling that tides were changing.[111] The Boston CESL followed up on this activism with another survey to find out how much the attitudes of the respondents had changed one year later, especially among Massachusetts graduates. Most of the alumni declared that they would back the college league, reflecting shifting attitudes among the college-educated population and hope for future success.[112] Massachusetts suffragists promoted the "door-to-door" recruitment and mass mailings of suffrage publications and postcards in various languages to investigate public opinion and invite locals to events.[113]

* * *

Trends in New York were like those in Massachusetts. Suffragists found in a survey of three thousand college alumnae conducted the previous summer that 77 percent of those polled supported woman suffrage, 13.5 percent were opposed, 8 percent were indifferent, and the rest came back undecided.[114] A survey conducted in the spring of 1914 had also shown robust support among those in higher education. "More college professors in this State are in favor of woman suffrage than against it," one report commented. Out of 400 professors polled, 258 declared that they supported the woman-suffrage movement.[115]

By 1915, Katrina Brandes Ely Tiffany had become president of the New York City branch of the CESL, and state suffragists prepared for another major grassroots campaign for women's right to vote under her direction. Tiffany, a graduate of Bryn Mawr College and wife of the wealthy Charles Lewis Tiffany, grandson of the founder of Tiffany and Co., seemed to be the perfect new leader. She maintained connections with higher education circles through her work with the Bryn Mawr alumni organization and had an active public life, being known for contributing to multiple charitable causes. She also had prominent connections to the business world through her family. The *New York Times* referred to her as "one of the best known of New York's suffragettes," her background making her supportive of the work that Jessie Ashley had begun with the league and of efforts to reach out to the workforce.[116] When speaking to the media about the CESL, she declared that the organization was made up of "particularly active women, the majority of whom are self-supporting," busy but ready to support the various New York suffrage organizations and their activities.[117]

Leading up to the state referendum, the CESL joined the Empire State Campaign Committee (ESCC), a coalition of local supporters united in the fight for woman suffrage in New York (as activists had seen the value in coalition building via the California example and of collaborating via their early work with Blatch and the ELSSW, despite tensions). They dedicated themselves to publicly calling attention to the injustice of female disenfranchisement.[118] Under the auspices of the ESCC, the CESL continued the goals of challenging electoral exclusion with new allies and of further urging government leaders to address the position of the suffragists right away. The CESL staged several headline-making protests under the ESCC's direction to underscore the hypocrisy of denying women the right to vote and to emphasize the urgency of the cause to improve women's conditions. As Santangelo writes, suffragists in New York "jockeyed for center stage" with political men via these initiatives. They worked like other NAWSA suffragists to turn the organization into "an institution more palatable to the general public."[119] The New York CESL increasingly did this, not only using more practical and democratic arguments but also, like others, creatively asserting a space for themselves in the urban environment and the male professional world. These actions helped to normalize the role of the politically engaged and publicly presented female citizenship via tactics used by suffragists in many cities, and especially prominently in New York. Santangelo comments that New York suffragists hoped their public campaigns would help to not only gain women the ballot but also "change their position in the metropolis."[120]

New York suffragists, like those in California, worked at different moments to recruit educators to the campaign, and the local CESL's efforts were only enlivened by outcomes in the West. The local CESL also realized that educators were a potentially strong group of supporters and hoped to spark and maintain their interest in the suffrage cause in the new era. As Santangelo notes, "Although far less wealthy than socialites, educators constituted a significantly larger pool of potential allies" in the New York movement. "Fifteenth thousand women taught in New York City public schools, constituting 87 percent of its instructional force."[121] CESL leaders realized that these women were an important target audience for their activism. They could help with larger mobilization efforts among these constituents, especially through work that involved emphasizing how the vote could increase pay for and promote greater gender equality in the educational sector. For example, the vote would help teachers push for other issues, including married teachers' rights and maternity rights.[122] In 1914, the National Education Association's resolution supporting woman suffrage bolstered the CESL's campaign among teachers nationwide.[123]

By this point, the NAWSA sanctioned a plan for new work in the educational realm (and even formed a special Committee on Education in 1907). New York activists followed suit to make sure that women were brought up in the curriculum, among other efforts aimed at reforming education to help socialize Americans from a young age into believing in a broadened definition of "citizen."[124] In January, the New York representatives of this committee (in a CESL-headed initiative) embarked on a campaign in the city (along with the People's Political Equality League of Kings County in the state) to get more schools named after key women to emphasize to the public that women had always been important players in shaping the nation. The CESL conducted research that showed that out of 250 schools in New York, communities named only sixteen after women, and then worked to produce a list of prominent women to present to the boards of education as names they should consider for schools. These names included female figures such as the writer Louisa May Alcott, the lighthouse keeper Grace Darling, the astronomer Maria Mitchell, and the nurse Florence Nightingale. Activists also lamented that among the schools named after men, too many took the names of military heroes, and hoped to include women who had made important contributions to society in other ways.[125] The CESL updated the list and edited it to share publicly with administrators. The ESCC commissioned the initiative, backed by Catt. The initiative had the potential to remind the community that women deserved the vote and to influence the minds of the younger generations who attended the schools.

* * *

As news of the onset of the Great War in Europe started to flood the American media and headlines in 1914, activists started to rethink their campaign. They included more protests that highlighted inequality and the hypocrisy of government policies, which flew in the face of foundational democratic values and made the country look weak to the international community. That summer, CESL members staged a dramatic demonstration when they marched to the Naturalization Court in New York City to make a theatrical plea for woman suffrage to local politicians. CESL members arrived in caps and gowns and suffrage sashes at the federal building, where immigrant men gained citizenship. New York CESL president Katrina Tiffany and her supporters entered the courtroom in silence. Merely observing, the league members wanted to stress to the state government and voters through their presence the "humiliation" that college-educated, native-born women felt by being denied equal suffrage "when the full right to the franchise" was "given to any alien" who would answer "a few simple questions" and "comply with a few requisites of residence."[126] After exiting the building, some CESL representatives spoke to the media about the silent demonstration, saying, "Less than three minutes to make a man a citizen, and he is a foreigner . . . and we women, whose fathers fought and bled and died for the U.S., work years in vain and must plead to this foreigner to grant us a voice in our own country. Could anything be more desperately unfair and humiliating?"[127] Reflecting an anti-immigrant bias and the ongoing ethnic and racial tensions in the city, this attention-generating protest questioned current laws and dramatically urged the state's leaders to reconsider the subordinate position of the intelligent upper-class female citizens in America, given the nation's history and chief ideals, especially at such an internationally compelling moment. It also highlighted the way that activists strategically changed their activism to relate and appeal to the audiences that they were hoping to reach at that present moment—in this case, elite White male politicians, and the voting public. It showed that sometimes activists took not just a racist but a nativist approach in order to win support by any means necessary, even if that meant at times alienating others, a major shortcoming of the movement. These types of divisions among women activists would only become more pronounced after the passage in 1920 of federal amendment legislation, preventing a unified and strong women's movement for decades into the future.

Not long after, the CESL signed a declaration created by the ESCC titled "An Appeal for Liberty" that targeted New York's men and ran in local newspapers close to the anniversary of the signing of the Declaration of Independence. The document, addressed to the men of New York State, employed democratic and well-known historical rhetoric to support women's voting rights. The CESL decried "taxation without representation" as "tyranny" and insisted that all people, including women, deserved a say in a government whose laws everyone was required to follow.[128] Still, reflecting a more elitist perspective, the league fell back on emphasizing female difference, mentioning that in most jurisdictions, the current electoral legislation grouped women with minors, aliens, and criminals. However, unlike many individuals in these categories who could eventually gain a political voice, female citizens could not. The pamphlet explained, "The minor receives his freedom at 21, the alien may be naturalized in 5 years, the criminal, the briber may be pardoned, and thus all escape from the dishonored class of the State's disfranchised, except women. For them, there is no open door to political liberty."[129] Returning to a more egalitarian tone, the document then called for suffrage on behalf of all female citizens, from college graduates and teachers to ordinary workers and mothers, not just upper-class White citizens. Alluding to the nation's founding, the document concluded, "Justice Gave You the Vote. In the Name of That Same Great Virtue, We Ask You to Give It to Us!"[130] The suffragists dramatized their appeal by visiting the Statue of Liberty and making a spectacle among the tourists to be sure to get into the newspapers and by using the holiday to dramatize their pleas for political change.[131]

The CESL of New York's significant final contribution to the 1915 state referendum campaign involved poll-watching activities to pressure local voters into backing woman suffrage, as in California. The ESCC sent CESL representatives to different parts of the city to stand in front of voting places and encourage men to cast favorable ballots. Some female college graduates handed out literature, while male alumni assisted the Men's League for Woman Suffrage by traveling to polling places to check on the work of election officials.[132] The local newspaper described the scene in Syracuse: "Dozens of gay society women—dozens of the earnest club women, many mothers and grandmothers, many women high in both women's and men's professions, were included." Suffrage headquarters

> buzzed with excitement as succeeding delegations of girls and women went to relieve others who had been for hours at the polls. Dozens of university women trooped to the headquarters to offer their services as "minute women," who were willing to devote as much of their day as possible to the cause. They were whisked to all parts of the city to stand in front of the polling places to urge the voters to vote for the amendment granting suffrage to the women of New York State. Banded together, these girls wore their suffrage colors and gave evidence of their affiliation with the College Equal Suffrage League. They were among the most enthusiastic workers of the day.

A fleet of "automobiles flying the colors of the Women's Political Union, purple, white and green and the campaign colors of gold and blue of the Empire State campaign committee, scurried to various parts of the city, carrying new workers to the polling places" to support their work. Members of the Men's League for Woman Suffrage assisted in helping the women and making sure that the public treated them with respect.[133]

Although the ESCC, CESL, and other local suffrage organizations encouraged voters to stand behind their cause, their campaigns were not enough, and the 1915 referendum in New York failed. Over 700,000 voters rejected the legislation statewide, including around 320,000 voters in opposition in "Greater New York."[134] Scholar Doris Daniels argues that suffrage activism was unsuccessful in part because the cause competed for attention with a proposition for a new state constitution, and this allegedly distracted voters.[135] Santangelo comments on the plethora of different suffrage organizations in the city alone and how much "interborough organizational rivalries" created divisions among activists. New York City campaigners further seemed to diverge from the wider vision of the NAWSA at times, with tensions among figures such as Catt, Blatch, and others.[136] These divisions affected campaigners' ability to create a united image and put forth a strong front. As seen in the CESL's early protest at the Naturalization Court, a certain amount of ethnic and racial tension did not completely disappear and kept some New York activists divided, possibly delaying progress in the city because the pro-suffrage front—despite becoming stronger—was not sufficiently united to be persuasive. In the aftermath, as Santangelo argues, suffrage leaders', such as Catt's and Blatch's, public statements included xenophobic comments that "blamed immigrant men," particularly Poles, Italians, and Germans, "for the loss."[137] Nonetheless, activists learned lessons from the 1915 campaign that they would successfully draw on in the future.

In Massachusetts that same year, the suffrage amendment to the state constitution also faced defeat again (two years in a row for activists), and this time by a margin of 132,000 votes, sending activists back to the drawing board. A total of 35.5 percent of voters supported the legislative change to enfranchise women, and 64.5 percent voted against it.[138] According to scholar Sharon Hartman Strom, by this point in the state, the amendment was supported by Socialists, Progressives, Democrats, the State Federation of Labor, and even the new Democratic governor, David Walsh.[139] One major reason for the state suffrage failure in Massachusetts was that the state harbored one of the best-organized antisuffrage campaigns. As in California, significant opposition came from men concerned about how voting women would influence the liquor industry. Strom calls Massachusetts "the eastern locus of anti-suffrage sentiment" despite it being "the home of a dynamic and politically sophisticated state suffrage movement."[140] Opposition was so strong that "suffragists in Massachusetts expected to lose the referendum battle" at the state level.[141] By November 16, 1915, two weeks after the referendum on November 2, Massachusetts suffragists held a conference at Faneuil Hall in Boston and decided to turn their efforts to activism to support the federal amendment campaign, an endeavor that NAWSA and Carrie Catt increasingly urged to the state's women.[142]

* * *

By the time of the 1915 referendums in New York and Massachusetts, college-educated African Americans joined the grassroots suffrage movement in almost every location, but they still faced strong discrimination from White organizers. Leading Black intellectuals, such as minister Francis J. Grimké (a relative of the famous southern sisters Angelina and Sarah Grimké, who supported women's rights and abolition in the nineteenth century), also took advantage of the historical moment. They played on the campaign culture to relay to African Americans that denying woman suffrage went against seminal documents such as the Declaration of Independence and the Constitution. He commented, for example, "To deprive her [a woman] of the right to vote is to govern her without her consent, which is contrary to the fundamental principle of democracy."[143] Grimké, a graduate of Lincoln University of Pennsylvania and Princeton Theological Seminary, worked as a pastor at the Fifteenth Street Presbyterian Church in Washington, DC, where he was recognized as one of the most influential local civil rights leaders, helping to found prominent organizations such as the National Association for the Advancement of Colored People.[144]

Black activists commonly evoked the legacy of prominent African American freedom fighters to bolster their cause. One New York Baptist minister wrote, "To force any class of citizens to pay taxes without representation is a scandalous subversion of the principles of American government, a principle for which Crispus Attucks and thousands of others willingly gave their lives."[145] Attucks, a multiracial escaped slave, became the first casualty in the conflict between the Americans and the British that would become the Revolutionary War when he was killed during the Boston Massacre. Black intellectuals framed the movements for women's enfranchisement and African American civil rights as part of a larger human rights struggle, even a global emancipation movement, dating back centuries. Through the prominent publication *The Crisis*, which he organized, internationally respected African American NAACP leader and Harvard University graduate W. E. B. Du Bois reminded readers that a larger campaign for the rights of all Americans, "without respect to color or creed," was at stake again with the woman-suffrage issue.[146] Scholar Garth Pauley wrote that several issues of the magazine backed his position and reprinted text from an NAACP resolution sent to the NAWSA for a joint campaign proposing that suffragists and civil rights activists unite because they were "fighting the same battle" against disenfranchisement.[147]

Debates over woman suffrage in the African American community sometimes turned into larger conversations about how the government needed to uphold the true meanings of long-standing post–Civil War-era laws, such as the Fourteenth and Fifteenth Amendments. These discussions spurred Black suffragists into bold action to challenge the denial of citizenship and voting rights. In 1908, the African American Equal Suffrage League of Brooklyn even sent a petition to the US Senate and House of Representatives, asking them to pass the controversial Bennet Bill, which was sponsored by a New York representative and would punish southern states for discriminating against Black voters by decreasing their representation in Congress.[148] Using decades-old "justice" or equality reasoning to support actions like this and declaring all existing disenfranchisement undemocratic, African Americans, inspired by the suffragists' work, renewed conversations about female voting rights in their communities, linking the battles against gender and racial discrimination. Their approach created a compelling rationale for college-educated African Americans, aware of and knowledgeable about existing controversies and past events that affected their race, to support woman suffrage.

African American alumni who backed the cause often also had their own unique motivations. They argued that all Black men should be key allies because they could relate to the political discrimination faced by women. For example, in 1915, Robert H. Terrell, a graduate of Howard University School of Law, prominent lawyer, judge, and educator from Washington, DC, and the husband of Mary Church Terrell, leader of the National Association of Colored Women, noted, "Of all the elements in our great cosmopolitan population the Negro [man] should be most ardently in favor of woman suffrage, for above all others, he knows what a denial of the ballot means to a people. He has seen his rights trampled on, he has been humiliated and insulted in public, and he has brooded over his weakness and helplessness in private, all because he did not possess the power given by the vote to protect himself."[149] Suffragists cautioned that African American men's failure to back women's voting rights would only reinforce White southerners' prejudiced suppression of Black electoral power and further "relegate the race to political slavery."[150]

College-educated supporters spoke out to ameliorate tensions between Black men and White women that might prevent endorsement. "We tend to oppose [woman suffrage] because we do not like the reactionary attitude of most White women toward our problems," Du Bois once commented.[151] "We must remember, however, that we are facing a great question in which personal hatreds have no place."[152] As scholars reason, to calm friction between the two groups, W. E. B. Du Bois framed his plea for the endorsement of the woman-suffrage movement by gently dismissing any racist activists as merely "misguided."[153] Du Bois pointed out that the discriminatory tactics and arguments of some suffragists in the White women's rights campaign drove the movement backward instead of forward.[154] He asked members of his race to rise above the prejudiced actions and attitudes of some White organizers and endorse woman suffrage for its potential to improve the lives of all Americans. He claimed that the denial of female political equality was as unjust as the denial of voting rights for African American men. Both were unfair prejudices that he believed all in the Black community should help stamp out.[155]

By the 1910s, eager to see victory secured, Black activists stepped up their emphasis on the numerous potential advantages to African American women of getting the vote and doubled down on claims that the entrance of this group into politics would uplift the race. Extending the franchise to Black women, they stressed, would weaken White supremacy because giving all African Americans the ballot would double the Black vote, increasing the likelihood of the government passing new civil rights legislation.[156] Scholar Garth Pauley comments that Du Bois placed educated Black women at the core of his "Talented Tenth," which referred to exceptional African American citizens whom he believed could lead the race and create improvements if given greater political power.[157] Some supporters stressed how many Black female philanthropists, social reformers, political activists, and respected teachers stood to gain the vote if new legislation succeeded, and these women could secure advances for African American communities.[158]

However, Deborah Gray White argues that Black women and men had different relationships with each other compared with those of White women and men. Gender dynamics between the races varied. More Black women viewed themselves as equal to men of their race earlier

Figure 2.4. W. E. B. Du Bois, a key leader in the Black community who spoke out on many issues, including woman suffrage. Photo courtesy of National Portrait Gallery, Smithsonian Institution.

in history. She writes, "This sentiment did not grow out of the tradition of enlightenment rationalism or the liberal tradition it spawned. Rather, it was based on the knowledge that Black women, just like Black men, had endured incredible hardships during slavery and that neither sex had gained any advantage in the nearly two and a half centuries of enslavement." Some Black clubwomen were very critical of Black men, whom they suggested had accomplished little to uplift their race. Thus, they asserted that the future of racial progress was in Black women's hands.[159]

The equal franchise would give Black women a more powerful voice in matters that affected their personal lives—matters White male politicians had previously decided for them. Suffragists of all races imagined that the right to vote could safeguard female sexuality and reproductive rights. NACW clubwomen were especially interested in the avenues Black women could take to secure greater protections against rape and illicit sex because club members viewed "moral purity" as central to African American social mobility; they felt their race made them even more vulnerable to attack than White women were. According to White, ideas about "moral superiority" were tied to conceptions of the Black middle class. White Americans rose in society through economic and professional avenues not always available to African Americans because of racism. As a result, in Black society, citizens gained "middle-class status" less through economic and professional standing than through a "style of life" or by embodying certain "manners," "morality," and "a particular mode of consumption," as well as through participation in "race work."[160] If the franchise were used wisely, it could bring African American women "the respect and protection" they needed by serving as a new "weapon of moral defense" to fight for fair treatment in the many sexual assault cases. They often lost because of racism, sexism, and political corruption. The vote would combat discrimination based on race and gender so common in the government and courts.[161] As one suffragist commented, the ballot promised to give Black women the political means to challenge the "men who place[d] no value on her virtue."[162] The vote could give Black mothers the authority to support other legislation that would also benefit their families and neighborhoods, such as stricter laws curbing public vices, including prostitution and alcoholism, by helping close barrooms and red-light districts.[163] These changes would benefit not only Black women but all African Americans.

Some college-educated Black citizens maintained that Black female voters would be more effective than Black men at the polls because women would be more resistant to the political corruption, bribery, and violence that hindered the electoral power of their male counterparts. According to this argument, history had shown that Black male voters were innately less moral and more likely to face coercion to sell their ballots than women would be. Suffragists who fell back on conventions about the superiority of all women asserted that because of their integrity, fewer female citizens would succumb to manipulation.[164] Suffragists also contended that African American women would be more likely to vote because their gender would protect them from the same electoral abuses and forms of intimidation used by Whites to block Black men from casting their ballots. White men pervasively employed overt violence to restrain Black men from voting in different areas, but suffragists argued that they were less likely to use these public assaults against African American women, even in the South, where racial violence was rampant.[165] Du Bois explained, "Even southern 'gentlemen,' as used as they are to the mistreatment of colored women, cannot in the blaze of present publicity physically beat them away from the polls."[166] Thus, if Black women gained the ballot, some African Americans believed that it would be more difficult to shut down their civic influence.

* * *

By 1915, a cross-racial initiative headed by the CESL's alumni leagues in areas such as New York again might have given the state campaign the boost it needed to move forward. However, the college association would not risk respectability by experimenting with this approach, and ultimately, they suffered. Because of the CESL's enduring limitations and exclusionary policies, the organization's city chapters of college graduates experienced problems. By the late 1910s, the league was not growing or expanding as much as other, more inclusive grassroots reform or political organizations. Frustrated with local campaigns and following the NAWSA's lead, many alumni leagues of the CESL gave up state suffrage drives and transitioned into federal amendment work.

NAWSA president Carrie Catt (reelected to replace Anna Howard Shaw in 1915 after returning from campaigns abroad) supported the push for the federal amendment. She traveled across the country to ask for support from local suffragists who lived in cities, such as Boston and New York, where woman-suffrage bills had not passed in their state and who were unlikely to prioritize work for the larger cause. The federal amendment became NAWSA's major focus by 1916.[167] At Ford Hall in Boston in February 1916, Catt met with local suffragists, including members of the CESL, to advocate strongly for national legislation. Her trip prompted the *Boston Sunday Globe* to officially announce that a "new campaign for suffrage" had begun.[168] Because of the event, the Boston CESL, joined by the MWSA and other local groups, planned mass meetings and conferences to support Catt's plan for a revitalized federal amendment movement beginning that year.[169] Later that month, the CESL held a meeting to discuss corresponding work in the state, and similar events followed.[170] After Catt's presentation, the Boston CESL's monthly gatherings included more speeches by guest lecturers on national, instead of state, organizing.[171]

New York suffragists, however, were reluctant to give up the grass-roots battle for state enfranchisement. Despite the 1915 loss and Catt's instructions, many women's rights activists remained hopeful for a possible 1917 victory. In 1917, the suffrage issue would appear on its own ballot, and other matters, campaigners hoped, would not distract voters. President Woodrow Wilson and all the major New York political parties now backed equal franchise, ensuring the cause's visibility among state leaders. Scholars note how the powerful political machine of New York City, Tammany Hall, even adopted "a position of true neutrality" toward woman suffrage by the latest campaign instead of outright opposition, fueling local optimism.[172] New York suffragists planned to take a different approach to the 1917 referendum campaign. After holding a reorganization convention following defeat in 1915, they decided that instead of focusing on winning support in the city, organizers would center their work on generating backing in rural areas and parts of the state previously ignored, following the example of activists in California.[173] As Santangelo has written, in this new campaign, state suffragists focused on "intensive work reaching every group of citizens."[174] This activism produced new awareness for the woman-suffrage cause across New York, and that year, the CESL held meetings in smaller urban centers and towns where they formed additional branches and headquarters in places such as Ithaca, Buffalo, and the Mohawk Valley.[175]

However, despite these efforts, after the 1917 referendum campaign had concluded, electoral statistics showed that it was the urban vote that drove the New York victory, unlike in California. Local activists had secured enough robust support, alliances, and public attention over the years to generate strong success in the city, which helped to carry the favorable tally and convince the state's men in other locations to support the cause. Victory in New York ended a seventeen-year grassroots campaign by the CESL and a nearly seventy-year battle waged by women's rights groups in the state.[176] Members of the CESL, NAWSA, and other women's rights organizations coast to coast celebrated a second major milestone in the campaign in the 1910s. After the suffrage successes in the large and politically powerful states of New York and California, more Americans, including those in higher education, viewed the victory as inevitable and opened their minds to reconsidering the cause.

* * *

At the state level, by 1910, not all NAWSA activists used a united rhetoric to get to this place, however. Expediency arguments to win the ballot focused on female difference and superiority, which became popular at the turn of the twentieth century among activists, but this was just one tactic used to sometimes convince elite audiences to support woman suffrage at the grassroots level. Northeastern suffragists in New York and Boston also often took a bolder approach to activism. This approach included using more sensational protests and practical rhetoric to advocate for equal franchise among diverse Americans. In the years leading up to 1917, as world war expanded, it just as often, if not more often, relied on what scholars would term "justice" claims to support the right to vote on the basis of women's equality with men and democratic principles.

In the West, where social reformers still dominated the women's rights movement in the early twentieth century, the CESL's organizing was more cautious. Although California suffragists bridged class divides in local campaigns, overall, they remained concerned about maintaining respectability and appealing to nativist male progressive politicians. Activists continued to advocate more often for a greater civic role for women based on the argument and tactics that underscored how suffrage was an inevitability, given the current realities that women faced. Suffrage represented a natural, fair right deserved by the modern woman who wanted to care for her family and community in the modern world. The state suffrage movement in California was particularly pathbreaking in other ways, however, setting precedents for later work in other areas such as New York and Boston because of its artistry and creativity. CESL cofounder Park lauded the work of this group and the model it created, which drew in diverse women and key allies such as teachers.

By the end of the first decade of the twentieth century, the CESL gained the acknowledgment of NAWSA leaders, appeared in the headlines of many newspaper articles, and caught the attention of alumni and the larger educational community nationwide. The grassroots popularity of the CESL's alumni branches and the league's successful city campaigns encouraged students to request that the leaders take their activism to college campuses and pushed NAWSA authorities to eventually invite the organization to join the group in the national political arena.

3

"The Obligation of Opportunity"

In April 1914, Barnard College faculty member and alumna Juliet Stuart Poyntz, who helped form the CESL's campus suffrage club, submitted a striking editorial to the literary magazine, the *Barnard Bear*. Poyntz noted a positive change in attitudes toward women's rights on the New York campus. The school's suffrage organization grew impressively from 1909 to 1912, rising from "ten or fifteen much abused members" to "one hundred and one highly respected members."[1]

By 1909, Columbia University, the school's male coordinate institute, had also formed a Men's Equal Suffrage League, whose membership was increasing.[2] Reflecting on the favorable sentiment, Poyntz remarked, "It seems difficult to believe that only seven short years ago it required considerable courage, or as the unfriendly might call it, 'nerve,' to take a decided stand for woman suffrage. This was conspicuously true even in such an enlightened institution as Barnard College." She continued, saying that when the school's first suffrage club formed, "The intrepid few who composed it were distinctly made to feel by the rest of the college that they were regarded as 'queer,' as lacking in balance and altogether abnormal." If "asked with withering sarcasm" whether one considered herself a suffragist, for most, this amounted to a "purely rhetorical question": "It was of course quite without the bounds of possibility that any decent, self-respecting Barnardite . . . could be a 'suffragette.'"[3] Poyntz's comments about a change in opinion toward woman suffrage did not pertain to Barnard College alone. These observations reflected larger national trends.

From 1905 to 1917, the CESL initiated a new level to their campaign for woman suffrage by moving from organizing alumni in urban centers to also rallying students on school grounds. In doing so, the league became a significant force for changing attitudes toward female political rights in higher education. Student suffrage clubs sprang up throughout the United States, inspired by the groups' campaigns. Some clubs remained separate organizations, and other clubs became official affiliates known as "college chapters." As Jana Nidiffer argues, these organizations were some of the earliest female political groups formed at colleges and universities in the United States.[4] Their members avoided marginalization and rejection by conforming to the academic culture. Through academic-style organizing, such as staging essay competitions, student debates, and guest lectures, and later strategically becoming part of existing college political traditions and events, suffragists used education as a tool to win support. They worked within traditional gender and class hierarchies on campuses to carve a place for the movement. At institutions where lasting student clubs inspired by the CESL formed in each region—such as Radcliffe College and Harvard University in Massachusetts, Barnard College and Columbia University in New York, Newcomb College and Tulane University in Louisiana, and the University of California at Berkeley—CESL campaigns contributed to the Nineteenth Amendment's passage by turning campuses into new training grounds and protest sites for the next generation of suffragists.[5] In the words of the Harvard Men's League for Woman Suffrage, the group helped to add "young blood" to the suffrage cause, which was at that moment "so welcome."[6]

By studying the CESL's campus campaigns at different institutions nationwide, this chapter challenges common depictions of early university women as largely apolitical and mostly self-involved. Considering campus campaigns outside the commonly examined northeastern women's colleges—at men's institutions and at coeducational public universities—reveals that women's rights activism was much more popular among students in higher education and influential on campuses nationwide by the early twentieth century than often argued. Female students were much more engaged in the causes that affected their communities and the larger world. The CESL's university organizing helped to politicize more second- and third-generation college women and strengthen their interest in government and reform. The vibrant activism that emerged at universities because of the CESL's campaigns changed the culture of higher learning and the women's movement in often-overlooked ways. This activism, for example, helped the CESL's alumni leagues to cultivate a scholarly, more respectable voice for equal-franchise organizing and set precedents for future youth mobilization for women's rights on

campuses. The campaigns fueled broader struggles against sex discrimination in the academy. Through their activism, in addition to sidewalks,
department stores, and government buildings, twentieth-century suffragists turned college classrooms into important protest sites for the
women's rights movement. They carved out an important new arena for
their organized campaign in higher education.

* * *

One reason why Park and Irwin's CESL faced opposition and why the
suffrage movement seemed so controversial on campuses in the early
twentieth century was that women's advancement in higher education
was still relatively new. Many people viewed association with this cause
as already controversial and radical and avoided adding to it by taking up another contested issue. Despite advances, some Americans still
viewed schooling for women as a frivolous and superfluous expenditure.
They believed that the nation's women belonged in the home rather than
in the classroom.

Certainly, they did not envision a place for women in politics and voting. Advances in thinking and opportunities emerged slowly. As many
historians highlight, in the colonial era, women's educational opportunities were restricted to the learning necessary to read the Bible and
to teach their children important knowledge, such as moral education.
In the aftermath of the Revolutionary War, some Americans supported
female literacy and learning to fuel the concept of republican motherhood, a role for women in the new nation wherein they would respon-
sibly cultivate their sons for good citizenship and promote enlightened
ideals in the household.[7] However, few formalized options existed for
women seeking an education in the United States before the Civil War.
Most local schools did not admit women until the late eighteenth and
even early nineteenth centuries in the United States. There were often
limitations on their attendance; for example, they were often only allowed to attend during certain seasons or months when men engaged
in other activities.[8]

The common school movement of the antebellum period, which
pushed opportunities for women's education forward, opened more
public schools (elementary and secondary) to women in different states,
but educational inequality between the sexes was still a reality in many

areas. Horace Mann, an educational reformer from Massachusetts and a leader of the common school campaign, helped to feminize the teaching profession and support training schools for women educators by arguing that women, whom he viewed as more moral than men, were natural teachers.[9]

The first institutions of female higher education in antebellum America were typically seminaries, normal schools, or religious institutions. They offered women advanced instruction for participation in theological or teaching careers. Scholars comment that these early institutions, primarily developed in the North and West, provided a limited curriculum to small numbers of admitted students working toward a specific career path.[10] Former first lady Abigail Adams once commented, speaking about the academic training available, that education for women in the best situations before the Civil War "went no farther than reading, writing, and arithmetic and, in some rare instances, music and dancing."[11] Adams and others suggested that the programs of study offered at many female seminaries, even premier institutes such as Emma Hart Willard's school in Troy, New York, Mary Lyon's seminary in Holyoke, Massachusetts, and Catharine Beecher's academy in Hartford, Connecticut, failed to measure up to similar institutions for men.[12]

Prospects for women's educational advancement also were bleak in the South. Upper- and middle-class White women seeking advanced instruction beyond developing basic literacy chose from a network of finishing schools. Other types of female academies were not popular in the region, and like their northern counterparts, they had limits. For example, scholar Christie Farnham explores how even exceptional institutions, such as Georgia Female College, created in 1839, which claimed to provide attendees with advanced training in writing, reading, arithmetic, science, foreign language, and various arts like music, fell short when compared to opportunities available for men.[13] One frustrated woman who attended a finishing school in Charleston, South Carolina, in the early 1800s commented that she felt that she came out with little beyond "knowledge of sixty different lace stitches."[14] More recent works by scholars reassess the value and significance of these early institutions. For example, Margaret Nash argues that early educational institutions helped to provide women with the important skills and knowledge to create the economic circumstances and lifestyles central to their increasing class and hierarchical mobility.[15]

Facing greater prejudice, African American women had to search even harder for facilities that offered scholastic preparation to their race and sex. During slavery, education for African Americans was minimal and often covert. Masters feared that it would inspire rebellion, and it was illegal to teach slaves to read. Blacks hoping to learn basic literacy skills either taught themselves or relied on sympathetic and progressively minded Whites. Much of this early education was informal, with some exceptions, such as Prudence Crandall's efforts to create a female boarding school and later academy that welcomed African Americans in Canterbury, Connecticut, in the 1830s. Opponents ultimately shut down the school. Abolitionists and Quakers established some integrated schools in northern areas such as New York, Pennsylvania, and Massachusetts.[16] There were few formal schools for Black southerners. Notable exceptions included opportunities created by civil rights supporters like John Chavis, a free African American, who organized classes for Blacks in the evenings when Whites were not at a local school in Raleigh, North Carolina. Other African American children managed to learn basic reading and writing from Sunday School programs and benevolent religious groups willing to teach Black slaves. After the Civil War, supporters of emancipation created Freedmen's Schools to educate African American citizens. Black women also enrolled in normal schools for teachers, institutions to train nurses, or special educational facilities like the Tuskegee Institute, established in 1881 to prepare young African Americans with the skills to establish other successful careers.[17] More advanced options, like Howard University (established in 1867) in Washington, DC, emerged in the late nineteenth century. Most Americans perceived women's entrance into these establishments as avenues through which to create better wives, mothers, and teachers, regardless of race, rather than as opportunities to cultivate ambitious female scholars who might later seek diverse public vocations or greater political rights.

Several colleges and universities experimented with new programs for women by the mid-nineteenth century, inspired by the early female seminaries and normal schools. In 1837 in the Midwest, Oberlin College became one of the earliest academic institutions to offer university training to young scholars of different races, classes, and genders. Scholars write that the school developed special routes for female pupils to enter higher learning by allowing women to enroll in the standard curriculum or take a "Ladies Course" tailored to their sex.[18] Antioch College became another of the earliest institutions to accept undergraduates of both genders into academic programs beginning in 1853. Administrators maintained a respectable public image by creating a policy that allowed male and female students to intermingle in the classroom but kept them apart in most other campus spaces.[19] The passage of new government legislation spurred the creation of coeducational public institutions open to women for the first time at midcentury.

The enactment of the Land-Grant College Act (Morrill Act) in 1862 provided federal funds to support the construction of agricultural and mechanical colleges, many of which expanded to include liberal-arts-type curricula for both sexes. Resources made available by the legislation assisted with the founding of public schools, such as the University of California at Berkeley in 1873, which approved women's entrance into academic programs early in the institution's development. However, as historians argue, the first college women faced rampant sexism on campuses because of the prejudiced policies and discriminatory attitudes of peers and personnel. When Berkeley opened, the university lacked undergraduate dorms or adequate facilities for extracurricular activities. College administrators prioritized events and services for men, marginalizing those for women because of the limited spaces and resources.[20] Female students chose to attend state and public institutions like Berkeley regardless of these restrictions because public universities were a more economical choice than most private academies. Scholar Andrea G. Radke-Moss argues that despite restrictions, Western women successfully managed to carve out a place for themselves on campus and challenge sex discrimination.[21]

Much scholarship explores how factors such as the Civil War, social and political activism, economic change, and international trends in education spurred the development of pioneering private women's colleges by the late 1800s in response to women's increasing bids for greater rights and entrance into the public sphere.[22] Historians assert that these single-sex institutions thrived in the eastern and southern regions of the United States, where prominent all-male schools had dominated the collegiate scene for decades. They offered an educational experience increasingly comparable to that given to men.[23] Well-respected schools for under-graduate women, such as the highly regarded "Seven Sisters," gained pop-ularity among the upper and middle classes. These establishments were careful to emphasize that they sought to preserve femininity while offer-ing vigorous academic training.[24] Schools like Radcliffe, Barnard, and Newcomb were some of the earliest private women's colleges to flourish in the late 1800s. Historian Helen Lefkowitz Horowitz writes that Rad-cliffe started as an annex in 1879, so that women barred from attending Harvard University, founded in 1636, could take college classes near the thriving urban center of Boston, Massachusetts. Administrators tried to keep the school as inconspicuous as possible by holding classes in a large, discreet residential building that looked nothing like a typical campus structure. The institution's success led to Radcliffe's expansion into a full-fledged college affiliated with Harvard in 1893.[25] Barnard had a similar history, founded as a separate educational institution for female students in 1889 and an educational home for New York women restricted from earning degrees at Columbia.[26] The development of Barnard differed from that of Radcliffe, however, in that administrators attempted to in-crease the institution's visibility as a marketing strategy, which would gain rather than deter new public support. Founders pushed for the school's affiliation with the men's university early in the college's development so that undergraduates could obtain access to numerous resources and na-tionally renowned instructors at the large men's campus.[27]

Lynn Gordon writes that the establishment in 1886 in New Orleans of Newcomb College, one of the premier options in the South for women, developed because of the campaigns of women's rights activists such as Susan B. Anthony and Julia Ward Howe. Anthony and Howe traveled to the city in 1884 for the Louisiana Cotton Exposition and gave speeches promoting female equality. Howe inspired local southerners to consider the ways in which women's production of art and crafts could offer a route to greater female independence. Two major organizations formed, inspired by their message, to make special training available to those women hoping to hone their skills: the Ladies' Decorative Art League and the New Orleans Art Pottery Company. Leaders pushed to institu-tionalize their programs for women at Tulane University, an elite educa-tional facility founded in 1884 that admitted only male students. When Tulane administrators first rejected their proposal, Ida Richardson, a local woman married to one of the school's trustees, convinced philan-thropist Josephine Louise Newcomb to fund the creation of a separate female academy. The institute that she helped to produce, Newcomb College, offered some of the most respected art education courses for women in the United States by the time it became an all-female affiliate school to Tulane.[28] The founding of prominent women's colleges like Radcliffe, Barnard, and Newcomb in the late 1800s revolutionized higher education by creating new options for women's academic advancement more equivalent to those offered to men. Most scholars dismiss or over-look these institutions as significant protest sites for women's rights in the late nineteenth and early twentieth centuries because of supposed disinterest among American college students and opposition from fac-ulty, staff, and administrators.[29]

Most scholars contend that woman-suffrage activism failed to gar-ner much undergraduate support before 1915.[30] The first-generation college women in the Victorian period supposedly came from mod-est backgrounds and sought skills that would allow them to get better jobs. They prioritized academics over other causes. Preoccupied with their coursework and with proving that they belonged alongside men in higher education, early college women avoided distractions like cam-pus political events. Scholars maintain that a lack of interest in women's rights activism continued among second- and third-generation female students. The large number of middle-class and wealthy women attend-ing colleges by the turn of the twentieth century, reportedly, perceived higher learning not as a necessity for starting a career but as an opportu-nity for attracting a partner. They concentrated on recreational activities and dating. When organizing for various social or political causes, their campaigns supposedly aimed at improving campus life rather than at external issues.[31] Scholars suggest that students interested in suffrage generally only came from certain places—particularly the Seven Sisters schools in the Northeast—where large communities of progressively minded female faculty and students made ideology about gender equal-ity fashionable in earlier periods.[32]

* * *

Most Progressive Era college and university campuses did in fact have no significant organized pro-suffrage presence in the nineteenth century.

After 1905, when the CESL started its campus campaigns, the college league helped to initiate a robust and often overlooked movement of support among students in varied places. The grassroots nature of the group's activism, which rarely made newspaper headlines given its educational form, supported state movements for the vote. Before the arrival of the CESL at colleges, many suffragists, including CESL members, dismissed or overlooked campuses as campaign spaces because of the apathy and opposition they expected. In Massachusetts, CESL leaders Park and Irwin experienced firsthand as did students themselves, how advocating for women's higher education was controversial enough to some people on campuses, without adding an endorsement for women's right to vote. An assortment of groups, from eugenicists and nativists to scholars and politicians, stressed that higher education for female students endangered the stability of society. College training led respectable young women into spinsterhood rather than into finding husbands and starting families. The data collected on the lifestyles of early alumnae from schools such as Radcliffe, Barnard, and Newcomb only raised the anxieties of Americans who opposed opportunities for women in the public sphere because they showed that university women delayed marriage and motherhood. Association with the women's rights campaign thus could further damage a student's or an institution's reputation, given suffragists' open and ongoing challenges to gender norms.[33]

Starting in 1905, Park and Irwin's perspectives about campaigning on campus changed when undergraduates from Northwestern University persuaded them to reconsider their avoidance. Northwestern undergraduates formed a suffrage club that year and asked to affiliate with the CESL.[34] The club's request (the first of its kind) to form a college chapter motivated Park and Irwin to pursue greater support at colleges and universities. They hoped to make similar recruits. Their campus campaigns engaged not only college women but sometimes even college men, creating an additional new constituency for the movement nationwide.[35]

One of the CESL's chief goals was to recast its activism in an academic rather than a political light to fit within the new campus environment. Park and others recognized that "the conditions of academic work" made it "desirable" for college chapters to focus on "educational rather than political" goals.[36] CESL members framed the woman-suffrage issue on campuses as a question for young scholars (both male and female) and characterized existing opposition as a matter of inadequate knowledge. Members promoted student clubs as study associations rather than political protest groups in order to gain institutional approval. Stella Bloch, a leader in the Barnard Suffrage Club, when planning the student organization, reassured skeptical New Yorkers that her association would avoid any "serious propaganda work," such as protests, rallies, or parades.[37] She sought to distance the suffrage club from rowdy and disruptive demonstrations since many citizens perceived these protests as distracting and inappropriate for college students, especially young women. When publicly announcing plans in 1910, to allay concerns, she reiterated the popular belief that "outside ideas should not trespass too much on studies."[38] Bloch stressed that participation in the Barnard Suffrage Club would not pull students away from academics but would enrich them. The names suggested for the group, including the "Club for the Promotion of Intelligent Interest in the Woman's Movement" and "Beyond the Ballot," reaffirmed the organization's educational focus.[39]

Newcomb College students similarly asserted their academic ambitions when they formed their campus association four years later, insisting that they would gain support through "steady, quiet, long-continued pressure and not violent, sensational measures."[40] The club would encourage an academic analysis of women's rights issues in a "sensible way."[41] Students at Berkeley announced in the school newspaper that they had created a suffrage "Study Club" and that "the purpose of the club is to study the question of woman suffrage in all its aspects."[42] "Membership in the society means not an assent to the doctrine of equal suffrage, but rather an interest in and knowledge of this big problem of the day."[43]

Early popular methods of activism on campuses were those that encouraged undergraduates to study campaign literature and cultivate their own positions on woman suffrage. College chapters aimed to promote the "self-education" of members by urging students to read important documents, such as the "classical arguments" and "recent records" of state and national activists. These activities included reviewing the reports from NAWSA conventions and copies of suffrage speeches reprinted in the newspapers.[44] Berkeley students even subscribed to the *San Francisco Call* and the *Woman's Journal* to read the latest suffrage news.[45] Newcomb students acquired "a large supply of literature of various kinds, even some anti-suffrage papers," to be sure that members could "read both sides of the question."[46]

From early years, the CESL planned scholarly activities for students to showcase their knowledge, such as campus writing and debate competitions that contributed to their efforts to cast their organization as instructional and in line with the academic mission. Suffrage essay contests took place in many formats. One early and well-publicized competition, sponsored by the Boston CESL alumni branch for college students in 1902, even before the development of the CESL's college chapters, invited undergraduates from local institutions, including Tufts College, Boston University, and the Massachusetts Institute of Technology (MIT), to submit essays between four and six thousand words. Participants selected from prompts, such as suffrage "as an influence on the home [or] the individual and the race" or "from the economic standpoint." The first-prize winner received seventy-five dollars.[47] Student groups also arranged smaller-scale contests to interest peers. At Radcliffe, college suffragists developed a competition asking for essays between five hundred and one thousand words to support female voting rights. Winners received less lucrative though still substantial prizes, such as $2.50 (around $70 today).[48]

Suffrage debates on campuses were diverse in style. CESL supporters encouraged, facilitated, and helped to organize competitions among students. Interested undergraduates from one club might form teams to take up different perspectives on woman suffrage to debate among peers or for an invited CESL or NAWSA representative. Students from several clubs might face off regarding each side of the question. Throughout the early twentieth century, Radcliffe students from the suffrage and antisuffrage chapters of the Civics Club participated in many oratory contests on female voting rights.[49] Student debates sometimes brought undergraduates from several campuses together for large, intercollegiate contests. In Northern California, where multiple institutions with active CESL college chapters existed in proximity, students from different institutions united. Berkeley's students developed teams that went up against others from nearby rival institutions, especially Stanford.[50] Triangular debates on suffrage among interested undergraduates from schools such as Yale, Harvard, and Princeton were popular in the Northeast and

covered in the media.[51] These oratory and essay contests helped legitimize the discussion of women's right to vote in higher education and
provided important opportunities to train young activists. Beyond focusing on the potential national effects of granting women the franchise,
suffragists challenged undergraduates to consider the state and local
outcomes. They asked students at Tulane and Newcomb, for instance, to
contemplate how woman suffrage would influence Louisiana women's
lives. At Radcliffe, suffragists used more personal themes, asking com-
petitors to respond to prompts such as "why I am a suffragist" or "why I
am an anti-suffragist."[52]

College debates and essay contests were distinct from off-campus
competitions because of the standards used to evaluate the participants.
Suffragists, like educators, viewed "matter and thought" as components
"more important than form" when assessing responses from the students. According to the CESL, one of the first steps to becoming an effective campaigner was developing the "ability to explain on one's feet
why one was a suffragist."[53] At an event in which Yale debaters faced off
against debaters from Harvard, the newspaper reported that in render-
ing their verdict, the judges decided not by the merits of the debate or by
the question itself. They focused on debaters' knowledge of the subject,
the logical sequence and skill in presentation of evidence, and the power
in rebuttal. They assigned no definite valuation to the style and convey-
ance of the speakers.[54]

Like other progressives and social reformers, suffragists staged public lectures, addresses, and presentations at colleges with professional
speakers to educate about their campaign.[55] The CESL's presentations
became supplemental avenues through which to learn about women's
political status since the existing university courses rarely addressed the
struggle for female voting rights in depth. The league's lectures picked up
for students where traditional avenues of scholarly inquiry often left off.
They offered an overview of women's current status, rights, activism, and
history.[56] The CESL leaders' strategic choice of lecturers helped to gain
respect for their addresses among academic audiences, given the obstacles that many scholars have identified as permeating the campus environment.[57] Suffragists who spoke on campuses conformed to an ideal
image of femininity and respectability promoted by the college league
and needed to exhibit suitable appearance, behavior, and credentials.

Activists strove to illustrate that "higher education and true woman-liness" were not "antagonistic."[58] They aimed to attract speakers who were "calm, gracious," and "essentially feminine" and who would help the CESL with efforts to "reflect credit upon Suffragettes as a whole"—speakers who would not give "just cause" for opponents to argue that "suffrage detracts from the womanly side of a girl's nature."[59]

Suffragists invited to campuses seasoned American speakers with impressive résumés. At Radcliffe, audiences heard presentations from highly regarded activists, leaders in NAWSA or state suffrage parties, such as Florence Hope Luscomb.[60] Luscomb was an alumna of MIT and executive secretary of the Boston Equal Suffrage Association for Good Government (BESAGG). Her feminine demeanor, articulate speech, and notable credentials made her an ideal campus speaker and a palatable role model for female students.[61] Luscomb was a committed suffragist from a young age when she attended women's rights presen-tations by Susan B. Anthony and Julia Ward Howe in Boston with her mother. Well known in Massachusetts for her work in the state, among many accomplishments, she helped gather ten thousand signatures on a suffrage petition to prove to local politicians that women wanted the franchise and mobilized workers to support the cause.[62] Luscomb orga-nized for the CESL while still in college at MIT (giving suffrage lectures and leafleting for the organization as an undergraduate) and adopted bolder protest techniques after graduation (participating in open-air speeches and marches). One of her most famous contributions was working for the *Woman's Journal* as a "newsie," distributing the suffrage publication near subway stations. She designed the suffrage bluebird symbol used widely in Massachusetts campaigns, which stood for "hope and optimism against great odds." Other activists later described her as the "youngest and most visible" of the suffragists in Waltham, Massa-chusetts, where she worked as an artist and architect.[63]

Suffragists were especially mindful of securing reputable orators when confronting college men, whose votes would be central to resolv-ing the equal-franchise issue. Harvard suffragists insisted that their campus group "must take pains that its guests are of the highest char-acter and intellect."[64] Campus suffragists recruited only "authorities in the field," including Anna Howard Shaw, a Boston University gradu-ate, medical doctor, and ordained minister who served as the NAWSA president from 1904 to 1915 and supported Park and the CESL for many years. She was a common college speaker. Madeline McDowell Breckinridge, a Kentucky social reformer educated in Connecticut at Miss Porter's School who had attended a Kentucky state college before becoming the NAWSA vice president from 1913 to 1915, was another key speaker.[65] Student leaders rejected candidates who failed to measure up, and their careful selection of speakers helped legitimize the women's rights movement in higher education.[66]

As the campaign progressed, leaders like Park, who, while on her NAWSA-funded trip abroad extensively studied the international conditions women faced, also recognized the benefits of highlighting global connections among suffrage movements.[67] An avid traveler, CESL leader Park encouraged students to consider the suffrage cause in a larger context to make it look less controversial. "Everywhere," she remarked on her return, "I found that there is an unrest and an aspiring after better things among women."[68] By 1909, the CESL had foreign suffragists addressing college students and held campus meetings with overseas lecturers to shed new light on suffragists' collective efforts worldwide. The CESL's primary international recruits represented non-militant women's rights organizations from England, who could reach college audiences in the United States by discussing British campaigns and providing contrast to reports of the violent suffragette protests. As one activist explained to Barnard students, "American newspapers have highly exaggerated the stories of suffragette riots; in almost no case have women performed the startling deeds attributed to them by the American press."[69] The Radcliffe Equal Suffrage Club similarly stated that it hoped its presentation "corrected many ideas concerning the 'suffragettes' which exaggerated and unfair newspaper accounts have produced."[70] A guest speaker at Newcomb focused on the "injustice of condemning a worldwide movement because of the indiscretion of a very few hysterical enthusiasts."[71]

By 1909, women's rights activists in the United Kingdom made headlines internationally for their controversial "war" waged against men for sex discrimination. The Women's Social and Political Union (WSPU), formed by social reformer Emmeline Pankhurst (educated at a ladies' finishing school in Paris) and her two daughters, Christabel (a graduate of the University of Manchester) and Sylvia (a short-term student at the Royal College of Art), adopted militant tactics to lobby politicians for the ballot. The WSPU promoted the slogan "deeds, not words" and used dramatic and sometimes destructive tactics to demand woman suffrage immediately. These tactics included breaking windows, burning and bombing buildings, hunger striking, and interrupting government proceedings and public events.[72] The WSPU campaigns, however, were the exception rather than the norm.

Most British undergraduates who were active in the woman-suffrage movement during the early twentieth century participated in less controversial activism. College students at the University of Cambridge formed the Women's Suffrage Society (CUWSS) in 1908, which developed from the smaller Newnham and Girton College equal-franchise organizations. The CUWSS affiliated with the National Union of Women's Suffrage Societies (NUWSS), an umbrella organization, like the NAWSA, that used an array of campaign tactics that were public and modern but not incendiary when compared to the WSPU's. Methods ranged from hosting guest speeches and participating in debates to organizing traveling tours and marching in parades. Approximately three hundred CUWSS members joined a suffrage procession in 1908. One of their banners included the words "Better Is Wisdom Than Weapons of War," which reflected the group's advocacy of education as their chief political tool. Students used school papers like Newnham College's *Thersites* to spread the news about their activism, and the group's membership totaled over six hundred by 1909.[73]

The English cousins Rachel Costelloe and Frances Elinor Rendel toured the United States extensively to represent the CUWSS and its work for women's rights to members of the CESL and NAWSA. Costelloe (later Strachey), a mathematics student, had been active in the campaign since 1907, when she participated in the "United Procession of Women," a peaceful London march planned by the nonmilitant NUWSS. Strachey and Rendel, school friends, attended events together. It was said that Rendel helped to get Strachey involved in the campaign.[74] At college and university lectures in the United States, they tried to improve the image of the woman-suffrage movement by emphasizing that the controversial suffragettes overseas were the minority in the United Kingdom. Most British activists mirrored their American counterparts in political style. Costelloe insisted to audiences at Tulane, for instance, that she was "a peaceful, ladylike suffragist" who had never stormed the House of Commons or courted arrest, contrary to popular images of many English protesters.[75] To establish credibility, Costelloe declared her preference for reason and persuasion over extreme demonstrations.[76] The women described instances of nonthreatening activism in Britain, including caravan rides through the English countryside.[77]

Costelloe argued that the media often overestimated the suffragists' culpability when trouble broke out. Usually, she argued, "A little woman would stand quietly at the end of the hall and exclaim: 'Votes for women,'" and a commotion followed.[78] Costelloe blamed this disorder on unruly onlookers and not the typical English suffragists. Despite being a more moderate suffragist, Costelloe noted that she still encountered her fair share of hostility when publicly campaigning for the vote. Regardless of her self-proclaimed amicable approach, she faced "rotten eggs, dead fish and decayed vegetables," all cast at her indiscriminately by spectators, just as they tossed these items at other suffragettes.[79] This image of the pleasant and reasonable British activists cultivated greater respectability for the CESL's mission.[80] In the aftermath, the *Barnard Bulletin* reported that the women offered "a breadth and sanity of outlook" and "practical knowledge of English conditions." They had "a bright and genial optimism" and were "delightful" guest speakers.[81]

American lecturers were equally cautious when framing their messages for college audiences. When challenged with explaining any foreign controversies to student audiences, these orators used their addresses as opportunities to recast notorious incidents and their orchestrators in a more respectable light. Shaw once told Newcomb undergraduates in 1910 that some suffragists in England went to extreme measures to make politicians aware of their positions because the situation for women in Britain was far worse than it was in America. The English government denied female citizens many freedoms of expression that their American counterparts enjoyed, rationalizing their behavior.[82] She noted the example of the notorious English organizer Christabel Pankhurst, known as "Queen of the Mob," with the hopes of explaining her actions.[83] Violence remained "the only thing left" for British women like Pankhurst because they were stripped of all political voice, even the right to petition by deputation. Under such stifling and harsh circumstances, she argued that for women like Pankhurst, "only stones could get into meetings" and make an impact.[84] American suffragists, Shaw insisted, did not need to resort to violent tactics because women in the United States had many more effective and respectable options for advocating their political agendas.

All suffrage lecturers encouraged students to support women's right to vote as a progressive and relevant cause that would improve their lives and the future. In 1909, when New York activist and CESL ally Harriot Stanton Blatch commandeered a physics lesson on contemporary technology at Barnard in a comical manner, she transformed the class into an opportunity to promote woman suffrage as a natural part of modernity. She showed up in the transmitter building during a demonstration for students studying "wireless telephony."[85] She spoke to the surprised academic audience, telling undergraduates, "I stand for the achievements of the twentieth century. I believe in its scientific developments, in its political developments. I will not refuse to use the tools, which progress places at my command. I will make use of the telegraph with or without wires, the telephone with or without wires, anything and everything, not forgetting that highly developed method of registering my political opinions, the ballot box."[86] Through such interjections, suffragists like Blatch connected their cause with innovation and progress. She emphasized that female citizens belonged alongside men in the public sphere in an advancing society and that a vote for woman suffrage represented a vote for the future. As one guest speaker told an audience of Berkeley students, "This is a problem about which no educated woman can afford to be ignorant."[87] At a suffrage meeting at Newcomb, suffragists similarly relayed that present conditions in urban areas like New Orleans were complicated and full of troubles. The vote would be the tool that the students needed to help them to survive and fulfill their duties in the modern world after graduating, when society expected them to "take an active part in solving social and economical problems."[88]

When arguments about the future proved ineffective, suffragists turned to the past and familiar academic subjects, such as US history, to bolster the cause. Suffrage speakers used the longer story of the women's rights struggle to appeal to undergraduates. For example, southern reformer and NAWSA member Kate Gordon delivered a 1911 address at Tulane to interested students, entitled "Millstones and Milestones," which sketched the history of women's changing position in society from the ancient period to the present. Gordon identified both milestones in female progress, such as women's entrance into higher education, and millstones (moments of ignorance and prejudice) that held them back. According to this history, activists accomplished much but much work also remained for the future.[89] Juliet Stuart Poyntz made similar arguments in 1912 when addressing Barnard students. She outlined the "rise of woman" from the 1300s to the present.[90] According to Poyntz, women organized for greater rights in all societies over time, and campaigns for political equality were not new. Ideologies that developed during the influential periods that students studied in the classroom, such as the Renaissance, shaped the women's rights movement. By recasting the current struggle in a broader historical framework, suffragists associated their present organization with a larger history of protest and reform.

The second component of college lecturers' academic appeals was a concept dubbed "the obligation of opportunity." Scholar Joyce Antler argues that at the end of the nineteenth century, female college graduates faced disillusionment when they came home and found that their families expected them to return to a domestic life. They argued that they had gained skills to serve the larger community and society, emphasizing a "social claim" to an expanded public role.[91] This philosophy may have informed the arguments for involvement in suffrage used by the CESL. Initially proposed by CESL cofounder Irwin, and consistently applied by Park, "the obligation of opportunity" argument (possibly the most popular and frequently used among the CESL's arguments) centered on connecting the movement for women's rights with the campaign for female integration into higher education. CESL leaders argued that college women owed their current academic opportunities to pioneering women's rights activists who came before them, many of whom were avid suffragists. They contended that female students should participate in the current suffrage campaign to repay earlier reformers for their efforts to open higher education to women.[92] As the *Times-Picayune* stated of Park's trip to New Orleans to visit students at Newcomb College, she intended "to awaken college women to the debt of gratitude which she feels every woman, who has enjoyed the advantages of higher education owes to the suffrage cause."[93] Park stressed at her Newcomb College address, "The advantage of higher education had been gained for woman by the continued efforts of the early suffragist."[94] College women should feel a special connection to the cause.

CESL speakers dramatized their bids for support using stories of hardships from the biographies of suffrage pioneers to emphasize what women in prior periods had overcome to allow them to enter colleges and universities and how indebted current students should be. At Newcomb in 1909 and 1910, for example, suffragists shared accounts of early women's rights leaders such as Lucy Stone and Elizabeth Blackwell, who overcame great adversity in their quest for university training. When Stone sought to enroll in college, speakers noted, "It was just as unthinkable as if she had aspired to be president."[95] Even after Stone was accepted at the progressive Oberlin College, one of the first universities to admit female pupils in the nineteenth century, she faced constant discrimination.[96] College leaders barred her from campus privileges, including reading a commencement address, because of her sex.[97] Blackwell came up against similar challenges when she pursued medical training in the nineteenth century. She applied to twelve programs before gaining admission to Geneva College in New York, where she confronted continuous prejudice.[98] Female students who lived in Blackwell's building refused to sit at the same table as she because they claimed she lacked "all womanly delicacy."[99] Early female students such as Stone and Blackwell faced a "social crucifixion" due to their efforts to create change for women.[100] Park and her supporters encouraged undergraduates to consider how far women's position in society had come because of early suffragists' endurance and hard work. The modern woman, they argued, had "not sprung Minerva-like into being." She was "the product of centuries of evolution," pushed forward by women's rights pioneers who "suffered" considerably to fulfill their goals.[101] Orators made compelling arguments for support based on notions of cross-generational sisterhood by evoking the groundbreaking efforts of the women who came before them.

* * *

The CESL did not directly exclude African Americans from this campus activism. However, much like its alumni leagues, college chapters did not actively take strides to campaign among African Americans or at Black institutions either. Their printed list of proposed campaign locations includes no such work, nor do reports of Park's travel itineraries mention trips to any Black colleges or universities.[102] The impetus for campaigns at White universities frequently came from off-campus groups like the CESL, but at African American institutions, movements to promote female voting rights commonly developed from within. Black students, faculty, and administrators led these movements in colleges and universities that were open to their race. Using educational activism to maintain a respectable image was particularly important to African Americans because the opening of higher learning was just as controversial for them as for White women, if not more so. Black college administrators encouraged institutions to uphold what scholars term the "politics of respectability" to achieve greater status for their race. African American schools created strict rules like curfews and dress codes, particularly for women. Scholars argue that to combat long-standing negative stereotypes, the upper classes urged women (and thus also Black female students) not only to be well educated but also to be sexually pure, moral and/or religious, invested in motherhood, and virtuous.[103] Dramatic or unlawful political protests at colleges and universities would not have gone over well in the larger communities and could have been dangerous given the rampant prejudice in White society.

During the early twentieth century, student clubs at Black institutions also invited suffrage speakers (White and Black) to campus to discuss the issue of female political equality under the auspices of many groups. By 1903, students from the Tuskegee Institute arranged their first appearance by NAWSA pioneer and aging activist Susan B. Anthony. She arrived with several White suffragists returned from a national convention in New Orleans, including Carrie Chapman Catt, then the acting president of NAWSA. The event, dubbed a "notable epoch" in the school's history, drew fifteen hundred listeners because of the speakers' national profiles.[104] Anthony spoke to African American students and faculty in the campus religious center, where she recounted her prior work for abolition with famous Black activists, including Frederick Douglass. Smaller events attracted student social and political activists who argued different perspectives on the woman-suffrage issue for classmates. Undergraduates at Howard University staged a discussion forum on popular political issues in 1912, including female voting rights, in the college's chapel. The meeting drew campus Republicans, Progressives, woman suffragists, Socialists, and Prohibitionists.[105]

Many historians write about how African American sororities furthered the campus suffrage campaigns because of their focus on improving society by bettering the plight of their race and gender.[106] On Black campuses, Delta Sigma Theta coordinated women's rights addresses with prominent members of respected social-reform organizations dedicated to the African American community, like the National Association of Colored Women. The NACWC's members were eager to serve as guest orators at the students' request since NACWC leaders like Mary Church Terrell viewed woman suffrage as essential for African American upward mobility—a goal they eagerly hoped to promote among both adults and youth.[107] Sorority sisters at Howard University heard presentations by NACWC representatives, including Black intellectuals such as the writer Alice Moore Dunbar-Nelson in 1916.[108] Dunbar-Nelson was an educator, writer, and activist from New Orleans who came from a mixed-race background. She graduated from Straight University (now Dillard University) in 1892 and worked as a teacher and later a summer faculty member at the State College for Colored Students (now Delaware State College). In 1914, she helped to found the Equal Suffrage Study Club for Black women in Wilmington, Delaware, and she also supported the work of the NAACP.[109] Howard's chapter of Alpha Kappa Alpha invited other political notables such as White congresswoman Jeanette Rankin from Montana. She talked about her experiences as a female politician and an equal-franchise organizer, and her message of supporting full voting rights for all women, regardless of their race, appealed to Black suffragists who were weary of marginalization in the White movement. However, Rankin's vocal commitment to Black woman suffrage, like that of many White women during the period, often changed depending on the audience. When the situation required, she quickly fell back on claims that supported White woman suffrage first.[110]

College civic and social clubs headed by African American faculty also took up woman suffrage as a key cause that merited further attention, helping to initiate their own events for those on campuses. The Woman's Club at the Tuskegee Institute, formed in 1895 by female faculty and administrators' wives, created an entire suffrage department in the organization with a library of literature available to the campus community about the women's rights movement. The club organized training classes to teach members about how the government and its various branches worked and to prepare them for engaged citizenship, as they believed woman suffrage was on the horizon.[111] As historian Rosalyn Terborg-Penn notes, leaders of the club became spokespeople for the campaign on campus, including Adella Hunt Logan and her daughter Ruth. The women planned student suffrage parades, sing-alongs, oratory contests, and presentations to engage the institute in the question of female political rights.[112]

Logan trained for a teaching career at Atlanta University. A light-skinned, mixed-race Black woman, she passed as White on many occasions and gained admittance to events and spaces often racially exclusive, including gatherings of the NAWSA. She learned from the group and shared with others of her race interested in the campaign. She once commented in a letter to Susan B. Anthony, "I am working with women who are slow to believe that they will get help from the ballot, but someday I hope to see my daughter vote right here in the South." She brought her daughter with her to suffrage events and promoted other causes, such as equal pay and reproductive rights.[113] With Logan's help, the Tuskegee Woman's Club held a "suffrage night" in 1915, which included a presentation on the history of the movement and a lantern slideshow with pictures of Black activists, such as Sojourner Truth.[114] Truth became famous in the nineteenth century as a touring lecturer on abolition, temperance, and women's rights. In a famous speech in Akron, Ohio, at a women's rights convention in 1851, she advocated for Black women's rights alongside those of their White counterparts, and she supported equal franchise. As Nell Irvin Painter comments, in White and Black activist circles her speech generated attention for its boldness.[115]

On other campuses, Black faculty and administrators also supported suffrage through the local activities of the National Association of College Women, which developed from the College Alumnae Club, a Black alternative to the mainly White Association of Collegiate Alumnae formed in 1910. The organization recruited African American alumni across the nation from White institutions that now admitted Black students and from the newly established, fully accredited Black universities,

such as Howard and Fisk. Members promoted female political equality alongside other issues, including supporting reading clubs for children, medical supplies for high schools, and career planning for Black
women.[116]

* * *

All colleges and universities (Black and White) were carefully controlled
spaces during the early twentieth century, and leaders scrutinized happenings. Columbia University screened new student clubs to limit the
unsupervised discussion of controversial topics on school grounds.[117]
Some administrators barred political addresses, activists, and organizations altogether because they feared creating forums for radicalism.[118]
Most college leaders agreed that families sent students to institutions of
higher education believing the academy would guard the young people
in their charge against "evil" outside influences. During the early twentieth century, many universities and colleges practiced a concept called
"in loco parentis." When young people were away at college, the institutions took on the responsibilities of their parents to protect them.
Administrators called the controls on student behavior "parietals," and
they took them especially seriously on women's campuses since people
viewed female pupils as more vulnerable than men. Scholars comment
that the system of in loco parentis did not crumble until the second
half of the twentieth century.[119] As Nicholas Murray Butler, president
of Columbia, once remarked, "There is no good reason why the youth,
who are committed to the care of a college or university, should be
turned over to any agitators or propagandists who may present themselves."[120] Suffragists, Prohibitionists, and Socialists posed particularly
potent threats in the minds of administrators.

Despite efforts to fit in, college suffragists sometimes found their
campaigns entangled with controversial issues on campuses that made
them stand out and put them at odds with the administration. One of
the most publicized examples of woman-suffrage advocacy fueling a
contentious showdown between administrators and students over the
broader issue of free speech occurred in 1911 when the Harvard Men's
Suffrage League tried to stage a presentation by the British suffragette
Emmeline Pankhurst, but the administration thwarted it.[121] After club
president Allen Olmsted heard about Pankhurst's plans to lecture in

Massachusetts, he wanted to bring her to Harvard. Most Americans knew Pankhurst for her militarism, but from Olmsted's perspective, she was an influential and experienced English organizer who could present a firsthand description of the movement overseas because of her status as a chief leader of the suffragettes. In the *Crimson*, to make Pankhurst seem less controversial, the students writing a description of her mentioned nothing about her militant activism, the suffragettes, or violent protests. The school newspaper dubbed Pankhurst instead as one of the "great leaders" from England whose campaigns helped to secure new political rights for British women. Before becoming active in the equal-franchise movement, as the *Crimson* pointed out, Pankhurst also participated in social reform.[122] She was a "well-educated woman."[123] Olmsted and other Harvard suffragists asserted that if anyone could dispel false rumors and offer a candid account of the radical campaigns in Great Britain, Pankhurst could.

Problems emerged after Pankhurst accepted the Harvard club's invitation and members sought a room in one of the college halls for her lecture. Administrators and antisuffragists challenged the request because they believed that having the school host a radical suffragette was inappropriate.[124] Members of the Harvard Corporation, the group that oversaw the college, emphatically opposed her visit with statements such as, "We don't want women in our halls. They weren't built for that"; "Our University welcomes free thought and free discussion, but it is clear that everything cannot be discussed"; and "Why don't you go to Radcliffe?"[125] Despite Olmsted's best efforts to convince the Harvard leaders that the suffrage campaign was "a man's and women's movement" and that college men could benefit from the talk, administrators denied him permission to hold Pankhurst's lecture.[126] The corporation urged the students to drop the issue and stop wasting time.[127]

Opponents of woman suffrage in the Harvard University community, the media, and the public supported the administration's preemptive decision to censor Pankhurst's speech. When suffragists would not relent in their campaign, antisuffragists spoke out about how the issue stood to disrupt university life. Pankhurst was known to deliver fiery speeches, and her opponents feared that her address could incite a dangerous uprising. Concerned academics asserted that the college had a responsibility to prevent threatening women who desired to "stir people up" from cultivating a riot or revolution.[128] Deploying popular gender stereotypes, challengers asked the public to think about impressionable young male students falling prey to the propositions of the female sex.[129] They did not want anarchists upsetting the peace at Harvard and using their womanly allure to target vulnerable university men. If Pankhurst spoke, her opponents asserted, it would set a dangerous precedent for future political lectures of all kinds.[130] The opponents advised college officials to do everything in their power to prevent the campus, a "place for serious study," from turning into "a theater, or a lecture bureau, or a circus."[131] University administrators worried that Pankhurst's talk could hurt the institution's reputation and spur parents to pull their sons and daughters from Harvard and Radcliffe "in horror."[132]

Student suffragists and state organizers who supported Pankhurst's presentation at Harvard confronted these unfair, archaic, and prejudiced policies, claiming that they limited the advancement of education and emphasizing undergraduates' right to learn about important contemporary issues, regardless of contentiousness. CESL leaders like Park took an active interest in the controversy. It provided an opportunity to attract new attention to the activism of the college league and broader work in Massachusetts. Park, a Radcliffe alumna, advised students and spoke to the press on behalf of the suffragists and her alma mater. She told newspapers that the "real reason" Harvard leaders blocked Pankhurst's address was their opposition to the equal-franchise cause.[133] Women's rights activists also pointed out that Harvard's outdated policies contrasted with the regulations of other universities across the nation. Cornell University had permitted NAWSA's Anna Howard Shaw to give a suffrage presentation to students the previous winter in the college's largest hall.[134] Equal-franchise supporters claimed that Harvard was not the conservative place that the university officials made it out to be. They insisted that the institution had "always had its share of radicals since the American Revolution" when "conspiracy and rebellion" ran "rampant."[135] Finally, suffragists maintained that the university should allow the Pankhurst presentation. Rather than being an unruly and irrelevant gathering, the meeting could have many important academic benefits, such as enriching the students' college training and helping them become well-informed citizens, one of the key objectives of higher education.[136] Cloistering the student body from outside issues would do unthinkable damage to the intelligence of future generations.[137]

Despite the suffragists' protests, university administrators prohibited Pankhurst's presentation and forced the lecture off campus to the nearby Brattle Hall.[138] Event organizers took many precautions to persuade the college leaders who opposed the address that they were wrong. To control the audience, suffragists limited the address to students, staff, or faculty from Radcliffe and Harvard and their spouses. They mandated that admission tickets be required and arranged for an on-duty police presence. The lecture did not become the full-blown riot that university administrators had feared, but it did not go as smoothly as the suffragists predicted. Some frustrated young people, denied entrance, tried to climb through open windows and banged on and scaled the walls outside the building. The crowd became rowdy—yelling, chanting, and cheering. Some antisuffragists attempted to interrupt the presentation altogether.[139]

Opposition remained strong when college suffragists and local allies continued to challenge campus restrictions because of the controversy and uproar at the event. However, the CESL and other suffragists lobbied and petitioned administrators until the Harvard Corporation relented and revised the rules. These early alterations became more exclusionary, and the school announced that it would no longer allow women speakers to make any addresses on campus unless extended an invitation by the Harvard Corporation.[140] Furious protesters forced college leaders to again reevaluate their rules, but the outcome did not help the suffragists' campaigns. In 1912, the institution adopted gender-neutral restrictive language: "The halls of the University shall not be open for persistent or systematic propaganda [altogether] on [any] contentious questions of contemporaneous social, economic, political, or religious interests."[141]

It was years before suffragists secured any significant victories against the Harvard administration. Harvard's equal-franchise club could not obtain any space for another lecture on campus until 1913, when college administrators approved a talk in a building in Harvard Yard by "nonmilitant" organizer Helen Todd, a teacher and settlement house worker from the San Francisco area interested in the vote, especially for how it could improve conditions of working women and children.[142] Todd was not a radical like Pankhurst. But the corporation's willingness to allow her lecture in light of past events and her ties to the suffrage and labor movements represented a key victory in the ongoing battles against censorship and sex discrimination in higher education.

The politics on many Progressive Era college campuses reflected larger state and national trends. Female students, for example, confronted other forms of censorship on campuses, including in student government, where they frequently faced the denial of the institutional franchise. University women, politicized by state suffrage organizing and angry about the inequalities they encountered, fought against sexist regulations by drawing on the rationale and protest techniques of local suffragists. In 1908, male students at Berkeley recommended amendments to the undergraduate constitution that would bar women from having a voice in the college government organization, the Associated Students of the University of California (ASUC). College women responded.[143] Female students reasoned that if the school blocked their participation in campus governance, the college should forbid the ASUC from using "associated students" in its title, as it would not be representing the entire college. Undergraduates who balked at the suggested policies arranged for a meeting with state suffragists. Concerned students hoped that upon hearing the message of the women's rights activists, indifferent or opposed peers might view passing woman suffrage as an important measure, even if only on campus.[144] The efforts of pro-suffrage students and outside supporters challenged the disenfranchisement campaign. Students voted down the discriminatory measure, further illustrating the influence of the women's rights movement on shaping the culture of higher education.[145]

Parallel activism occurred at other institutions, including the Teachers College of Columbia University, where female students, politicized by the women's rights campaign, fought for a full voice in campus elections. Undergraduate women wanted a say in appointing members to the Columbia Student Board of Representatives in 1912 and rallied university leaders using many tactics of state suffragists, including confronting administrators and electoral clerks to inquire about their exclusion.[146] Despite female students' repeated petitioning for participation, college leaders refused to change the existing rules that privileged male power and denied female students' voices. Columbia's college leaders encouraged the women demanding greater authority in student government to become more involved in campus life at Barnard—the institution's all-female affiliate—and allow Columbia—a historically all-male college—to continue catering to men. Female students fighting for full enfranchisement at Columbia failed to secure the changes they sought. Their efforts to promote women's political rights in academia, however, awakened their peers' interest in improving female status beyond national government and laid the groundwork for future campus campaigns for women's rights.

University students also used what they learned from NAWSA activists and CESL members to challenge discrimination based on factors other than gender, such as age. Some college organizations excluded underclassmen from membership. Campus leaders banned first-year students at Barnard from its suffrage club because of their youth and supposed immaturity. In 1912, outraged first-year students petitioned to change the regulations prohibiting their acceptance, pointing to outside trends. They reasoned that state suffrage organizations incorporated women of all ages, even pupils in high schools. Mirroring the rhetoric of women's rights activists, first-year students demanded the right to join the suffrage club by spinning popular arguments about women's proper place in higher education. They stated, "We are intelligent enough to do credit to this right, interested enough to exercise it, and it would not take up enough time to drag or entice us out of our proper sphere—the sphere of Mathematics A and Roman Life!"[147] The young lobbyists emphasized that participation in the suffrage organization would not distract them from their studies. By 1914, because of relentless campaigning, the group was accepting pupils of all academic levels.[148]

* * *

As negative attitudes toward suffrage activism softened at colleges and full voting rights for women nationwide seemed more likely, during the first few years of the 1910s, female students asserted their equal status on campuses. They became more active in university political events and rallies (seen as preparation for the future). Columbia undergraduates staged a mock Republican National Convention in 1912 to inspire student civic engagement and prepare students for adult responsibilities in the modernizing world. Barnard College suffragists showed up and were not hesitant about interrupting the proceedings by shouting things such as, "How about votes for women?" and forcing men to grapple with the equal-franchise issue.[149] This mock convention is just one example. Encouraged by supporters of the vote, many female students who took part in these collegiate political activities went to great lengths to study, learn about, and re-create government processes. Undergraduates at Barnard, for instance, who advocated a larger role for women in civic affairs, staged campaign festivities to raise interest in elections among others of their gender. Students organized an elaborate presidential rally in 1912 in which women masqueraded as members of popular governmental factions. After the event, undergraduate suffragists encouraged female students to cast ballots for the candidate that they felt was strongest, much as they would after listening to actual contenders if given the franchise off campus.[150] The activities coupled the students' interests in drama and theater with suffragists' goals to teach undergraduate women more about casting ballots, political culture, and government processes.

Female students started to familiarize themselves with the voting process in other ways, such as by participating in campus elections and straw polls, viewing the franchise as inevitable for their sex over time and wanting to practice these methods of political engagement. Columbia and Barnard students now both regularly participated in campus surveys of important political issues, including those related to woman suffrage. Poll results consistently favored the movement by 1915 and 1916, illustrating the shift in attitudes. During the fall of 1915, after a recent positive vote on the question of female enfranchisement, the student newspaper, the *Columbia Spectator*, even declared, "Columbia Goes Suffrage." Out of 560 voters, only 129 cast ballots against woman suffrage. In 1916, another poll showed that only 297 students out of 1,537 voted against the cause.[151] Through these college political events, which were opportunities to learn about how government worked, suffragists conditioned female students to view themselves as the country's future leaders alongside men of their social class and educational background.

The overall tone and character of suffrage activism on college campuses still contrasted with heightened protests outside of academia, where campaigns in many populous states were more sensational and sometimes even contentious in the 1910s. At most institutions, even when students now turned to pageants or protests, they avoided aggressive demonstrations in favor of creative displays or practical jokes that drew on the artistic or theatrical talents typical of college students. After Harvard administrators forced a young male suffragist to remove a placard supporting women's rights from his dorm window, Radcliffe students sewed him a "monster sofa pillow" with "Votes for Women" in bold lettering to replace it.[152] They encouraged him to put the pillow in public view where the school authorities forced him to take down his poster. The gesture was an amusing but nonthreatening way for students to object to the censorship that Harvard leaders tried to impose. Activists may not have considered this tactic in earlier periods but reflected the larger use of public space, advertising, and media in the national and state movements.

In 1913, other innocuous yet entertaining demonstrations to support woman suffrage occurred at Columbia and Barnard. In early May, someone hung a "Votes for Women" sign on the arm of the Alexander Hamilton statue at Columbia, and a group of men tore it down. Rumors swirled that responsibility for the sign rested with three "moderately militant crusaders" from Barnard. However, no evidence to support this is available. Not long after, someone broke into the locked corridor of Columbia's West Hall to paint "Votes for Women" crudely on the wall in eighteen-inch black letters.[153] The newspapers blamed the Barnard suffragists, who continued to deny their involvement, perhaps because they feared punishment or damage to their respectable reputations.[154]

Pro-suffrage open-air speeches and parades, which were common in state campaigns by the 1910s, were still unusual at most colleges and universities. When they did happen, they were typically smaller in scale and organized by state suffragists and not student campaigners. The Era Club of New Orleans secured permission to give several "street meetings after the English fashion" at Tulane in 1910.[155] Five years later, the club held a suffrage rally at the school's Gibson Hall. Besides opening the event to the public, Era members issued special invitations to faculty and students.[156] The Newcomb Equal Suffrage League offered support by attending, but it orchestrated no major protests of its own at the school.

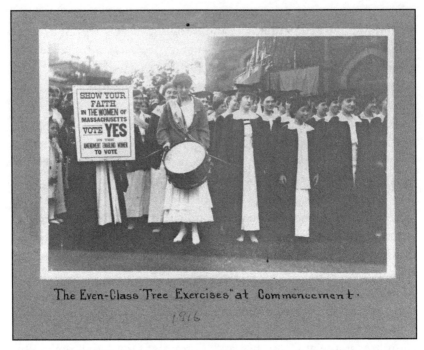

The Even-Class "Tree Exercises" at Commencement.
1916

Figure 3.1. Mount Holyoke students carry suffrage banner in parade on Class Day in 1916. Photo courtesy of Archives and Special Collections at Mount Holyoke College.

Suffrage marches, which were expansive and frequent in urban centers, were less common at colleges and universities. Several Barnard students once paraded around, displaying flags and banners as they headed to a political rally at Columbia, and at Mount Holyoke College, one Class Day, students staged a rudimentary campus parade in which they wore sashes, blew horns, and beat drums to get attention for, among other things, women's voting rights.[157] However, these actions were exceptions rather than the norm.

As off-campus suffrage campaigns intensified, most university supporters of female political rights responded with larger and more professional educational tactics, such as holding extracurricular courses to train interested women in political organizing. In 1917, Radcliffe students arranged a noncredit class to teach street speaking as part of the Civics Club's winter agenda. Students practiced lecturing on issues such as "Earliest Demands," "Women's Rights," "National Suffrage," "The British

Empire," and "Testimony as to Results" in front of veteran organizers. Participants learned how to improve their arguments, vocal projection, posture, and facial expressions to better equip them for active campaign roles.[158] Campus speaking classes sometimes evolved into larger "schools" for training suffragists with more expansive all-day or even multiday programs (like conferences). These events were run by state suffrage associations during the summer or winter breaks and were sometimes held on campuses to teach interested students and other participants about how to be effective activists, often with the help of national or state women's rights organizations, including the CESL.[159] By developing formal speaking classes and courses, members of the college league created new ways to cultivate student campaigners, many of whom would become leaders in local and national movements after graduation.

By 1914, woman suffrage came up regularly in social settings, classrooms, club meetings, and school competitions at African American institutions like Tuskegee but did not result in contentious publicized activities on campus.[160] Students at the all-Black Lincoln University in Missouri started a suffrage petitioning campaign in 1915, a new tactic for the campus movement. Two undergraduates, Auvelia Hayden and Lue Vence Franklin, interviewed peers about the cause during their free time and gathered signatures from their senior class. While drawing more attention to the issue on campus and encouraging others to learn about the campaign, this tactic was neither contentious nor sensational.[161] Influential Howard University leaders—such as English professor Coralie Franklin Cook and her husband, George William Cook, an administrator, professor, and trustee—openly endorsed women's right to vote in their public statements by the late 1910s, providing a model and motivation for interested student and faculty involvement, but avoided advocating protest demonstrations.[162] Black students and faculty persistently engaged with the issue, but dramatic challenges to political inequality were still uncommon on campus, especially given the hostile racial climate of the Progressive Era that educated African Americans sought to mitigate.

* * *

By working to fit in, suffragists of both races, though divided, successfully carved out spaces for their campus campaigns and made recruits among students nationwide to promote female enfranchisement. Their activities shaped the campaign for women's right to vote by pushing it forward among the college-educated population. They also changed the culture of higher education by introducing organized women's rights activism to campuses, setting precedents for future activists, and opening more opportunities for women's equitable leadership in student government.

From 1905 to 1917, the CESL helped to gain greater acceptance for women's rights activism in institutions of higher learning nationwide. At American colleges and universities, CESL members used education and academic culture as political devices to aid in student recruitment for the equal-franchise movement. On campuses, the college league adopted campaign tactics that did not directly challenge gender or racial norms, remaining mindful of the existing social attitudes and customs at universities. Despite a cautious approach, by the 1910s, college activism had done much to change the culture of the women's rights movement and higher education by cultivating new stages and training grounds for younger generations of equal-franchise campaigners.

During the Progressive Era, the equal-franchise cause politicized more male and female students. Although campus campaigns prompted few sensational demonstrations for national or state voting rights at universities, they prompted many tempered grassroots educational movements for the ballot and several fervent fights for other causes, such as academic free speech and gender equality. As a result, the CESL's college organizing set important precedents for later women's rights activism in higher education. The campaigns made organizing a more legally, politically, and socially accepted pastime for female university students, changing policies toward campus political action and bringing greater attention to institutional sexism on campuses. The CESL's tactics and the effects of the equal-franchise movement also shaped educational instruction by helping to usher in a new era of improved civics training at American colleges, especially for female students. The group introduced more conversations about women's status and women's history into the classrooms. The thousands of women who became suffragists through their involvement in the CESL's campus campaigns or by witnessing college chapters' university events gained an early education in US government, politics, and lobbying not available to them previously at most Progressive Era academic institutions.

4

"New" Womanhood Denounced

If Massachusetts activists Maud Wood Park and Inez Haynes Irwin were the most prominent leaders of the woman-suffrage campaign among college-educated Americans, then outspoken New Yorker Annie Nathan Meyer was one of their chief adversaries. Meyer possessed many qualities that would have made her a desirable suffrage organizer, but she chose the opposition instead. She supported a more conservative vision for contemporary womanhood and posed a formidable threat to suffrage campaigners. First, Meyer was well educated, with some college training, and of about the same age as Park and Irwin. She received early collegiate training in a special program for women at Columbia College long before the institution developed into a university or admitted female students into its degree-granting programs. She dropped out upon marriage, viewing this as an appropriate step for a respectable new wife.[1]

Second, Meyer harbored an elite and expanding social network that many woman suffragists would have coveted. Her husband, Alfred, helped the couple establish a distinguished position in their local community through his work as a physician, while her sister, Maud, introduced Annie to the world of social and political reform while serving as New York president of the Consumer's League. Third, Meyer's talents contributed to her success as an activist. Much like Irwin, she achieved national fame for her writing, which included three Broadway plays, helping her to craft propaganda against suffrage parties effectively. She acquired a reputation as a valuable fundraiser because of her relentless drive to gather resources for the founding of Barnard College. As one of the school's most active trustees and a leading spokesperson for women's education, Meyer played a significant role in shaping the university.

Despite her advocacy for women's entrance into higher education and her endorsement of other seemingly progressive issues like equal access to divorce, Meyer never considered herself a suffragist nor a feminist.

She drew a line at promoting certain changes to women's status, such as full female enfranchisement. Like other opponents, she believed that American women were better suited to working for political reforms from behind the scenes rather than through direct routes like casting a ballot. Meyer's opposition to woman suffrage transformed into activism when the National League for the Civic Education of Women (NLCEW), an antisuffrage group from New York, recognized her potential as a state organizer and appointed her to lead their College Committee. The committee challenged the issue of women's right to vote among elite, educated Americans throughout the region and on college and university campuses.[2]

Promoting woman suffrage on Progressive Era university campuses and among Americans with higher education was difficult for groups like the CESL, especially before 1915, because of the attitudes and efforts of antisuffragists like Meyer and the organizations to which they belonged. Antisuffragists effectively undercut campus support for women's enfranchisement for many years through well-organized political campaigns that were just as persuasive and public as their opponents'. Recent scholars have illustrated that while suffragists worked hard to promote changes to established gender norms, antisuffragists strove just as diligently to maintain them. On campuses, college men defended male privilege and dominance in the academy and society, while female students fought to maintain the more traditional image of "true womanhood," or the notion that the ideal woman should be a contented homemaker, just as antisuffragists did off campus. But they placed special emphasis on how suffragists stood to ruin female and male students' futures. Opponents also emphasized students' immaturity and unreadiness to tackle the issue of women's right to vote.[3] In the 1910s, as campus suffrage campaigns became more popular, opponents abandoned on-campus challenges to equal franchise based on older Victorian ideas about age, male superiority, and gender essentialism. They used new arguments that drew on the emerging perceptions of equality between the sexes, claiming that new female voters would not improve the electorate enough to justify their franchise. These arguments captivated the academic community with evolving and more progressive ideas about gender and the equivalence between men and women. Leading up to 1920, antisuffrage (like suffrage) activism in cities and states took on new forms. At universities, the struggle over suffrage became an even more open competition between men and women related to gender ideals and political power. Supporters of the "true" and the "new" woman icons faced off for the allegiance of college-educated Americans within the university in boisterous public demonstrations that most suffragists would have shied away from, especially on campus earlier in history. The Nineteenth Amendment's passage in 1920 marked victory not only for woman suffrage as a political amendment but also increasingly for the new, independent, and civically engaged feminine ideal beginning to emerge at colleges as well as outside of them.[4]

Although the antisuffrage agenda failed as equal-franchise legislation succeeded, scholars note that opponents' public protests caused the women's rights movement to, most notably, "sharpen" its focus and arguments. Antisuffragists forced suffragists to work to reform and remake their image and the image of their campaign several times over the decades in order to stay relevant. In doing so, antisuffrage activism contributed to a better-organized, broader, and more professionalized women's movement and, more broadly, improved liberal and conservative political movements in the United States. Their tactics and arguments influenced other campaigns.[5] On campuses, antisuffragists helped to create a space for new, female-directed, socially accepted, conservative political organizing. As antisuffragists continued their efforts, their increasingly vigorous and prolonged public campaigning further normalized women's activism for social and political causes, engagement in the public realm, and involvement in conversations about government within higher education and beyond, regardless of partisan leaning.

* * *

The climate on most university campuses was at first supportive of antisuffrage, which made it initially easy for antisuffragists to gain support. State activists opposing woman suffrage traveled to institutions of higher education nationwide, broadcasting their message to receptive audiences with few restrictions in the late nineteenth and early twentieth centuries, unlike their suffrage adversaries. Opponents of women's right to vote created groups for university men and women by the 1910s, like and sometimes in response to the CESL, to try to halt its progress in academia, which administrators, who did not support the movement, welcomed at first. In 1911, the New York organization against female enfranchisement, called the NLCEW, developed a special committee for college work, viewing the campus as an important arena for the campaign after witnessing the efforts of Park and Irwin.[6] Not long after, a College Anti-Suffrage League (CASL) organized and affiliated with the larger Massachusetts Association Opposed to the Further Extension of Suffrage to Women. Like the CESL, the CASL's campaigns began among alumni, university leaders, and parents, before moving to undergraduates.[7] African American antisuffragists organized at Black colleges and institutions and challenged woman-suffrage supporters. These opponents of female voting rights posed a formidable threat to women's rights activists in higher education, and suffrage clubs on most campuses faced off against antisuffrage clubs by the 1910s. Over time, like suffrage organizations, these groups had the support of both male and female students and often the leadership of bold women, whose activism against the vote scholars have only begun to recognize for its formidability compared to the work of suffrage parties.[8]

Antisuffragists and their organizations were in a privileged position because they often had the support of key allies: administrators and faculty who from the beginning had been concerned about the suffrage movement's infiltration onto their campuses. Hostile administrators and faculty, who felt that women's rights campaigns harmed educational institutions and the youth attending them, endorsed their campaigns and created easy openings for their presentations. During the Progressive Era, many college leaders still wanted to maintain respectability and approval from the public by striving to prevent their schools from becoming hubs for liberalism. Although some educators recognized that advanced academic training broadened students' worldviews, many more Americans saw schooling of any type as another tool for socialization, conformity, and assimilation. Working against the status quo was something many college leaders avoided, as maintaining a positive reputation was particularly important to administrators at White women's colleges, who already faced criticism for opening higher education to female students.

At Radcliffe, influential figures—from deans Agnes Irwin and Mary E. Coes to founder Stella Gilman—backed the opposition to women's right to vote. They tried to stifle equal-franchise activity on campus to uphold the integrity of their institution and project the proper appearance of cultivating the modern "college girl," a woman whose college training made her into a better wife and mother, not a contentious feminist. As one antisuffragist stressed, "Feminism is the theory of individualism."[9] It went against the family and was often a concept that discouraged women from being content with their roles as mothers and wives. White men's colleges also discouraged suffrage advocacy in order to preserve male supremacy, power, and dominance in all areas of American life, including in higher education. For example, Harvard president Charles Eliot remained an adamant, long-term antisuffragist, opposing pro-suffrage activism at the university in his statements and at every turn and challenging suffragists when misquoted on the issue, to be sure to distance himself from the cause.[10] Male administrators like Eliot were reluctant to see women infringing upon their authority at colleges and in other traditionally masculine spaces.

White coeducational institutions also sometimes bolstered the antisuffrage position initially, backing opposition to the campaign on campuses despite their progressive action of accepting students of both sexes. Coeducational schools, under attack for the controversial decision to allow women into their universities, were careful about who and what they allowed at their institutions, to avoid further criticism. At the University of California–Berkeley, president Benjamin Ide Wheeler and his wife, Amey Webb, considered themselves avowed enemies of the woman-suffrage movement. Wheeler declared, as often as possible, "I'm opposed to it. . . . I think the women of California are too good to be thrown into the turmoil of politics."[11] His wife held a position as honorary vice president of the Northern California Association Opposed to Woman Suffrage, creating a united antisuffrage image and affirming to the public the leaders' stance.[12] As with the administrators of all-female and all-male colleges, leaders of coeducational institutions feared that association with the suffrage campaign would heighten public criticism of them. They were concerned that suffrage activism could cause alumni to withdraw support or parents to hesitate to send their children to campus.

African American educators, already worried about their institutions' respectability in the harshly racist and nativist US culture that supported White privilege, often avoided open advocacy for woman suffrage to maintain their institutions' credibility and safety, just as these other institutions did. Given the controversy surrounding the enfranchisement of Black men and the extension of higher education to African Americans, some college leaders dodged the woman-suffrage issue to protect their institutions not only from sexist but also from racist attacks. Some prominent Black advocates of higher education—such as Booker T. Washington and his wife, Margaret—eagerly supported many progressive causes, but they took more calculated positions on women's right to vote. Washington, a leader of the Tuskegee Institute, sidestepped the issue with vague statements. Notably, he commented that he favored "every measure" that would "give to woman, the opportunity to develop to the highest possible extent, her moral, intellectual, and physical nature."[13] But he did not think that women needed the ballot to advance in society. However, he argued that because "the women know better than men," he was "willing to leave it to their deliberate judgment."[14] Margaret, educated at Fisk University, conceded that she supported women's right to vote but that the cause never "kept her awake at night."[15] She viewed woman suffrage as inevitable, so she reasoned that any time wasted on campaigns would not be "well-spent."[16] She suggested that African American women should learn about how the government worked and prepare for any new citizenship duties to come, instead of actively politicking.[17] Some African American college administrators were far more blatant in their discouragement.[18] The prevalence of antisuffrage sentiment at coeducational Howard University, for example, led the District of Columbia Association Opposed to Woman Suffrage to discuss fostering a campus group.[19]

Antisuffragists won support among college leaders and even parents of all races by using popular and common gender- and age-based stereotypes about students' (especially female students') immaturity and need for protection against outside influences. During the nineteenth century, scientists and medical professionals developed theories to substantiate ideas about women's difference and inferiority that justified their subordination to men in society and in academia. Some people continued to emphasize how women differed from men in anatomy, physiology, temperament, and intelligence, and to argue that this influenced their academic and public aptitude.[20] These theories resonated into the twentieth century, creating a culture in which many Americans still viewed women as vulnerable and in need of oversight by men.

Opponents like Meyer asserted that suffragists manipulated female students who were unready to tackle the equal-franchise question for personal and professional reasons. These opponents argued that advocates of the vote were expert exploiters of female youth who tried to capitalize on the naivety, ignorance, and vulnerability of college and university women.[21] In 1909, Meyer, for example, argued publicly that shrewd suffragists took advantage of the "untrained emotions and the highly aroused sex-consciousness" of university students. They strived toward "catching the suffragist young" so they could easily manipulate her because of her delicate nature.[22] Suffragists could easily cajole female undergraduates into making "themselves conspicuous on the streets" in "ridiculous" and "undignified" protests since, antisuffragists asserted, female students lacked the advanced educational training and maturity necessary for tackling important public issues and followed along blindly.[23] As one opponent commented, "The college girl is not an educated person. She is undergoing the process of being educated. Her mind is still unformed, and she is extremely sensitive to all kinds of impressions."[24] Meyer recommended that students avoid taking a position on female political rights until after graduation, when their academic preparation was finished and they developed stable, mature identities. She commented, "Do not be ashamed of having no feeling whatsoever on the subject. It is really no disgrace for a college girl to leave some questions to be faced after her graduation," and she called for thought on the issue to be "postponed for later, mature consideration."[25] By referring to female students as "girls" rather than "women," antisuffragists further denigrated support for equal franchise among undergraduates in their speeches, statements, and literature, and made the young women seem juvenile and insignificant. Opponents advised female students to leave women's rights issues to older, wiser generations.

Antisuffragists also appealed to administrators and students by contending that suffragists threatened college students' education. Suffragists' "disturbing" propaganda disrupted university life and took focus away from coursework.[26] Learning about government would infringe upon time spent on subjects more relevant as female students did not enter school to "argue politics."[27] The government was a predominantly

Figure 4.1. Annie Nathan Meyer as a young adult.
Photo courtesy of University Archives, Rare Book &
Manuscript Library, Columbia University Libraries.

male realm, and women should devote their energies to learning about matters more realistically useful for their futures. Opponents charged equal-franchise activists with trying to "bend the women's colleges to the purpose of educating suffragists."[28] They urged administrators to consider how women's rights campaigns on campus would conflict with their establishments' central goals. As Meyer wrote, "I think I may say that there is growing opinion among the authorities at Barnard that there is danger that outside interests are being pressed too closely upon our students' interest, and that they have all they can properly do to study their lessons and enter into sufficient amusement to keep the proper balance of work and play."[29] She asserted, "The study of suffragism has no place in the curriculum of Barnard College" and would take away from these suitable elements. "The young women do not go to college to argue politics or to let the subject intrude upon their studies. It offends them. It hurts the standing of the college. Its intrusion and the disturbances and distraction that ensue are harmful," she continued.[30] Another antisuffragist similarly questioned whether modern universities are "institutions to educate young men and young

Figure 4.2. Annie Nathan Meyer as she would have appeared during the antisuffrage campaign. Photo courtesy of the Barnard Archives and Special Collections.

women in the spirit of learning without partisan bias, or do they exist to train the student bodies, according to the tenets of some faith or cult?" Would the "propagandist ideal of education," which included preaching about equal franchise, prevail at modern colleges?[31] What was the purpose of contemporary colleges? Opponents urged university administrators to consider that students' parents needed to know what they were "putting up their money for" and take a stand, hopefully against the issue.[32]

Antisuffragists drew greater attention to their cause when they vocally expressed public concern after female students engaged in off-campus events to support full political rights, using this engagement as an opportunity to rally support for their perspective. They bombarded administrators and the media with statements arguing that university women's proper place should be behind closed doors in the classroom, not out at demonstrations for the vote, potentially damaging the reputations of their institutions and themselves. In May 1910, after Barnard undergraduates appeared in a New York suffrage parade, for example, Meyer responded by trying to launch a nationwide ban on university regalia at such processions, conventions, and open-air meetings. She encouraged alumni organizations to take up the cause and pressured administrators to create new rules permitting people to wear caps and gowns only for academic purposes. Meyer hoped her campaign might deter students from future participation in women's rights protests by disassociating colleges from the movement and putting in place new regulations with real consequences for campus affiliation. Commenting on her efforts to reporters, she asked, "Cannot something be done to instill into college graduates something of the reverence for the cap and gown which is felt for the flag of one's country?" She stressed that the cap and gown should be "suitable only for academic purposes."[33] Soon after, concerned parents backed Meyer's activism and showed up at Dean Virginia Gildersleeve's office to demand that Barnard block all college students from suffrage parades. As one fearful woman argued, if the students continued to participate in the marches, it "would be a shocking and shameful thing" that would "injure the college greatly."[34]

Three years later, in 1913, antisuffragists and Radcliffe alumni similarly bombarded school leaders with letters after learning of students' plans to enter a suffrage parade in Massachusetts. Outraged alumni worried that their participation would imply Radcliffe's support of the women's rights agenda and feared the effects of the school being "advertised" in the march. As in New York, opponents reiterated that undergraduates' involvement in protests might cause harm not only to the students but also to the college's reputation through "association in the minds of the public with the violent socialist and suffragist propaganda."[35] The march, they insisted, could also be "bad for girls, physically, mentally, and morally."[36] College and university leaders, already under fire for extending higher education to women, wanted no additional negative attention, and these types of incidents often only jarred them into expanding opposition or evading the campaign.

To deter support, antisuffragists also stressed that endorsement for woman suffrage was the exception rather than the norm at colleges and universities. Most respectable men and women on campuses did not back the suffrage movement, opponents argued, citing evidence that equal-franchise groups struggled to attract members. In 1910, Meyer noted that the Barnard suffrage club provided desperate forms of encouragement for students to join, such as claiming that it was one of the "cheapest" organizations in which to participate.[37] Pointing out the alleged desperation of suffragists to attract backing was a common tactic of the opposition. "Everything is being done to drag out students into the movement," Meyer lamented, even the creation of false and embarrassing claims about high levels of pro-suffrage support.[38] Antisuffragists emphasized that attendance at suffrage events was typically low, with an average audience of barely fifty students at Barnard gatherings. Members of the suffrage club supposedly chased people through the halls to increase turnout for their presentations, so their guest lecturers would not be "insulted" by a thin audience.[39] Many newspaper articles, Meyer pointed out, noted the lack of backing for women's right to vote at colleges.[40] One write-up stated that suffragists asked college men to add their names to a contact list after a university presentation, and almost all students hurried away, suggesting that the advocates had not sold the audience on their perspective.[41] Meyer pointed out data from Barnard showing that the class of 1910 "formally voted against woman suffrage," and that in 1911, the Barnard suffrage club only had twenty-one student members.[42] Later statistics from a straw poll showed that out of over 800 students, only 354 had polled in favor of women's right to vote, meaning that less than 50 percent of students supported the cause.[43] By claiming that few pupils sympathized with the campaign, and by sharing these embarrassing accounts and numbers, opponents denied the suffrage movement's viability on campuses, ostracized advocates of the vote, and deterred potential recruits from their organizations.

Antisuffragists easily won support from many undergraduates opposed, or at least apathetic, to campaigning for female political rights because of concerns about how endorsement might further affect their personal and professional futures. Some female students already avoided the issue because they felt they did not have time for women's rights associations, and antisuffragists supported this approach. Opponents suggested that there were too many important, popular, and respected campus groups deserving their attention. By the Progressive Era, many institutions, especially women's colleges, boasted an array of activities for female students that increasingly mirrored those offered to men. Opponents reminded that campus suffrage organizations competed with other well-established extracurricular committees, clubs, and associations that required their involvement to uphold university traditions.[44] College women could participate in many activities less contentious and more suitable for members of their sex, including drama, art, athletics, and philanthropy. Unlike campaigning for suffrage, these pastimes were acceptable to parents, alumni, and administrators. Antisuffragists encouraged women's engagement on campus and in the community with avenues that did not overtly challenge traditional gender norms, which they highlighted as better options for students. Even if female students avoided becoming avid antisuffragists, their initial lack of active support for the equal-franchise campaign and willingness to avoid woman suffrage in favor of other college activities helped advance the opponents' position.

Apprehension about how involvement in women's rights campaigns might influence students' social lives and experiences outside the classroom in other ways—particularly how it could affect their fitness for marriage—remained a central impediment to the promotion of equal franchise among college students. Antisuffragists rallied undergraduates by arguing that participation in the movement unsexed women, making them more like men and, therefore, less desirable partners. As one NLCEW speaker noted, extending suffrage "would cause women to more or less lose their feminine graces and natural refinement, and tend to make them masculine, while this usurping of masculinity by women would exert a bad influence upon men in the opposite direction, making them less masculine, and consequently more effeminate."[45] Southern antisuffragists from Tulane similarly asserted, "We believe that the grace and high station of Southern womanhood is seriously imperiled by this suffrage cloud."[46] Many female students assumed that men would have "no use" for a suffragist, and opponents played on this apprehension.[47] In one 1914 article, for instance, activists against the vote wrote that "like murder," association with the movement could adversely affect a woman's ability to find a husband.[48]

Fighting for female political rights was a publicly controversial cause partly because it encouraged women's independence and acquisition of greater liberties.[49] Promoting equal suffrage would be another strike against the character of college women, already under attack. As one opponent commented in 1911, a "large army of spinster ladies" already existed in the United States.[50] "What young man . . . would marry a girl who is both a college graduate and a suffragette?"[51] Men, opponents claimed, would consider these qualities as signs of an unfit personality, and would question such a woman's prospects of becoming a good wife and mother. A Barnard graduate argued, "There is a fixed opinion in the mind of the average man that his wife should be a clinging vine and should not have any desire for an independent personality."[52] She continued, "Men flee in fear from an Amazon or a strong-minded woman" and seek "consolation in the arms of a fragile creature."[53]

During the Progressive Era, women still received mixed messages about gender ideals. As historian Cindy Sondik Aron writes, for generations "women had been told to behave like the clinging vine, not the sturdy oak. . . . Self-reliance never held out the same promise for women that it did for men."[54] Society expected men to be strong protectors and providers, in essence, the "sturdy oaks." Women's natural position was submissive and subordinate. Many people viewed challenges to these ideals as "deviant" and "unnatural."[55] Given these enduring attitudes, antisuffragists garnered a sizable following among university women who were fearful of change and rejected the appeal for an extension of female voting rights, still grasping to traditional Victorian ideas about gender.

Some university men avoided women's rights activism for similar reasons. They worried about how endorsing the movement might affect their reputations.[56] Whereas women feared that supporting full political rights would have a "defeminizing" influence on them, men were concerned that openly backing the suffrage movement would have an emasculating effect. Besides influencing their ability to find wives, some college men feared that supporting women's enfranchisement could diminish their employment opportunities and, therefore, their ability to reign supreme over the family.

Americans in government and big businesses challenged woman suffrage. Leaders of the railroad, oil, manufacturing, and liquor industries held a special disdain because they contended that women's right to vote might disrupt their employment practices by spurring a crackdown on unethical labor regulations. Opponents viewed woman suffrage as a tool toward other reforms that Americans asserted were harmful to industry, like additional Prohibition, child labor, and welfare legislation.[57] College men feared managers would not hire a known suffragist. Some Americans strove to dissociate from males who supported equal franchise because they viewed them as outright traitors to their sex.

Endorsement of woman suffrage could spur the criticism of friends, family, and neighbors, leading to embarrassing and harmful public shaming. For example, during a New York suffrage parade in 1912, male students from Harvard, Princeton, and Yale faced unrelenting ridicule as they marched through city streets. Onlookers attacked the men's masculinity with comments like, "Can't you fellows get a wife?" Bystanders referred to the male paraders as "the bearded lady," among many other demeaning things, to humiliate them and undercut their authority.[58] These attitudes, perceptions, and actions supported the antisuffrage position among college students, giving opponents greater fuel with which to capitalize on the anxieties of the younger generations.

* * *

Black citizens had much more at stake when determining their politics than White people did. Given the rampant White-on-Black violence during the Progressive Era, concerned African Americans explicitly warned against entanglement in controversial causes like woman suffrage because campaigning might lead to increased lynching, assaults, vandalism, and attacks from groups like the Ku Klux Klan on and off campus.[59] Opponents of women's voting rights contended that Black people should let White people battle over female enfranchisement among themselves, protecting their race from unnecessary repercussions. Other college-educated African Americans who opposed woman suffrage maintained to academic audiences that it distracted from the higher priority of fighting against racial injustice. Kelly Miller, dean of the College of Arts and Sciences at Howard, emphasized that the struggle against racial discrimination should take precedence over support for female voting rights. Many college-educated African Americans like Miller saw fighting White politicians for female enfranchisement as trivial compared to supporting larger civil rights campaigns beneficial to the entire race. In 1914, Miller wrote, "The question of granting women the right of suffrage affects but feebly the foundation principle of the proposition to relegate a part of the people to an inferior caste."[60]

The African American community was still trying to secure full access to the ballot for Black men. While national legislation officially granted them the franchise, in practice, White people often denied them access to the vote. To college audiences, opponents maintained that guaranteeing Black men the ballot was the priority and should come first. African American antisuffragists highlighted fears that, because of its radical reputation, association with the suffrage campaign could hinder the mainstream struggle for civil rights by hurting the respectable image of the movement for racial equality that the upper classes worked hard to cultivate. Later, scholars would argue that alliances with White suffrage activists undercut the strength of civil rights campaigns and hindered the struggle for African American rights.[61]

Opponents encouraged African American college women to ignore suffragists and embrace racial solidarity over "sisterhood," or gender alliances. Black antisuffragists asked African American women in the academy to consider the discriminatory comments, policies, and proposals of White suffragists closely and stay away. White women had not welcomed African Americans into major organizations or at many of their equal-franchise events. According to *The Crisis*, not all college-educated African American women were ready to back White woman-suffrage efforts, given the historic mistreatment of Black activists in their associations. To some African American women, supporting the movement would gloss over the long-standing mistreatment of their race and reward White female campaigners for their discriminatory actions.[62]

KELLY MILLER, A. M., LL. D.
Dean of the College of Arts and Sciences, Howard University, Washington D. C.

Figure 4.3. Kelly Miller, a prominent dean at Howard University, did not strongly support woman suffrage as a primary goal and instead advocated for racial uplift first. Photo courtesy of the Schomburg Center for Research in Black Culture, Jean Blackwell Hutson Research and Reference Division, Digital Collections, New York Public Library.

Other Black opponents asserted and reasserted to various communities that the amendment would fail to improve the status of female citizens of their race. Drawing on historic trends and current events, they predicted that after the victory, White people would pass "grandmother" clauses to prevent African American women from voting.[63] On and off campus, by connecting their rationale to larger race, class, gender, and cultural struggles of the Progressive Era, both Black and White antisuffragists made their campaigns to college-educated audiences about more than just rejecting equal franchise.

* * *

Regardless of activists' background, new antisuffrage tactics to bolster the universally appealing argument that women's political involvement would unsuit women for motherhood were taken up with vigor by the opposition, and drew on popular campaign and cultural trends. By the early twentieth century, antisuffragists emphasized to academic audiences this common perspective and the "scientific" theories and findings, past and present, that claimed that enfranchisement would turn women into negligent parents.[64] Carefully framed research compiled from noted medical figures of the nineteenth and early twentieth centuries was effective propaganda to counter the suffrage campaigns on campuses because it seemed to substantiate the "natural" differences between men and women. This research demonstrated that suffrage could endanger female health and reproduction in an age when eugenics, concerns about demographics, and competition among races and ethnicities were hot-button governmental issues. Speakers tried to convince audiences that the sexes were destined for different duties by "tracing the [supposed] origin of the natural differences between men and women from their earliest manifestations in the lowest forms of life" and showing that "this differentiation between the sexes is marked in every stage of development."[65]

Antisuffragists commissioned well-known and scholarly opponents of extending the ballot, such as Dr. Max G. Schlapp, to warn college audiences that as more women took on duties outside the home, such as engaging in politics, the nation's fertility rate would drop. Schlapp had a national reputation as a doctor and worked as a professor of neuropathology in the Post-Graduate Medical School and Hospital of New York City, where he was also the director of the Children's Court Clinic. He studied mental health and crime, in addition to his other work, and spoke out against "radical women," arguing that they contributed to "insanity," "divorce," and "race suicide."[66] He tried to argue that pro-suffrage sentiment was the result of neurological disorder and called suffragists

"THE ENEMY AT THE GATE" in his articles.[67] "The suffrage movement," he argued, "was probably first started by katabolic women, women who had lost some of their secondary sexual characteristics and had acquired some of men's." Suffrage was "a craze" just like those that inspired "witchcraft" or other types of "hysteria."[68] Schlapp showed audiences diagrams of US "birth curves" over forty years to illustrate his predictions that equal franchise would contribute to spinsterhood and childless families, particularly White childless families.[69]

The NLCEW made related assertions in its broader campaign literature. To evoke fear, it presented arguments that frequently played on racist and nativist ideologies about the end of the White race and of true "Americans." In 1915, NLCEW propaganda pointed to a recent US Census Bureau report on decreased birth rates among White women, warning that all White women must give birth to four children for the race to survive. Women's political engagement would distract them from their responsibilities as mothers of future generations, jeopardizing the country's future by ushering in race suicide for White Americans.[70] Suffrage stood to destroy the nation, according to some proponents.

Arguments that equal franchise and its proponents would "radicalize" the female sex became popular in the early twentieth century, especially as World War I broke out in 1914 and people feared subversives and outsiders with greater fervor.[71] Antisuffragists asked audiences to consider the links between women's rights activists and other controversial groups: spinsters, divorcées, Prohibitionists, labor organizers, Socialists, Communists, polygamists, and coeducationists. All these groups aspired to make far-reaching changes that threatened traditional gender norms and disrupted the traditional family.[72] As evidence in higher education, antisuffragists pointed to campus alliances among these parties. Student suffragists received support from many contentious associates, particularly college Socialists and labor organizers endorsing more egalitarian gender relations. To opponents, the suffragists' willingness to form these questionable unions was further evidence of the harmful effects the equal-franchise campaign could have on society.

Antisuffragists' claims about the radical nature of the women's movement were only bolstered by reports of suffragette violence in the international news media. Antisuffragists highlighted the negative connections between campaigns in the United States and fierce suffragette activism in Europe to exploit the fears of college communities and counter the work of their adversaries. Meyer lamented the suffragists' claims that the suffragettes in the United Kingdom were "martyrs," instead arguing that they were "unladylike hooligans" who played upon their sex, and "international carpetbaggers" who came to the United States to "try to lead our women with their tales."[73] Much of the information that on-campus men and women received about the movement was gathered from descriptions in newspapers, magazines, and books, which included sensational stories about controversial protests and events. These accounts covered shocking occurrences, like the male suffragist who attacked English leader Winston Churchill with a dog whip in 1910 and the female activist who chained herself to a tree in 1912.[74]

In 1913, newspapers widely reported on the death of Emily Davison, a notorious suffragette killed when she ran onto a racetrack during the Epsom Derby (presumably to attach a suffrage flag to the king's runner) and a horse trampled her. Journalists speculated whether Davison sought publicity for the vote or wanted to kill herself. Her stunt inspired copycat incidents. At the race for the Ascot gold cup in 1913, a man named Harold Hewitt jumped a fence "with a suffragette flag in one hand, and a revolver in the other." He reached out and grabbed a bridle, knocking a horse and rider down, and received a skull fracture.[75] The college-educated population, some of America's most avid readers, devoured sensationalist stories about radical, violent, and unlawful suffragists in amusement, shock, and horror. Many female students distanced themselves from the campaign because of these reports. These stories depicted women's rights activists as irrational and extreme, out-of-control women.

Concerned about the growing suffrage threat, especially to higher education, opponents sometimes went beyond rallying administrators and students to endorse their activism and appealed directly to parents in a way that the CESL did not by arguing that they had a special role to play in the antisuffrage campaign. Parents, especially mothers with traditional Victorian sensibilities, could counter the suffrage menace by becoming more involved in shaping the worldviews of their sons and daughters.[76] In 1916, the chair of the CASL of Massachusetts warned women, "Before your daughters, at a plastic age, go to boarding school or college, see to it that they have been well-influenced by our sane ideals!"[77] Mothers, Meyer once emphasized to counter the CESL, should remind their college-aged daughters that they did not owe the equal-franchise movement their support. Female students should not feel they needed to take up activism to prove "loyalty" to their gender. She commented, "The appeal of woman suffrage to college woman is usually the appeal of loyalty to sex rather than any personal desire to vote. The college woman is quick to feel a sense of obligation, or noblesse oblige, which, while having its admirable side, also makes for a certain sensitiveness dangerously near self-consciousness. Loyalty to woman does not demand allegiance to the cause of suffrage." She publicly called pushing for woman suffrage "a greedy reaching forth."[78] Rather, she contended that college women could support the "highest interest of womanhood" by fighting against or ignoring the suffrage campaign.[79] Meyer argued that parents should tell their college-aged daughters that, rather than looking for "new duties," they ought to take up the "neglected duties" of past generations as the best measure for uplifting their sex.[80]

Antisuffragists made other compelling claims to mothers, declaring that equal franchise would be an unnecessary burden for their young daughters after college, when new graduates should return to the home to help their families or, at most, become involved in more respectable reform or charity work. Voting, Meyer stressed, was a serious responsibility requiring attention paid to government events, issues, and arguments. If enfranchised, all women would need to become "professional politicians" and keep up to date.[81] Making informed and educated political decisions would entail a distracting "eternal vigilance" because exercising the vote required more than simply dropping "the ballot in the box."[82] Meyer suggested that parents should remind current generations of female students that they should be "glad" they did not "have to concern" themselves with topics like "business interests, the regulation of trusts, of interstate commerce, and the niceties of the tariff." These issues would pull them away from personal and social interests.[83] Instead, once female students completed their degree, they could focus on raising their children and caring for their husbands and communities, as she had done.

Meyer led a campaign against the presswork of the suffrage movement. For example, in 1915, Meyer tried to rally opposition among students against the editors of *Barnard Bulletin*, to pressure them to publicize the debate around the woman-suffrage question in a more equal way. Meyer claimed that the *Bulletin* was an "organ for suffrage" rather than a nonbiased student newspaper that included information that represented the entire student body. She spoke out against a full-page poster in a 1915 issue, which included the message "Use Your Influence for Woman Suffrage" in large bold letters on a single page. Meyer argued that if the flyer was paid for by the suffrage activists, it should have noted clearly that it was an "advertisement" for a particular organization. The way the paper displayed it, she argued, made it seem that the poster was "news or editorial advice" coming directly from editors. Meyer encouraged students to push to get more antisuffragists elected to the school newspaper board so that the press equally promoted their campaign. Meyer commented that she hoped that the *Bulletin* editors were not "too square" to believe that "all thinking women must be for suffrage."[84]

* * *

Ironically, by the 1910s, White antisuffragists employed many of the same campaign strategies and public work they had previously condemned, including visible protests, to bolster and dramatize arguments, especially on campus.[85] College men supporting antisuffrage used overt tactics that played on the fears of the public and the academic community to position themselves as defenders of the family, the government, and, more significantly, American civilization, with little concern for propriety. They theatrically asserted their masculinity and dominance, countering the suffrage threat in higher education through bold demonstrations that undercut the authority of the woman-suffrage campaign in highly publicized ways, with little fear of censure. Their efforts to protect patriarchy were consistent over time. Both on campus and off, their activism became welcomed and accepted initiatives by those in sympathy with their campaign.[86]

The media covered these methods with enthusiasm. For example, in 1913, antisuffrage students from several US colleges and universities banded together to plan an ambush of suffragists headed to Washington, DC, for a parade on March 3. Reports leaked to the local press that undergraduates planned to release about two thousand mice and rats during the procession. The press covered this news as an entertaining front-page story to engage readers and further the opposition's cause.[87] The students allegedly aimed to turn the orderly suffrage procession into a public mockery.[88] The antisuffrage club at Tulane similarly planned to taunt supporters through various tactics that gained publicity in city newspapers for the group's primary goal of "check[ing] the tendency of the fair women of the South to meddle in politics."[89] In the spring of 1913, Tulane men opposed to equal franchise boldly posted a flier on the lawn of a women's dorm at Newcomb College that invited undergraduates to attend a rally. The flier openly and humiliatingly depicted all suffragists as "unsatisfied old maids" that university women should want to distance themselves from.[90] After the event, which stirred up more interest in the voting-rights controversy on campus, Tulane men continued to challenge equal-franchise supporters at the school and in the city to informal debates in dorms, lunch halls, and college classrooms. Write-ups on these challenges appeared in campus and local newspapers. Sometimes, clashes between men on both sides resulted in aggressive threats. For example, one confrontation in the cafeteria between antisuffrage and pro-suffrage men spurred the on-campus leader of the opposition, Lionel Meyer, to challenge the head of the suffragists at the school, A. W. Montague, to "come on outside," to the dismay of the administration, who feared a fight breaking out at the university.[91] Tulane antisuffragists relentlessly harassed the city's primary female reform organization, the Era Club, which held meetings at the university. Opponents stormed the organization's gatherings and repeatedly issued invitations to debate. The Era Club declined, repeatedly, dismissing the undergraduates as foolish children.[92] Despite the club's attempt to ignore opponents at Tulane, the active antisuffrage presence that emerged on the campus in the 1910s remained a constant threat to the equal-franchise movement at the university and in the nearby urban center.

At Tulane, antisuffragists waged a ribbon war with their opponents to advertise their cause among college students.[93] Antisuffrage activists, like their pro-suffrage counterparts, developed an array of insignia and badges to distribute to students who opposed women's enfranchisement. The most common suffrage symbol adopted by undergraduates was the deep red ribbon, which offered a dramatic contrast to the blue worn by the suffragists around campus.[94] In addition to attaching blue ribbons to their clothing and book bags, members of the suffrage party decorated their belongings with gold pins reading "Votes for Women" in bold black lettering.[95] To counter these tactics, antisuffragists responded by creating new posters: one of the group's designs included an image of a "suffragette" head with a hatchet raised to strike it.[96] This aggressive image reflected decisive antisuffrage ambitions to rid the campus and community of support for suffrage, sending a clear message that the antisuffragists hoped to squash challenges to them on campus. Antisuffrage men staged a variety of other ambushes and attacks to increase visibility for their movement on campus and used new accessories. In 1913, antisuffragists allegedly and controversially "recruited" women to join their campaign by cornering them in college halls, giving short addresses, and then swiftly pinning them with red ribbons, the symbol of support, declaring that they had been converted.[97] By using these ribbons, pins, and images, student supporters created a stylish means of promoting their cause among fellow students and visually challenging each other for control of the collegiate scene.

The strongest resistance to woman suffrage in the early twentieth century came from "elite" southerners in conservative areas like Louisiana, both on and off campus.[98] In the South, the livelihoods of the upper classes, including members of the college-educated population, often depended on well-established, long-standing, and deeply ingrained family businesses that practiced the exploitative labor policies female reformers and political activists opposed. Strong southern kinship and community ties spurred powerful coalitions and factions that challenged the woman-suffrage movement, which many viewed as a threat to their way of life. College politics and demonstrations against the vote reflected these stances.[99] After the Civil War, White southerners had perceived female enfranchisement as another attempt by northerners to undermine their culture, in which elite White families derived authority from strict notions of gender difference and prescribed roles for men and women. According to scholar Lorraine Gates Schuyler, like opponents and skeptics in other locations, southerners also feared that woman suffrage would create a sense of competition between the sexes, lower the marriage rate, and detract from important elements of femininity like "modesty," "dependence," and "delicacy."[100] White southerners, more than others around the country, feared that enfranchising women would influence the economy, undermine White racial supremacy, affect politics by contributing to a larger uneducated voting bloc, and lead to a loss of elite White male privilege. Wealthy White southerners especially did not want more African Americans or lower-class White people involved in government.[101] These ideologies did not fade over time.

Southern antisuffragists made various unique threats as political strategies to defend their power that created a sense of hysteria and fear of the campaign, including insinuations that female enfranchisement would lead to a rise in miscegenation and sexual assault. They argued that women entering the public sphere to perform new civic duties would be more vulnerable to illicit interracial relations.[102] Through these racialized tactics, especially popular in the region, opponents continued to evoke the anxieties of conservative people in their communities who worried that equal franchise would dismantle traditions and the structure of society. Their attitudes trickled down to the younger generations. The confrontational antisuffrage campaigns on southern college campuses and the media attention they generated reflected these sentiments.

College and university men in other regions sometimes used rowdy protests to underscore the damaging effects of the proposed woman-suffrage legislation on modern American society, but different influences and objectives shaped these. In the North and West, antisuffrage activism among male students sometimes mimicked aspects of European "charivari," in which young men would stage noisy demonstrations in the streets to challenge unacceptable behaviors or threats to social conventions. Charivari, later known as "rough music," was a European tradition dating to the late thirteenth century, wherein young men banded together to create noisy and theatrical public performances, often to express disapproval for challenges to gender norms. Participants took to the streets in loud protests against controversial marriage arrangements, partners who defied conventions, or undesirable behavior in relationships, such as infidelity, illicit pregnancy, and domestic abuse. The charivari was a way to oppose deviance, enforce conformity to social standards, and display male authority.[103]

In the United States, this tradition's influence was especially evident during events like the 1913 antisuffrage demonstration staged by sophomores from Columbia University, who planned an outrageous campaign in which college men dressed in costumes and held an imitation suffrage parade in New York City. The procession included many symbolic elements negatively portraying the suffragists and their movement. The goal seemed to be humiliation and the delegitimatization of the cause. It started with an undergraduate posing as well-known New York suffrage leader and Vassar graduate Inez Milholland, who had headed several local parades, riding a "mule" rather than her traditional white horse. Around two hundred students followed, adorned in white apparel, and carrying handmade banners, which included phrases like "Votes for We-Men, Women Can Wait."[104] Undergraduates rang bells and used loud noisemakers to call residents into the streets. They danced, "waved veils," and sang their own derogatory versions of suffrage songs.[105] At one point, students even mocked the actions of the British suffragettes by chanting, "Assassination is vexation; / And murder gets my goat; / But arson, it is glorious; / It's sure to get the vote!"[106] Students also used theatrics during the procession to support their primary opinion and most visible argument that woman suffrage would disrupt motherhood and negatively affect the next generation. In one example, a group of men dressed as women carrying imitation children and pushing baby carriages followed a large sign stating, "No Votes, No Babes."[107] When these marchers reached 100th Street, each "mother" paused in front of the onlookers and declared that she was tired of dragging along her child. Demonstrators pretended to quarrel about abandoning their babies or leaving the parade.[108] After voting to stay, they cast off their props—buggies and children—and burned them in "nice little bonfires" along the route for the next two blocks. Some protesters even used baby dolls as torches.[109] The procession ended at the gymnasium on Columbia's campus, where participants paraded into the athletics center to rally to raise morale. Dramatic events like this occurred at colleges more often in the last decade of the antisuffrage movement, as male opponents led final efforts to block equal-franchise legislation in new, attention-grabbing ways. They hoped to make the front pages with their campaigns, just as the suffragists did with their marches and demonstrations, countering the suffragists' presence in the press.

* * *

The arguments antisuffragists offered to support their perspectives underwent some transitions as the campaign matured.[110] Discussions of Victorian gender norms began to fade among White activists, especially as women's higher education gained greater acceptance. More White antisuffragists altered their messages on campuses to appeal to college and university audiences who reflected the increasingly equitable ratio of male and female students. Although opponents did not completely abandon early contentions based on male superiority and gender essentialism, these arguments diminished in favor of more egalitarian challenges. By the 1910s, many opponents opted for a new rationale centered on ideas about women's equality with men that would appeal to the intellect of the current generation. According to this new schema, antisuffragists declared that giving women full enfranchisement would fail to clean up corruption in modern American society because female citizens were no more moral than men and would not, therefore, make sounder political decisions. Antisuffragists commented that promoting woman suffrage was selfish as it would "multiply by two the present ignorant and unconscientious vote."[111]

Women would not be the mothers of the nation that suffragists promised. They could not fight vice and impropriety any better with the ballot than without it. As Meyer commented, women had no greater "conscience or humanity" than men.[112] "I see everywhere among the suffragist a blindness to the faults of women," Meyer stated. Suffragists "speak as if every woman voter, every woman legislator, would quickly stop [corruption]."[113] She asserted that many women, like men, participated in criminal and shameful actions. Men did not run the White slave trade alone. Men did not cheat on their wives and break up families by themselves, either: Meyer argued that mistresses were equally to blame for the rising divorce rate.[114] As another NLCEW speaker argued, the vote would extend the influence of the good but also the "bad and corruptible women" who would easily fall under the control of insincere politicians and be willing to "do their dirty and corrupt work."[115] Meyer asked the most educated group of Americans—given their knowledge of current events and the culpability of both sexes in contributing to society's ills—to consider what real advancements would come with women getting the ballot. Voting could not fix all the world's problems and stood to only increase the country's issues.[116]

Antisuffragists also pointed out that, contrary to suffrage leaders' claims, states that adopted equal franchise early were no better off once women started casting ballots. They were particularly fond of citing the report by CESL representative Helen Sumner that suffragists published in 1909, in which they encouraged college girls to read "carefully and critically" for the "blatant prophecies of what can be accomplished by the vote."[117] The CESL of New York commissioned the document, hoping that it would support their campaign; it reported on the effects of woman suffrage in Colorado, where female citizens gained the ballot in 1893. New York suffragists expected the study to show positive results but learned that the findings fell short of their expectations. Most importantly, the pamphlet showed that, as predicted by opponents, once women gained the vote, salaries for female workers did not improve, major reforms sometimes failed, and crime did not decrease.[118] Meyer encouraged campus audiences to study the Sumner publication to learn more about the dismal influence of woman suffrage on society.[119]

Opponents presented their own statistics on suffrage states like Colorado, highlighting further negative trends. According to their findings, woman suffrage had been a "potent factor on the side of the most degraded element of local politics" and had thus "helped to perpetuate evil conditions."[120] Meyer cited, for example, research from the census that supposedly showed that from 1890 to 1900, the divorce rate in and around suffrage states increased almost 50 percent and had also increased in the United States nationally almost 40 percent since women had been enfranchised in certain locations.[121] Opponents pointed out other data of concern from the West. For example, one activist asked, "Why are there more Mormons [thus polygamists] in the four suffrage States than in all of our other States put together?"[122] Opponents argued that woman suffrage supported the Mormon agenda and that Mormon women often voted along the same lines as their husbands, which, in the minds of some Americans, made their entrance into the electorate dangerous. However, ultimately, their arguments and tactics failed.

As more states granted woman suffrage and the Nineteenth Amendment seemed inevitable, the opposition adjusted its goals from defeating to curbing the impending legislation. In an attempt at a partial victory, some antisuffragists suggested that voting should be a privilege for select Americans and not a right given to all people.[123] In 1910, antisuffrage students from the University of California–Berkeley won a debate by proclaiming that politicians should extend the franchise, but only to those Americans whose participation could contribute in some meaningful and novel way to shaping the US government, which they argued most women could not do.[124] On campuses, desperate antisuffragists promoted a limited or restricted franchise, usually based on race or class differences. White elites who hoped to prevent woman suffrage reemphasized their position as the nation's natural leaders and tried to resubstantiate their privilege over the masses. US-born, middle- and upper-class Americans contended with vigor that they knew what was best for society and, as the most civilized class, should continue to have authority over lesser groups, including African Americans, Native Americans, and immigrants, no matter what new legislation passed.[125] Some college-educated antisuffragists insisted that if women won the vote, the government should institute educational requirements to weed out undesirable electors. In 1911, one Radcliffe antisuffragist asserted, for example, that "giving women the ballot now would be as injurious to the country as was freeing the slaves," which had, in her mind, created social and political problems because most African Americans were unprepared for freedom, just as most women were not ready for enfranchisement.[126] Thus, opponents claimed that politicians should delay suffrage until more women were better educated, or else limit the vote to female college graduates qualified for the duty.

Some antisuffragists, including Meyer, went as far as to argue that antisuffragists were women's rights advocates, too. However, they urged the maintenance of a different, conservative female citizenship. According to this strategy, opponents like Meyer suggested that they wanted not to deny women's rights but to protect the rights they viewed as most helpful to the female sex.[127] Over time, some antisuffragists conceded that women should have a greater public role, but they did not agree that changing the laws or the political system was necessary to expand female influence. Opponents heightened their statements about how women could effectively shape civic life without the vote by using other channels.[128] Female candidates, Meyer and others claimed, could gain government positions by writing or asking leaders for local appointments.[129] But if the country's leaders chose enfranchisement, women would be ushered into political factions, weakening their valuable nonpartisan power. As one opponent reminded the public, current female reformers could back candidates from the group that best suited their goals without worrying about alliances.[130] Meyer commented that women could use the influence they had and "do more to better conditions" by their current methods of influence "than by swamping an already overloaded electorate with millions more votes no whit better in the aggregate, no whit wiser in the aggregate, no whit less being able in the aggregate than those of the men."[131] Equal franchise would encourage women to join parties, thus weakening their social, philanthropic, and educational campaigns by steering them in particular political directions. Government groups often did what was best for themselves rather than what was best for society. "Do not," opponents of equal franchise warned women, "put on the shackles of political slavery."[132] Opponents similarly argued to Berkeley students, "Not a single important interest would suffer were the suffragists to disband," continuing, "The greatest reforms of today are being carried on by women without the aid of the ballot. They think that suffrage would undermine their work instead of aiding it."[133]

* * *

Within the Black community, a shift away from justifying female disenfranchisement primarily based on Victorian ideas about gender difference did not occur to the same extent, nor did bold antisuffrage campaign tactics as the campaign progressed. Many college-educated African Americans who challenged women's right to vote continued to use traditional arguments and avenues of opposition that highlighted, in writing and public speech, how the ballot would distract women from their duties as wives and mothers. Viewing the maintenance of traditional gender norms and ideology as still important in gaining respect for their race, some middle- and upper-class African Americans who had bettered their circumstances by subscribing and conforming to White Victorian gender roles did not want to destroy the cloak of gentility from which they gained power.

Scholars write that, to gain power and respect in broader White society, some Black men and women challenged popular stereotypes about their race by behaving in ways that were contradictory to or the opposite of expectations. For example, White society stripped Black men of power by arguing that they were weak, effeminate, and in need of protection. Black men responded by displaying characteristics like physical strength and hypermasculinity, asserting their right to a patriarchal position. Some African American women—who were viewed as dominant, aggressive, and overly sexual—countered these perceptions by illustrating submissiveness, femininity, and chastity.[134] Consequently, in their activism many African American antisuffragists refused to adopt new Progressive Era ideologies about women's equality or "sameness" with men or participate in protest tactics that would undermine traditional gender decorum, despite the reality that most Black families did not, or could not, conform to older White conventions because of various factors limiting their positions in society. Some among the upper classes held that the only way to sustain any authority in the White world was to maintain respectable behavior by avoiding controversies like the battle for enfranchisement or even by opposing it in boisterous ways.[135]

For example, late in the campaign, Dean Kelly Miller of Howard publicly maintained that giving the ballot to women would distract them from their family obligations, especially raising children. Like early White activists, Miller held that women were not physically or mentally suited to politics. Further, the next logical step after gaining equal franchise—women entering government office—would make granting female voting rights too "risky" because of its disastrous effects on the family.[136] To help maintain authority for other "elite" Black citizens, Miller defended male dominance in society with persistence, and promoted the image of fragile women needing male supervision.

Prominent African American women persistently stressed that the suffrage issue threatened to distract them from focusing on the home, which they continued to emphasize as essential to the upward mobility of their race and gender. Black mothers were central to the well-being of African American communities because they had all the same duties as their White counterparts and more. As well as more conventional lessons, Black mothers in particular had to teach their children about racism, tolerance, and resistance.[137] African American writer Sarah Dudley Pettey asserted, for example, that Black women could do more to improve society and future generations by taking advantage of their authority in the "home environment" than by participating in political activities like their White counterparts.[138] By maintaining that African American women should concentrate more on their important family obligations than the campaign for the vote, some Black women upheld conservative gender ideals for their race with the hope of continuing to contribute to a more respectable image for African Americans within mainstream society.

* * *

As White antisuffragists realized that they were increasingly losing support, they focused on finding new ways to refute the accusation that their position was outdated. Antisuffragists furiously circulated lists of prominent twentieth-century women who did not want the ballot, including educators, nurses, social reformers, civic leaders, and high-ranking members of popular associations both on and off campuses. These women, they noted, championed antisuffrage while backing improvements to state hospitals, public safety, urban reform, schools, local government, and many other progressive issues suffragists supported. Opponents noted that antisuffragists led many well-known groups that were popular among middle- and upper-class college-educated women, including the Young Women's Christian Association, the Women's Municipal League, the National Federation of Day Nurseries, and the Board of Health, Lunacy, and Charity.[139] If anything, opponents stressed that suffragist activism "detracts from charitable enterprises and relief work" and pulled women away from these important causes.[140] By making these connections, they rejected stereotypes that they were "drones," "parasites," "old maids," or "butterflies of fashion" and "indifferent to the needs of society," as the suffragists claimed to targeted audiences. Instead, they were "thoughtful, intelligent women who are sincerely concerned in studying and seeking to solve many of the big social and human problems of the day."[141]

To improve their reputation, opponents continued to leverage the support of high-profile academics and advertise their endorsement to female students throughout the campaign. Meyer and the NLCEW planned a special event, College Days, for students from New York and Massachusetts, to hear presentations by antisuffrage advocates in the field of education, like Smith College professor Mary A. Jordan.[142] Antisuffragists called on well-known figures for support—including Caroline Hazard, president of Wellesley College, and Heloise Hersey, English professor at Smith College, and others—for regular campus lectures and presentations.[143] They utilized the campus media and press to highlight the endorsement of key figures in the academy. For example, in 1915, Meyer wrote to the *Barnard Bulletin* to highlight and reemphasize the many outstanding women in higher education—like Radcliffe's first president, Elizabeth Cabot Agassiz—who endorsed antisuffrage.[144] Such tactics bolstered the credibility of the antisuffrage movement among college students, demonstrating that antisuffragists were not some distant and archaic enemy but the figures seen by students every day. As one antisuffragist stated, "Suffragists and their sympathizers are constantly declaring that no man or woman of intelligence and broad views could oppose woman suffrage," and asserted that that could not be further from the truth.[145] Another antisuffragist similarly asserted that "educated, progressive women in very large numbers oppose woman suffrage in Massachusetts and elsewhere."[146] Their campaign tactics aimed to underscore these points to students and alumni.

In the twentieth century, antisuffragists made their movement look more contemporary by starting campaigns to reach even younger Americans, and sometimes with more success and in a more organized fashion than suffrage advocates. If they could influence people earlier in their academic training, they could better reframe their image as modern. Antisuffragists mobilized high school students alongside their college counterparts in organized youth clubs that sometimes affiliated with state suffrage organizations. For example, the New York State Association Opposed to Woman Suffrage formed its Junior League in 1910.[147] Massachusetts antisuffragists took similar steps after about 150 teenagers showed up at one of their gatherings. Many high school students wanted to join the state organization, but leaders initially turned them away because of age restrictions.[148] Not wanting the children to fall under the suffragists' influence, Massachusetts opponents also created a junior branch of the state association in 1911.[149] Antisuffragists appealed to teens in church groups and student clubs at public schools to head off the suffragists' campaigns, and seemed to place more focus on this activism and its importance and offer more resources to it than the pro-suffrage movement.[150]

Student recruits participated in philanthropy and fundraising to aid more than just the battle against equal franchise and maintain the positive image of their campaign in the community. Through their organizing, opponents hoped to further highlight that their women advocates

were progressive, cared about their societies, and took an interest in issues outside the home. In 1914, at the Food Fair in Boston, antisuffragists recruited nearly fifty Radcliffe, Wellesley, and Smith students and
Junior League volunteers. The college and high school women served
as ushers and guides, sold red roses, and handed out antisuffrage literature.[151] The New York City branch of the state's Junior League staged a
large benefit ball at the Plaza Hotel two years later. This event included a
fashion parade and raised around eight hundred dollars for the National
Aeroplane Fund to train two male pilots in 1916 for future war service.[152]
Not long after, the group held a similar event called Fête de Vanité at the
same location, featuring young debutantes dressed in "fashion poster
costumes."[153] Funds raised went to care for victims of infantile paraly-
sis. The celebration ended with a student antisuffragist dressed as Lady
Liberty, surrounded by Junior League members. The patriotic, dramatic
display conveyed to Americans that the antisuffrage position, endorsed
by youth, aimed to protect rather than harm the nation and was in line
with modern tenets.[154] Youth activism continued until US entry into
World War I.

However, despite these tactics for gaining new supporters, with increasing numbers of states giving women the vote by 1917, a world war
raging, and the political climate in the country shifting, woman suffrage
eventually seemed even more imminent. Support for the opposition and
active organizing against the ballot was declining among all Americans.
Despite a decrease in backing, Meyer and some followers still tried to
maintain some level of activism against the ballot, refusing to give up
hope in the face of growing opposition. In a last major effort, Meyer
proposed a nationwide boycott of the vote by female conservatives in
the states that enfranchised women. She asserted that to block the federal amendment, antisuffragists should not cast ballots in areas where
they had full electoral rights. Then, subversive suffragists, feminists, and
Socialist women would dominate the electorate and the extreme consequences of their political participation would further dramatize the antisuffragists' arguments on the national stage. Meyer expected this protest
to increase opposition to the federal amendment and end its promotion for the last time. She commented, "I for one earnestly declare that
the duty of the anti-suffragist is to refuse the vote and thus do her part
in revealing to the entire nation before it is too late the true quality of

woman's vote. . . . By having a city or State where women's votes go over-whelmingly pacifist or socialist, the conservative woman who refrains from voting can help."[155] However, World War I made these final efforts by women like Meyer, which distracted attention from the military crisis, seem unpatriotic. Many suffragists and antisuffragists alike viewed continued political protest of any kind during the war as destructive to the nation, believing that women's primary duty should be supporting the home front.

Like those off campus, most antisuffrage campaigns among college students came to a halt during the post-1917 period. Many antisuffragists joined efforts to support the home front and the war effort instead, expecting that suffragists would do the same and hoping that the issue would fade during World War I as it had during prior military conflicts, leaving them as the ultimate victors. Opponents like Meyer and others on and off campus never would have anticipated that World War I, and the last three years of the suffrage movement, would be the most crucial. This would be the period in which the suffrage movement would gain the most ground among Americans of all backgrounds, leading to the passage of the Nineteenth Amendment in 1920.

* * *

Scholars debate the causes of the failure of the antisuffrage movement in 1920. Some studies suggest that antisuffragists' use of more public protests in the twentieth century contributed to their eventual defeat. As these historians argue, antisuffragists' methods produced "confusion" in the late 1910s because opponents advocated that women's proper place was in the private sphere; yet, they were out in public campaigning against the vote in ways that often matched the equal-franchise supporters' actions. Consequently, their tactics frequently undercut the message they promoted.[156] Other scholars contend that antisuffragists failed to block women's voting rights because they could no longer outwit their counterparts ideologically. Time had proven many arguments against extending the franchise to be inaccurate, and the rationale of the challengers outdated. According to historians, another weakness proved to be the movement's narrow appeal. Although the suffrage campaign included more working-class and Black women in the final ten years, antisuffragists maintained relatively strict racist attitudes and a greater unwillingness to bridge class boundaries.[157] On college campuses, various factors—including the growing acceptance of women's higher education and women's rights, changing gender norms, a broadening of the equal-franchise movement, and the onset of World War I—all combined to defeat the antisuffrage campaign in the second decade of the twentieth century.

Studying the opposition to female political rights at colleges despite this loss sheds light on the challenges that women's rights activists from groups like the College Equal Suffrage League faced when campaigning for the franchise on many Progressive Era campuses. Gaining suffrage support was not easy in the collegiate realm. From apathy to opposition, suffragists confronted diverse obstacles to their activism in higher education. Most notably, by the early twentieth century, representatives from the CESL came up against a formidable antisuffrage force led by women like Meyer, which led organized protests that often paralleled campaigns advocating for equal enfranchisement. Antisuffrage activism at colleges gradually shifted from a focus on challenging women's right to vote based on Victorian notions of gender, age, and sex difference to a more modern rationale centered on ideas about male and female equality. It also became more public and bolder.

Although antisuffragists lost their battle against the ballot, their activism had important implications for female political organizing in the period that followed. Throughout most of the twentieth-century campaign, for example, opponents of woman suffrage kept advocates of equal franchise on the defensive, encouraging them to strengthen their arguments and tactics to keep up with the opposition, which was also evolving, and helping to maintain support for a "conservative" form of female citizenship both inside and outside the academy. Confronting the battle over female voting rights at colleges urged more men and women of the younger generations to consider questions of American civic participation, citizenship, and government in new ways, regardless of their political leanings. In doing so, the antisuffrage campaign had the unintended effects of helping to engage greater numbers of students, especially women, in civic questions and of encouraging further acceptance for future female political organizing in higher education.

5

"How the Vote Was Won"

From October 15 to 21, 1908, leaders of the College Equal Suffrage League (CESL) gathered in Buffalo, New York, for the fortieth annual meeting of the National American Woman Suffrage Association (NAWSA). The event memorialized the sixtieth anniversary of the historic 1848 Seneca Falls Convention, where women's rights activists endorsed the Declaration of Sentiments, which outlined their goals for female advancement in a male-dominated society. NAWSA's fortieth annual meeting also marked the official formation of the CESL's umbrella body, the National College Equal Suffrage League (NCESL), a NAWSA affiliate that leaders had been planning for nearly two years. As a part of the conference's festivities, university women met for a special session known as the College Evening.

The meeting included presentations by prominent orators and esteemed figures in higher education. These speakers stressed the significance of equal franchise to enlightened womanhood. The NCESL's first national president, M. Carey Thomas, declared at the event, "It is unthinkable that women who have learned to act for themselves in college and have become awakened there to civic duties should not care for the ballot to enforce their wishes."[1]

Thomas and other NCESL members reasserted, as Park and Irwin had many years earlier when founding the organization, that as astute and influential citizens, university women should be at the forefront of the movement for the vote. Thomas encouraged attendees to continue recruitment work on and off campuses and at the federal level. Work in Washington, DC, would be particularly crucial to persuading politicians to support the Nineteenth Amendment, which more activists increasingly viewed as the goal of their campaign.

The NCESL's activism, and the support of the NAWSA during the early twentieth century, helped transform the woman-suffrage movement. The NCESL worked to further professionalize woman-suffrage organizing, guide federal amendment activism, and contribute to NAW-SA's wartime mobilization, thereby casting the cause in a more favorable light in the national arena. As Sara Hunter Graham illustrates, Carrie Chapman Catt, during her NAWSA presidency from 1900 to 1904 and again from 1915 to 1920, was concerned with the professionalization and uplift of the suffrage campaign. In 1915, Catt introduced the "Winning Plan," with several new elements. First, it marked a shift in activism from state campaigns to national campaigns. Second, it gave greater power to the leaders of NAWSA to oversee grassroots branches. Third, it focused on attracting more upper- and middle-class supporters. Fourth, it helped to change NAWSA from a suffrage organization to an unofficial female political party or lobbyist group.[2]

From 1908 to 1920, in places where primary national organizing occurred, such as Washington, DC, and in key states where campaigns shifted focus to the Nineteenth Amendment by the late 1910s, the NCESL and its grassroots sections fueled leadership change in the modern women's rights movement by bringing more college-educated Americans to the front lines of the campaign. By providing the younger generations with leadership opportunities in federal amendment protests, which placed them front and center, the NCESL's campaigns visibly and directly challenged antisuffragist claims that university students (influential citizens of the future) opposed granting women the right to vote. To combat the image of the woman-suffrage campaign as an irrelevant and outlandish cause supported by a few radical spinsters, the NCESL contributed to NAWSA's larger efforts to turn the campaign into a mainstream political movement endorsed by most Americans—especially the youth. A youthful and respectable image, achieved in part by recruiting more college students and graduates to aid in the campaign, was one factor central to suffragists' success in 1920.

Another key to suffragists' success in 1920 was their ability to make the equal franchise a political issue for more Americans. Sara Hunter Graham argues that NAWSA's work to make the movement appear more respectable, for example, led new women to endorse full suffrage, including female citizens who, until that point, may not have been interested in active civic life. Nevertheless, she concludes that during the NAWSA's campaign to gain greater upper-class support, the women's rights movement became more exclusive rather than inclusive. By the late 1910s, however, a closer examination of NAWSA and its affiliates, such as the CESL, showed that the organization did not always form upper-class alliances at the expense of the working class or a more diverse backing, although in certain campaigns, levels of prejudice characteristic of the leaders, culture, and location resonated. Oftentimes, efforts to reach the upper classes simply represented yet another move to recruit a target audience. Racial and ethnic divides, while present, were less clear-cut at the local, state, and national levels after 1915. Many women of different backgrounds and political ideologies came together at varying moments in the final years to contribute to the common goal of winning the vote and overcoming differences, especially when it came to supporting the Nineteenth Amendment.[3]

The college league's focus on encouraging the younger generation to participate in the modern women's rights movement helped alter long-standing trends in female political organizing. Prior to the twentieth century, as scholars note, women middle-aged or older typically headed Victorian reform efforts, club activism, and charity work, while they relegated younger women to secondary roles. By the beginning of the modern American period, however, many younger women, including students and recent college graduates, inspired by the older women's examples and their culture of progressive reform, had risen from subordinate positions to become campaign leaders. Considering student and alumni protest for woman suffrage during the Progressive Era makes clearer the vibrant youth following for women's rights in the early twentieth century, challenging the stereotype that suffragists and their leaders were all staunch, older women.[4] The college league facilitated the rise of college-educated women, especially students, to the top of the women's movement. It set important precedents for future women's rights activism in the later twentieth century, when younger women, especially those on campus, would lead other campaigns commonly covered by scholars. These included movements such as the movement for reproductive rights and the sexual revolution during the 1960s and 1970s, often seen by scholars as centered around the university campus.[5]

* * *

Thomas and the NCESL embarked on their first efforts to professionalize college and university activism for women's rights and gain greater influence for students and alumni in the woman-suffrage movement in 1908. Thomas was an interesting choice as NCESL leader. Her values and bold personality at times put her in conflict with others, but her status and power in academia cultivated respect among women of her educational standing. Thomas was known for her challenges to sexism and patriarchy, especially within education, where she opposed figures such as Charles Eliot of Harvard for his statements against women. In a particularly famous speech directed at him, she stated, "As progressive as one may be in education or other things there may be in our minds some dark spot of medievalism, and clearly in President Eliot's otherwise luminous intelligence women's education is a dark spot."[6] Eliot did not feel that women were intelligent enough to tackle the curriculum at men's colleges. Reflecting on her feelings about women's position in society and attitudes like his, she later similarly remarked, "I was terror-struck lest I, and every other woman with me, were doomed to live as pathological invalids in a universe merciless to women as a sex."[7] She continued, "Now we know that it is not we, but the man who believes such things about us, who is himself pathological, blinded by neurotic mists of sex, unable to see that women form one-half of the kindly race of normal, healthy human creatures in the world."[8] Thomas had come from an educated background with family that supported her intelligence and independence. Her work helped establish Bryn Mawr College and oversee its administration while the suffrage movement took off. Its message appealed to her. However, some people might have found off-putting her racist and antisemitic statements, and her discouragement of African American and Jewish entrance into the college and politics. Nonetheless, she was a strong advocate for the college league because of her administrative experience and strength in changing the opposition.[9]

As leader of the NCESL, Thomas initially focused on expanding recruitment and regulating the work of branches to help professionalize the organization and get the attention of NAWSA leaders. She recognized that the NCESL could be a critical campaign vehicle within NAWSA and reach the college educated, whom she saw as an asset to the movement because of their network, intelligence, and resources. Early in her tenure as head of the organization, Thomas directed the league to petition for support from various previously untapped academic organizations that

Figure 5.1. M. Carey Thomas, NCESL president.
Photo courtesy of Special Collections, Bryn Mawr
College Libraries.

traditionally opposed or ignored the campaign for women's right to vote, hoping to shift their perspectives and gain new allies of different generations in higher education. During the 1910s, NCESL members lobbied the Association of Collegiate Alumnae (ACA), composed of socially and politically engaged graduates, the National Fraternities, and the National Pan-Hellenic Council, among other academic groups, for backing for the federal amendment. During the early twentieth century, prominent organizations that included large numbers of college-educated Americans, such as the ACA, were reluctant to publicly support equal-franchise legislation, not only because of the controversial nature of woman suffrage but also because the leaders of the group worried about straying from the organization's chief goals.[10] League representatives were particularly aggressive in their ACA activism, recognizing the group's respected status in higher education. They bombarded ACA state presidents, college councilors, and members in nonsuffrage states with letters asking for support. The NCESL viewed representatives of the large female alumnae organization as essential comrades.[11]

Thomas and her team of NCESL executives also developed a standardized campaign plan to address nationwide work toward NAWSA's larger efforts. The college league's leaders tried to regulate the activism of the student and alumni branches. The NCESL's executive secretary, for example, was tasked with securing and vetting the speakers for local chapters (rather than the chapters themselves performing these tasks), ensuring that qualified orators up to meeting the national leaders' criteria visited grassroots sections and that all members received the same messages.[12] During the mid-1910s, the NCESL had nearly a dozen traveling presenters, approved by national leaders, from which local affiliates could choose.[13] The NCESL further attempted to become a clearinghouse for campaign literature sent to college campuses, which influenced the suffrage education that students received. NCESL leaders reviewed documents from the National Woman Suffrage Publishing Company, sending to its members only material they deemed in line with the group's goals—promoting nonradical educational activism that taught women the major arguments and context for the voting-rights campaign.[14] In addition to using selected materials donated by NAWSA, Thomas and the NCESL executives kept their members updated about collegiate campaigns by printing and distributing their own literature on campuses and in cities focused on campus activism. For example, the group distributed copies of its meeting minutes and significant convention addresses to grassroots affiliates.[15] In 1915 alone, the organization produced around twelve thousand leaflets for eleven college campuses.[16] The NCESL, under Thomas's leadership, prepared a suffrage bibliography that listed suggested reading materials for students, and the organization created traveling libraries stocked with popular books and articles on women's rights sent to college and alumni chapters.[17] By delivering literature to and suggesting material for smaller branches, Thomas and the NCESL tried to ensure that members remained united in the group's mission, work, and goals.

Thomas sought opportunities for members to participate in national and international woman-suffrage events to improve the NCESL's position and influence in NAWSA. By helping the NCESL become actively involved with conventions, Thomas transformed the CESL into one of NAWSA's most visible and influential affiliates. Under Thomas's direction, the NCESL held annual meetings during the NAWSA's conferences and thus made the group's gatherings an official part of the widely circulated national program. This move encouraged a high turnout among university students and graduates eager to travel to meet and network with some of the most well-known suffrage leaders and celebrities, as well as to explore a new locality to which they might not otherwise have been able to travel. Conventions not only represented an opportunity to learn more about the campaign. They were also an avenue for personal social and cultural advancement. By 1915, the NCESL sent one of the largest participating delegations to the NAWSA conventions, typically drawing forty to fifty members, and thus filling the NAWSA gatherings with the new voices and votes of younger college-educated women.[18] The organization developed an international presence in global women's rights circles and similarly sent representatives to suffrage meetings abroad, including the conferences of groups like the International Woman Suffrage Alliance, heavily supported by key NAWSA leaders like Carrie Catt.[19] The NCESL's participation in these national and international assemblies raised its status among women's rights groups and increased its power in the United States and overseas.

During NAWSA events, Thomas and NCESL leaders not only sent representatives but also sponsored programs and offered volunteers to staff important positions needed to make the programs run. Thomas and colleagues organized "college days" at NAWSA conventions to further entice academics with special addresses, presentations, and lunches tailored to women with higher education.[20] In 1912, the NCESL staged a suffrage debate open to conference delegates and the public, in which two teams of university students faced off to illustrate their knowledge of campaign issues, arguments, and tactics.[21] These activities helped raise the group's profile and visibility among NAWSA suffragists, within academia, and with the public, and led to increased media coverage. The NCESL made its presence known among other NAWSA branches and members by mobilizing students and alumni to assist the group's leaders in entertaining and educating its guests. The NCESL aided the Congressional Committee (CC) for the Nineteenth Amendment in Washington,

DC, a special body of NAWSA dedicated to federal amendment work that had been established around 1910 (taken over by Alice Paul and Lucy Burns in 1912), with plans for a suffrage "school" to train campaigners attending the NAWSA's convention in 1913.[22] At the request of Thomas, college students supported NAWSA's annual convention by acting as ushers and guides, greeting guests, answering questions, running information booths, and conducting local tours, all of which helped to raise the NCESL's visibility among other women's rights activists.[23] The NCESL highlighted college-educated Americans' support for the women's rights cause by positioning university women in these jobs as the first representatives whom conference delegates met, which helped students and alumni to become the new face of the suffrage movement.

* * *

By the mid-1910s, CESL grassroots branches progressively moved from state to national organizing in the direction of the NAWSA and the NCESL. A large impetus for this change had been key success both on and off campus in recruiting new members, the state suffrage victory in California, and the growing belief in possible national legislative victory as a result. In cities and at colleges nationwide, most alumni and campus chapters now followed the NCESL's policy of "making friends instead of making enemies" to gain backing for the suffrage cause, which paralleled NAWSA's larger vision of being generally nonthreatening, educational, and focused on garnering a positive public reputation through engagement in both suffrage and social reform.[24] The DC alumni branch of the CESL, which formed with the purpose of recruiting more politicians to the cause, primarily worked among Washington's well-educated and upper-class citizens, seeking for an endorsement of the Nineteenth Amendment among the Americans most likely to have powerful positions in government. Leaders of the DC branch of the CESL hoped to form alliances with other progressive reformers in Washington, the families of government leaders, and respected grassroots activists with whom they could introduce the equal-franchise movement to Congress and sway greater political favor toward suffrage.

To do this, the DC branch of the CESL joined forces with the upper and middle classes in various popular urban campaigns heavily covered by the media. For example, the group participated in a coalition of five hundred women, including many politicians' wives, in a citywide campaign to clean up the streets of Washington and address the local pollution and rubbish issues.[25] During the campaign, the CESL phoned and sent cards to DC residents, asking them to cover their trash cans and keep their yards orderly. They worked with the city police and street cleaners to set new service schedules.[26] They hoped these actions would lead to a safer and healthier climate for local children and families, illustrating that suffragists and college women cared about their communities. CESL members of the DC branch also assisted with programs specifically aiming to improve the lives of women and mothers in the capital, distancing college women and suffragists from spinster stereotypes. In 1916, the CESL helped plan the local baby week by sponsoring exhibits and presentations on infant welfare for the general public.[27] The league invited renowned speakers like Julia Lathrop, head of the Children's Bureau, to give talks at CESL events, which were covered by the press given her national reputation, to illustrate that family and motherhood were compatible with the civically engaged woman.[28] This activism in DC further challenged the negative depictions of women's rights organizers and female university graduates as narrow-minded, self-centered, and out to destroy the American family.

The DC CESL sought to win greater backing among Washington's professionals, such as teachers (as had campaigners in California and New York), and encourage engagement in political equality among the youth by helping to create greater gender equity in public education. For example, the DC CESL formed a special committee that examined public school programs for evidence of sex discrimination and bolstered the efforts of female teachers enraged over prejudiced practices in their field. The committee, headed by educator and scientist Clara Ludlow, examined the history textbooks used in the city's schools from grades five to twelve for references to female figures to find out what students learned about women's contributions to the past and where gender stereotypes originated. Starting with the typical fifth-grade text, David Henry Montgomery's *Beginners' American History*, for example, CESL representatives located only seven references to women, and they noted that the book rarely used the terms "women" or "woman" at all.[29] Suffragists found that the texts used in subsequent grades were no better. The books often portrayed female figures as bystanders, victims, or people of insignificance.

In *Elementary American History*, the most common sixth-grade text, Montgomery allegedly downplayed female resourcefulness and agency while discussing women's roles during key moments in the country's past, such as the American Revolution. During the War for Independence, the text said, American men went off to fight, leaving behind "wives and children at home who did not know where they were to get bread to eat."[30] Such descriptions left students with the impression that female citizens had done little of importance to shape society or the nation's most significant moments. Horrified, the CESL and local educators argued that changing the works used in the classroom or students' "chief source of instruction" would induce more academics and students in the capital to correctly view men and women as partners in building the nation.[31] These types of educational shifts could not only lay the groundwork for woman suffrage but help set the historical record straight.

The DC CESL, eager to support local education in order to generate further support for equal suffrage, also assisted in a citywide protest against a controversial policy, Rule 45, despised by female teachers.[32] According to this rule, if a female teacher married, the district would automatically drop her from the payroll and change her status to "retired" because administrators expected a woman to give up her public role of work and turn to the domestic sphere upon taking a husband. School leaders created a loophole that allowed female teachers who lost their jobs because of Rule 45 to take an exam to protect the city from losing some of its best educators. If they passed, administrators could reinstate their positions.[33] Suffragists spoke against the policy to the local media, arguing that it discriminated against women by unethically infringing upon their personal lives and was hostile to popular values. Rule 45 discouraged women who hoped to keep their jobs from getting married, even as the country's leaders endorsed the importance of unity, family, and domesticity as the cornerstones of the nation. The CESL gained greater backing among more progressive academics in the city by standing with the DC teachers as they fought for administrators to evaluate local educators on the basis of their professional performances rather than their personal lives.[34]

The DC CESL gained visibility within local suffrage circles by networking with other national suffrage leaders pushing for federal amendments in Washington, DC, as well, including representatives from NAWSA, and assisting with their campaigns in the city. The DC CESL contributed to the NAWSA and the Congressional Committee's congressional lobbying campaigns designed to persuade politicians to back the Nineteenth Amendment. Elsie Hill, the DC CESL's president, a French teacher and Vassar graduate originally from Connecticut, became a leader in these initiatives and joined with CC leaders Alice Paul, a Swarthmore graduate, and Lucy Burns, also a Vassar graduate, in planning activism in the capital during the 1910s.

Hill backed the CC's work on political pressure, recognizing that the CC included many college-educated women, potential allies and recruits to the CESL. In 1913, the CESL sent a large delegation to the CC's first mass suffrage parade, planned for the day of Woodrow Wilson's presidential inauguration. The presence of CESL members in their caps and gowns highlighted the support for equal franchise among college-educated Americans to the incoming president and the city's residents. At the CC's invitation, the CESL joined a deputation, composed mostly of college alumni, to meet with President Wilson and urge him to recommend the Susan B. Anthony Amendment to Congress that year.[35] Hill and the DC college league further illustrated endorsement of the CC's national agenda by creating speaking opportunities for CC organizers at CESL gatherings. The DC CESL hosted CC leaders like Lucy Burns, who discussed details about the future of local campaigns, including plans for a hearing before the House Judiciary Committee and demonstrations in the capital in 1914.[36]

Although NAWSA leaders in organizations like the CC welcomed the backing of the CESL's upper- and middle-class, college-educated White women in their federal amendment activism, Black university women faced the same hostility at the national level as they had in state and local campaigns. Fearing a loss of support, White leaders did not want Black faces (especially at the helm of the equal-franchise movement, and particularly in Washington, at the national capital and so close to Virginia and the South), regardless of their educational standing. African American alumni and college students confronted challenges when hoping to be included in national public demonstrations for equal voting rights led by White activists, such as the federal suffrage parade on March 3, 1913. This parade would garner significant attention from White voters, mass media, and the country's leaders because of its timing and location.

According to *The Crisis*, NAWSA members often dismissed African Americans interested in participating in major activities and tried to discourage their involvement. While planning the 1913 suffrage march, White activists allegedly turned Black campaigners away by "coolly" deterring "callers" who came to inquire about the procession, offering them ambiguous directions or unclear advice to deter their involvement.[37] The CC sent African American women intent on participating to "registry clerks" when the staff was unavailable so no one would be there to sign them up.[38] Once it became clear, however, that Black women would not back down despite attempts to curb their enrollment, CC leaders tried to appease racist Whites by segregating these Black women in different sections of the march.[39] Then the CC suppressed the news of their involvement as much as possible until the date of the procession.[40]

Despite facing overt racial discrimination and mistreatment at the hands of White suffragists, more than thirty African American women from northern and western states, including many college students and graduates, marched in the 1913 national demonstration. In doing so, they promoted equal franchise and challenged prejudice in the women's rights movement.[41] Twenty-five Howard University students in caps and gowns made up the largest delegation of African American marchers to endorse suffrage in the 1913 parade. African Americans from many classes also joined the Illinois, Michigan, New York, and Delaware sections. African American artists, teachers, musicians, nurses, and PhDs represented upper-class and well-educated professional Black women.[42] Their presence indicated that the new Black female electorate would include many women from the African American community's upper crust; their enlightened and responsible participation would help rather than harm the country. African American suffragists struggled for fair treatment in the NAWSA and CC, but their relentless fight slowly broke down barriers and attained representation for their race in the campaign.[43]

As events in Washington, DC, captured headlines, many college suffragists—Black and White—outside the city followed the lead of DC's suffrage organizations. CESL alumni leagues and campus chapters in other locations became important forces in advancing the federal amendment alongside the DC group and the larger NCESL. In the North, from 1915 to 1916, CESL alumni branches, for example, held lectures to educate members on how to lobby the government for the first time. The Boston league contributed to Washington campaigns by aiding with preparations for the NAWSA's Conference on Congressional Work and sending telegrams to local politicians, pleading for national legislation to support equal suffrage.[44] Although few CESL branches had gotten off the ground in the South, university students and alumni inspired by CESL and state suffrage organizations remained active in the equal-franchise movement, using outlets of their own. The Tulane University campus was a crucial site for equal-franchise activism to support the federal amendment in New Orleans after 1915, and state suffragists frequently allied with local educators to stage events at the school, including a federal amendment parade in 1916 that ended with a mass meeting at the college. At Tulane, suffragists held rallies and presented speeches supporting the national equal-franchise cause.[45]

However, southern suffragists, including representatives of the CESL, continued to face a unique set of roadblocks when mobilizing for equal franchise in the region and faced especially stringent opposition regarding rallying for federal enfranchisement. Many southerners of all classes, backgrounds, and loyalties rejected national legislative change on the voting rights issue, and other similar causes, and preferred to keep the equal-franchise question as a state's rights issue to allow for greater local control of voting procedures in the region. Some southerners feared that passing the Nineteenth Amendment would challenge state power, and others remained concerned about how it stood to dismantle White supremacy—the deeply ingrained part of southern society that underpinned many aspects of public and private life.[46] State suffragists tried to counter this hurdle by attempting to convince interested locals that if women hoped to obtain the ballot, seeking a federal amendment would be far more expedient than campaigns for grassroots change, or that even if national organizing succeeded, it would not be a simple "shortcut to liberty."[47] Suffragists would still face the challenge of state ratification, ultimately leaving the new national legislation's fate in local hands to make a final decision on the issue.[48]

* * *

As more diverse groups took up the suffrage cause nationwide, divisions in agendas and strategies among activists continued to increase, pushing and pulling activists in different directions. Given her other aspirations and growing reputation, Maud Wood Park, for example, moved more toward the larger NAWSA in the movement's final years. Catt invited her to lead the Congressional Committee in 1916, after the departure of Paul and Burns. She believed in confronting politicians in Washington in a direct manner, dubbed "Front Door Lobby," to convert them or spur them to greater action peacefully and rationally, one by one. These responsibilities pulled her further away from the CESL, leaving the group to Thomas and others.[49]

Other factors altered national activism for woman suffrage among college women and within the larger NAWSA. America's entrance into World War I and the New York referendum in 1917 transformed the federal-amendment drive nationwide as suffragists now saw an even clearer opportunity for victory. Many studies have argued that World War I created an important political opportunity for suffragists to argue for the right to vote.[50] During the war, suffragists of all backgrounds and from all organizations disagreed over appropriate action but viewed the war as an opportunity. Some leaders advocated abandoning equal-franchise activism altogether in favor of mobilizing on the home front; they considered continued agitation for women's voting rights during the military crisis to be unpatriotic. Many more suffragists viewed American involvement in the war as an opportunity to bring positive publicity to the equal-franchise movement by supporting the war effort and taking patriotic actions that demonstrated female fitness for full citizenship.[51] They also recognized that it was a moment when their chief opponents (antisuffragists) focused on the military campaign and stepped down. Radical suffrage protesters argued, in contrast, that World War I was a chance to escalate the battle for woman suffrage by using democratic rhetoric, egalitarian sentiment, and the changing political climate to their advantage. They favored ignoring women's war work and instead putting their time and resources into bolder demonstrations that played on the wartime culture and rhetoric to challenge the country's leaders to live up to the ideals they promoted globally and deal with domestic issues such as discrimination and inequality in the United States.

Despite contemporary and past debates about women's participation in the war effort, some scholars suggest that female contributions to the military crisis on the home front "made no practical difference" in the outcome of the war or on the effects of the conflict's aftermath. At home, the government asked many Americans to do their part as a "vital" measure to aid the crisis, but the psychological benefits of such participation, rather than the actual material effects, were more significant. As the country's leaders recognized, assisting with war mobilization fostered the sense of unity and heightened morale among the American people necessary to maintain public support for the military campaign. This study provides more evidence to illustrate, however, that women's war work in the United States was much more important to shaping the economic, political, social, and cultural aspects of the conflict than some early studies claimed. Suffrage war workers provided essential services on the home front to both civilians and the military, helped to construct the war's legacy by influencing social aspects like traditions, material culture, and memory, and shaped domestic politics during the conflict by adding to the ongoing conversations about American ideals, citizenship, and civic rights.[52]

Differences in campaign ideology and methods continued to trickle down to influence the CESL's activism. By this period, Inez Haynes Irwin's active CESL leadership faded alongside that of cofounder Maud Wood Park, but for different reasons. Park's political style gained her a prominent position in the larger NAWSA, but Irwin's aligned her more with the CC and eventually the NWP. Park garnered respect among NAWSA's elite because of her feminine image, her gracefulness in conducting all dealings, and her knack for working within the current political system to achieve the desired results. A young journalist described her first encounter with the Massachusetts leader in Washington, DC, near the end of the campaign: "It was a hot summer night," she recalled, and activists met in the capital for a gathering in a local theater.[53] While helping backstage, she ran into Park, struggling to ready herself for a speech. "Would you mind pinning up this wisp of hair for me?" Park asked.[54] The young woman remembered being surprised, since Park had a reputation for being such a shrewd lobbyist. But unlike the more radical activists, who got pleasure out of defying gender stereotypes in every way possible, including often in their personal dress, cultivating a womanly and even traditionally feminine appearance seemed important to Park.[55] Writing an article on the prominent Massachusetts suffragist several years later, the young woman reiterated this short anecdote to color her description of Park's political philosophies. "When Park talks about her ideals for women," she reported, "there is no bitter denunciation of 'sex slavery,' no battle cry for wholesale uprisings."[56] Instead, like Catt and others in NAWSA, Park believed that "sanity and moderation" served as the most important factors in effective campaign work.[57] This characterization of Park as calm, patient, and reasonable in her ambitions contrasted radically with that of her coworker, Irwin.

Irwin's demeanor was darker and much more overtly fiery, as her great anger toward women's unequal position in modern society only increased once she reached adulthood and drew her away from a "sane" and "moderate" political approach as promoted by Park and NAWSA. She commented in her writings, "I regretted bitterly that I had not been born a man."[58] She recalled later that growing up, she wanted to be everything from a sailor to a soldier. "I wanted to go to prizefights," Irwin wrote, reflecting on her mindset. Outings to places such as "barrooms; even barbershops and smoking rooms" seemed to offer the potential for "a brisk, salty taste of life," which was denied to those strictly confined to the domestic realm.[59] Reflecting on the lives of the female friends, family, and neighbors all around her, Irwin commented that they "degenerated" into two types, either "the fretful, thin, frail, ugly scold" or "the good-natured, fat, slatternly slut."[60] She wanted to be neither. Newspaper reports of the British suffragettes, who violently challenged women's unequal position overseas by carrying out actions like smashing windows and lighting fires, invigorated her as her dissatisfaction with a more strategically conservative lifestyle and groups like NAWSA heightened alongside others' during the period. "I became very impatient with the slowness of a struggle waged on such scrupulously polite lines," Irwin commented. "And when the first militant in England threw the first brick, my heart flew with it."[61] She became a "firm believer" in these types of forceful tactics and started to pull away from the more conventional NAWSA and CESL, eventually supporting Alice Paul and Lucy Burns's more radical vision for activism.[62]

During World War I, the NCESL and CESL alumni and college branches advocated the intermediary approach advanced by the NAWSA. Members began war work to aid the military while improving the perception of the equal-franchise campaign. Like other NAWSA affiliates, the CESL argued that activism to support the international crisis would simultaneously impel Congress to pass the federal amendment by earning the respect of patriotic Americans. Suffragists framed the war's end as an opportunity for the federal government to do justice to American women politically by granting them the franchise and for the country's current leaders thereby to make up for past actions, including the failure of politicians to grant women the ballot after the Civil War.[63] DC suffragists continued to set the tone for grassroots chapters nationwide by seeking new opportunities to lead mobilization on the home front and, through these efforts, win increased support for equal franchise. Members backed US troops, stirred emotions, and generated public favor by acting as mothers to soldiers with little family, "adopting them" and sending letters and gifts overseas.[64] The CESL took other traditional and socially acceptable steps to bolster the military effort, like donating food for Red Cross fundraisers.[65]

CESL alumni and college branches outside Washington followed the DC league into wartime activism. In Boston, from 1917 to 1919, the CESL staged fundraisers for the military and entertained the troops, assisting the work of the United Canteen by participating in programs meant to raise the spirits of visiting military men: every weekend, suffrage workers were sent to socialize with members of the armed forces. The Boston CESL offered the use of its writing and waiting room in the local Suffrage Coffeehouse to any American soldiers who stopped by.[66] The CESL participated in food drives and bake sales in Copley Plaza to raise money for the war fund.[67]

University students joined this war work and used school newspapers as forums to promote passing the Nineteenth Amendment as a "war measure."[68] On campuses, undergraduates argued for equal franchise by drawing on their peers' sense of nationalism. In 1917, one Barnard student, Edith Morgan, commented that traditional "war work is taking most of the time that is not given to academic work—but I don't think it should be so. I think we ought to care tremendously about the vote, now more than ever."[69] The military crisis only made the suffrage cause more relevant to some students. Morgan continued, "Politics has been brought more vividly into our homes by the war, but wouldn't it be even more our war, if women had the vote and could help decide what 'sacrifices' were needed . . . ?"[70] A Radcliffe student wrote, "The Senate seems to have forgotten that we are living in 1918, not in 1908. It is to be expected that a

Woman Suffrage Resolution would be defeated 54–30 in 1908, but in 1918, such a vote was behind the times, against the times."[71] She encouraged students to write to politicians and explain their "sentiments" regarding equal franchise as a progressive cause that would better the nation during the military conflict, improving democracy.[72] By the late 1910s, many members of the CESL made similar appeals, portraying support in favor of the suffrage issue as timely and fundamental to the country's future.

Despite this continued grassroots activism for the federal amendment and engagement in the suffrage issue on and off campus, the college league was facing interorganizational challenges. The NCESL voted to disband in December 1917 because of issues with finances and tensions among the group's leaders. Not wanting to harm the group's reputation, leaders publicly claimed that the national section disbanded only because the executive branch felt that the NCESL had achieved its primary goal of raising awareness about suffrage for women in higher education. As one press report declared, "The educational work for which the league was formed, that of making suffragists of college women, has been attained."[73] NCESL leaders asserted that continued equal-franchise activism in academia was unnecessary because most university women and men supported female voting rights. The organization pointed to other major academic groups advocating for woman suffrage, including the Association of Collegiate Alumni, as evidence of this success, and it used these associations' conversions to support the disbanding of the NCESL. Campaigners noted that after extensive NCESL lobbying, the ACA's perspective on equal franchise had shifted from disapproval to enthusiastic endorsement; it had even passed several pro-suffrage resolutions from 1915 to 1917.[74] The NCESL insisted that the respected academic organization's actions were proof of suffrage victory in higher education. NCESL leaders also cited its impressive membership figures. When the NCESL disbanded, its top three alumni branches—Boston, New York, and Washington, DC—had strong numbers for such a restrictive, special-interest association: approximately seven hundred, four hundred, and two hundred members, respectively.[75] By 1917, the NCESL supervised fifty-one college and alumni sections and encompassed over five thousand suffragists nationwide.[76]

* * *

Although the NCESL appeared successful, many unpublicized internal factors contributed to the disbanding. According to reports, the NCESL needed about five thousand dollars to cover its annual activism expenses in 1916, but the league had problems coming up with the money.[77] Vice presidents and executive officers skipped meetings because of internal schisms over the group's organizing, which weakened leadership on all levels and even influenced local cohesion.[78] Comments from state leaders indicated that the war took a toll on recruitment. According to the Boston secretary's report, from 1918 to 1919, mobilization had stalled in certain locations. "In the [Massachusetts] Colleges," she wrote, "the undergraduates' time outside their regular [course] work has been entirely taken up with War Work. So as also with the college graduates, the great majority have given up everything to devote their time to the branches of War Service."[79] Not all students and alumni supported the dominant wartime agenda of the NCESL, which resulted in difficulty attracting members and maintaining activism after 1917.[80]

Upon disbanding, the NCESL encouraged local chapters to fold into state suffrage associations or to become federal amendment clubs on campuses to support the grassroots activism of other, more mainstream equal-franchise organizations. Some CESL sections, however, refused to take this advice. Members argued that they could still contribute to the women's rights cause without abandoning the CESL title or negating the group's original aim of rallying more university support for equal franchise. The Radcliffe Suffrage Club did not dissolve until June 1920.[81] The Washington, DC, and the Boston alumni branches also continued until the Nineteenth Amendment passed. As one newspaper report commented, "When the National College League disbanded last December, the local chapter [DC] was undecided on what course to pursue. There was so much interest shown in the society here that the women kept up the work and retained its name."[82] Some grassroots branches refused to step down, remained independent from state suffrage parties, and began new federal amendment campaigns for women's right to vote under the CESL name.

After 1917, enduring local and state chapters of the CESL remained an active force in renewed efforts to bombard politicians and electors with requests for national equal-franchise legislation support. In Boston, the

CESL's alumni branch flooded congressional representatives with letters and telegrams inquiring about their stance on woman suffrage and pressuring the men of their class to endorse equal franchise.[83] In New York, during the spring of 1917, league members distributed literature to approximately forty-two hundred university men graduating in the state, hoping to secure new allies.[84] Through these actions and similar initiatives nationwide, the CESL's resilient grassroots sections made college-educated men, a crucial voting body within the electorate, consider the woman-suffrage question more closely.

In the South and other areas without organized branches, the influence of the CESL's sustained activism and the increased discussion that state suffragists generated on equal voting rights led prominent men in higher education, including local administrators and professors, to reconsider their positions; at times, new statements of public support were issued. In Louisiana, endorsement of the vote generated by visiting CESL representatives and local suffragists at Newcomb spurred Dr. Brandt Van Blarcom Dixon, president of the college, to declare his advocacy for equal franchise in New Orleans newspapers. Dixon stated, "I am for women's suffrage because the time is ripe for it." He continued, "Woman has taken so important a part in the world war, has filled places of responsibility so efficiently and conscientiously; she has shown such endurance and stability in trying situations; she occupies positions in every walk of life, even in the scientific laboratories. I consider it unfair that she should serve longer without a voice in the affairs of the world where she plays an important role. . . . Today is the day—the world is ready for unrestricted franchise."[85] Nationwide, the work of alumni both within and outside the CESL won further backing for female voting rights among greater numbers of the country's "elite" male electors.

Many of the CESL's remaining campus branches helped alumni sections to lobby politicians and prominent men for equal franchise after the NCESL's demise.[86] In 1919, Radcliffe suffragists obtained signatures on a petition to send to Congress that emphasized Massachusetts's support for the federal amendment.[87] During the late 1910s, students carried out other initiatives for national legislation, such as keeping abreast of current political attitudes toward women's right to vote in their local communities, writing reports about their findings, and publishing statistics

Figure 5.2. Radcliffe students go door to door handing out suffrage literature. Photo courtesy of the Schlesinger Library, Harvard Radcliffe Institute.

to inform the public, the nation's leaders, and other activists about the status of the equal-franchise campaign.[88]

* * *

During the final three years of the movement, college-educated African Americans reinforced federal amendment activism conducted by White suffragists by using their educational training and professional connections to construct compelling pleas for women's right to vote tailored to the upper classes. African American newspapers became an especially powerful tool: well-educated Black citizens used them to reach influential members of their race—particularly in the South, where high rates of racial violence suppressed outright protest, public demonstrations, and more overt organizing.[89] African Americans wrote numerous articles—published anonymously to protect suffragist identities—discreetly backing the campaign for female voting rights in the area.

World War I provided a key opportunity for middle- and upper-class Blacks to link the patriotic wartime culture that embraced ideals like active citizenship, democracy, and freedom with the causes of racial and gender equality. During the military crisis, a greater number of college-educated African Americans turned to the written word as an outlet for challenging White opposition, particularly related to politicians in the Jim Crow South who campaigned against the Nineteenth Amendment on the basis of discriminatory claims that extending the ballot to women would harm society by doubling the African American vote.[90] In 1918, the *St. Louis Argus* printed quotations from leading southern legislators like John Sharp Williams of Mississippi about Black women's voting rights. Williams attacked the Nineteenth Amendment using aggressive racial assertions. He claimed that although he "loved the President personally, perhaps better than any other man in the Senate," he was "unable to follow him in suffrage."[91] He further stated, "When the President says we can't lick Ludendorff, scare Bulgaria, and reconquer Palestine because Nigger women in Mississippi can't vote, I decline to agree with him."[92] By printing his comments for the Black community to see, the *Argus* discredited Williams's position. Furthermore, it followed its overview of his most outrageous remarks with stark criticisms about how the entire foundation for his desire to block women's right to vote relied on a "traitorous banner of race hatred," rather than any genuine claims.[93]

Upper-class Black suffragists writing in newspapers encouraged other well-educated and politically informed African Americans, especially those who could vote, not to endorse politicians like Williams, hoping to undercut support for and raise questions about the fitness for leadership of such prejudiced government figures. One Black citizen declared in the *Argus*, "Men like Williams of Mississippi, Reed of Missouri, and their miserable followers are too little to hold high places of trust either in state or national government. The spirit of race hate, which seems to actuate their every puny effort, unfits them for the big things that are required of real red-blooded Americans in the present crisis."[94] By using the media as their mouthpiece, Black suffragists publicly shamed elected officials. They labeled these officials "obstructionists" because they blocked the passage of the Nineteenth Amendment using racially charged rhetoric, encouraging divisions between Americans during wartime, when the country's people most needed to come together. In 1918, African Americans commented in the *Argus* that, given Black contributions to the military crisis—about three hundred thousand African American soldiers fighting to make the world "safe for democracy"—White politicians should take Black citizens' appeals for equal franchise much more seriously.[95] While Black men were legally enfranchised by federal amendment after the Civil War, grassroots politics and loopholes often left them excluded. "Denying a man participation in the government he fights to uphold, whose flag he carries upon its battlefield, whose institution he exposes his life to defend . . . may find justification" with some people, African Americans maintained, "but not with those who believe in RIGHT." The authors of the article continued, "The Colored women are doing their full care, giving their sons freely to their country's cause—answering every call of their government, as true women have done throughout the history of the world" and, thus, deserved full citizenship.[96] In pro-suffrage commentary during World War I, upper-class African Americans, including many college students and university graduates, used their writing, debate, and analytic skills creatively, fueling women's enfranchisement and discrediting any racially prejudiced campaigns against equal franchise by focusing on Black contributions to the war effort.

During the final years of the woman-suffrage movement outside the South, college-educated African Americans also lobbied politicians for female political equality and interviewed government leaders about their positions on equal franchise. In 1918, prominent Black suffragists from New Jersey, including members of the local branch of the National Association of Colored Women's Clubs, signed a petition pressuring Congress to pass the Susan B. Anthony Amendment.[97] In early 1920, members of the Women's Republican League from New York traveled to Washington, DC, to meet with state senators and ask their perspective on the suffrage amendment.[98] Throughout these campaigns, African Americans continuously reminded hesitant White leaders challenging women's right to vote based on race that by preventing equal franchise, they deprived White women the vote as well as Black women. As one suffragist wrote in the *New York Age*, "This is the irony of the whole Negro problem: 'The white people . . . have to deny themselves many of the good things they need and want because they are not willing for the Negro to have them too.'" White women, they continued, "evidently would like to have the vote, but their Senators must fight against the national enfranchisement of women"—all because they do not want "colored women" to join the electorate.[99] Black suffragists even alleged that perhaps some White politicians only used racial arguments to justify female disenfranchisement to hide the sexism central to their disapproval; they did not favor granting the right to vote to any woman, regardless of her background.[100]

Leading up to 1920, an increasing number of both Black and White suffragists expressed discontent with the campaign tactics and arguments espoused by mainstream women's rights organizations and pressed for change. Some restless White and Black college students and alumni claimed that most suffrage groups were not going far enough to promote equal voting rights. Some of these discontented suffragists were especially reluctant to take up traditional forms of women's war work to raise support for equal franchise. They viewed this manner of campaigning as a step backward and contradictory to the cause of women's rights. As disapproving campaigners pointed out, they were lobbying the government for greater equality between the sexes, yet the wartime agenda, promoted by major organizations such as the NAWSA, ironically mirrored the decades-old types of female civic engagement they had since outgrown. For some women, supporting the armed forces also meant backing sexist military institutions and programs that rarely saw women as equal to men.[101]

* * *

During the last years of the campaign, some frustrated suffragists switched their memberships to the NWP, the militant equal-franchise organization formed in 1916 by Alice Paul and Lucy Burns, former college graduates and CC leaders. Scholars have debated whether the NWP or NAWSA's campaigns were the most central to legislative success.[102] Whereas American social reformers, clubwomen, labor organizers, and politicians heavily shaped the NAWSA's methods, the NWP's activism was molded by the work of international feminists like the suffragettes in the United Kingdom. Although the NAWSA favored educational, orderly, controlled, and lawful agitation, the NWP preferred headline-generating, emotion-stirring, theatrical protest for women's rights that directly challenged the government.[103] These differing approaches reflected a larger generational divide between some older activists, who viewed these controversial demonstrations as unsuitable forms of political lobbying for women, and some younger women inspired by feminist ideology and current events to take up aggressive demonstrations to advance equal franchise.

Despite being known for their more contentious approach, most NWP supporters, such as CESL members, did not stage militant or fierce demonstrations for woman suffrage on college campuses. Instead, they reserved these tactics for political spaces within cities and cultivated federal amendment backing at universities in more subdued ways. The overt nature of the NWP's activism kept it distinct from the CESL. Representatives from the NWP marketed the group to university women as an organization created for and by the youth. The group held explicitly political events to attract students on campuses without attempting to mask or hide the truth behind their tactics and campaign goals—the NWP wanted to change the government.[104] Anita Pollitzer, a Columbia alumna and college professor, helped to organize a "Federal Suffrage Mass Meeting" at the University of Virginia, where she worked as an art instructor in the final years of the equal-franchise movement. She blatantly publicized the suffrage gathering through streetcar posters, "handmade slides at movies," and fliers produced by some of her students. Unlike CESL members, NWP suffragists like Pollitzer did not cloak their tactics in education; instead, they openly encouraged direct activism, getting students involved in lobbyist work that asked state senators, including Virginia's Thomas Staples Martin, to support the Nineteenth Amendment.[105] One particularly spirited campus meeting at Ohio University headed by NWP members in 1918 even resulted in a direct written appeal to President Woodrow Wilson asking for the passage of the national woman-suffrage legislation.[106]

Off campus, university women carried out the NWP's mission of urging the president and other politicians to support woman suffrage. Many college students and graduates participated in the NWP's federal amendment demonstrations in Washington, DC, in which suffragists highlighted inconsistencies between Woodrow Wilson's political platform and position on suffrage to make him look foolish, unjust, and hypocritical for denying the franchise to women. Wilson advocated an active and involved citizenry, so suffragists responded by more aggressively taking their campaigns to plead for female voting rights to the streets and government halls.[107] By helping other NWP members organize picketers outside the White House gates holding banners and signs that advocated woman suffrage, some university women became central to bolder demonstrations that frustrated politicians and captured headlines in the capital. Scholars have commented that World War I created a public market for sensational stories and journalism. Suffragists recognized that shocking actions would generate media headlines and publicity for their cause. Thus, the more outrageously they behaved, the more Americans would read about woman suffrage.[108]

Besides joining regular picket lines during the NWP White House protests in 1917, students and alumni demonstrated on special college days, urging government leaders to pass the equal-franchise amendment by emphasizing the support of well-educated Americans and youth.[109] NWP members affiliated with universities wore suffrage sashes that noted the names of their institutions and turned the sidewalks outside the White House into their own "pulpit" to promote women's right to vote among others of their class and academic standing.[110] At one event early on February 3, 1917, students and graduates showed up representing more than a dozen different schools; the largest delegation came from Goucher College, which one of Wilson's daughter's had attended.[111] The

Figure 5.3. A typical "College Day" on the protest line during the NWP picketing of the White House. Photo courtesy of the Library of Congress, Manuscript Division, National Woman's Party records.

presence of university support in DC for women's right to vote challenged some of the antisuffragists' most popular claims, including that female college students and members of the next generation were apathetic about American politics.

American entry into World War I, however, made NWP's public demonstrations for suffrage more controversial. NWP members faced harsh criticism from colleagues, families, and authorities because of their picket signs and speeches. The NWP's campaign material often quoted the president's comments on democracy, and the public and politicians no longer considered the protesting women carrying NWP banners as harmless attractions to ignore; instead, female protesters were considered radical, even anti-American, demonstrators.[112] To quell NWP picketing, the government arrested protesters on bogus charges, attempting to intimidate the suffragists into giving up their campaigns. President Wilson's administration believed that pressing charges would reduce backing for the NWP's equal-franchise activism among women fearful of facing formal punishment for their actions.[113]

These arrests only fueled the equal-franchise movement, especially among young women on campuses looking for adventure and a meaningful avenue to make a difference before and after graduation. As a result, many female students and recent alumni filled the jails. Their presence only drew greater public and political sympathy to the plight of the imprisoned suffragists, often respectable middle- and upper-class women. The NWP recognized that university students were key recruits. They could afford to protest on the front lines and had much less to lose physically, professionally, and socially, given their young age, than middle-aged or older women. After the media announced that the picketing suffragists would face punishment in places like the Occoquan Workhouse in Virginia and the local DC jail, many people rallied behind the young protesters and argued that the government was taking their response too far.[114] The involvement of college women in the NWP demonstrations only made it harder for male voters and political leaders to ignore the suffrage platform. Now, women of their own classes and from their own families were protesting and ending up in prison.

Little is known about the participation of African Americans in the NWP picketing and demonstrations except that NACWC activist Mary Church Terrell and her daughter took part in the protests outside the

White House. Other African Americans may have also been involved, although the NWP had a reputation as discriminatory. Suffragists and newspapers may not have documented the participation of certain people because of their role or race. As Doris Stevens comments in *Jailed for Freedom*, many women demonstrated but faced no punishment. Authorities arrested some picketers, but they never went on trial. Still other demonstrators encountered convictions, but the judiciary overturned their sentences. Unfortunately, the NWP recorded only the women who served jail time.[115]

Even from jail, college women were significant leaders and political actors protecting the rights of arrested suffragists. Students and graduates used their literacy skills and civic knowledge to challenge unfair treatment and build morale among NWP members. University women drafted petitions to the guards and authorities to improve the treatment of incarcerated suffragists. Elizabeth McShane Hilles, a recent Vassar graduate held in the DC jail for taking part in the campaigns, became a particularly powerful figure during her sentence. Hilles worked tirelessly to persuade the police to treat the NWP activists as political prisoners rather than common criminals. She demanded that the guards allow the women certain exceptions to the rules, including permission to wear civilian clothes, send and receive mail, have outdoor exercise, meet with visitors, and access food offered for sale or as gifts and donations.[116]

For younger college-educated women like Hilles, the stories of older alumni like Burns, Paul, and others of their academic standing, who refused to give up campaigns in the face of punishment, inspired continued engagement despite difficult conditions. Burns was a chief source of motivation for women like Hilles. Burns was an NWP leader, college graduate, and key leader in the picketing campaign. Stories about her dramatic experiences spurred on students and other alumni. Burns spent more time in prison than any other suffragist. First arrested in June 1917, she initially faced a paltry three-day sentence for her transgression; however, repeated clashes with authorities led to longer punishments, including a sixty-day jail stint that fall. After her release, Burns returned to the picket line instead of backing down until police finally curbed her demonstrating with a six-month sentence.[117] Nonetheless, Burns's actions and determination were an important example to younger campaigners of the NWP's core values. She became an icon for college women and was legendary on campuses.

Hilles often mentioned Burns in her writings and noted her impassioned suffrage activism alongside Paul, her NWP cofounder. Fueled by Paul, Burns, and other rabble rousers promoting contentious causes throughout history, Hilles continued protesting for women's right to vote. She, along with other jailed suffragists, participated in controversial hunger strikes to challenge the injustice of their imprisonment, refusing to eat until guards forcibly fed them. Speaking of the motivation for her extreme tactics, Hilles repeated that she was "trying to keep up courage by thinking of Christian martyrs, Alice Paul, Lucy Burns, and the general history of persecutions."[118] Encouraged by Burns's relentlessness in similar circumstances, Hilles said she viewed her as somewhat of a mentor. When authorities moved Burns from the Occoquan Workhouse in Virginia to the Washington hospital in the local DC jail where Hilles was serving her sentence, Hilles said she remembered feeling "so excited" to talk to Burns about the campaign.[119] "Finally, this p.m.," Hilles wrote, "Lucy Burns was carried in on a stretcher, looking like a corpse with her beautiful hair gleaming against her white, white face. Of course, we rushed to her cell, on the first floor, and knelt about her, breathless to see if she really lived. She has been 7 days without food and was forcibly fed through the nose in the hospital today. But, in spite of her looks, her spirit is as strong and cheering as ever. The whole world looked different when she began to speak."[120] When Hilles experienced her first force-feeding during a hunger strike, she was "outraged, hurt, and insulted" and went to Burns for support and "to weep hysterically on her shoulder."[121] Despite the concerns of health officials and encouraged by Burns's actions, Hilles remained on hunger strike and endured several more force-feedings. At one point, she took ipecac smuggled into the jail to induce vomiting, not wanting to be a traitor to the cause by ingesting any food.[122] The political precedents set by older college women like Burns deeply affected the activism of the younger generations.

After the picketing concluded, despite arrest and imprisonment, many university women remained at the forefront of the NWP's intensified protests to challenge female disenfranchisement. College women were crucial to other major events, such as a 1918 mass meeting for woman suffrage in Washington, DC, at the statue of the Marquis de Lafayette, a Frenchman who became a war hero of the American Revolution. The meeting drew nearly one hundred spectators and connected the founding principles of the country to the debates about female political inequality.[123] University students and alumni also participated in the NWP's "watch fire" demonstrations, during which members burned copies of the president's speeches in urns on the sidewalk outside the White House and other political spaces to draw attention to the equal-franchise campaign. During the protests, suffragists gave compelling and controversial talks that charged Woodrow Wilson, as the leader of the party in power, with "obstructing democracy" in the United States by denying women the ballot.[124] To further connect equal franchise and revolutionary ideals, the NWP used wood from a tree in Philadelphia's Independence Hall for the fires. College women were among the NWP members who received five-day sentences for taking part in these shocking and symbolic demonstrations.[125]

* * *

The continued agitation, education, and protests for woman suffrage by the NWP and the NAWSA in the late 1910s, however, eventually generated political change. By 1918, suffragists had convinced Woodrow Wilson to back the Nineteenth Amendment by openly exposing the "contradiction" between the president's principles and his administration's actions. If Wilson did not back equal-franchise legislation, he threatened to undermine his political "integrity" in the minds of the American people. With Wilson's backing, female enfranchisement became a more viable political issue and even a "democratic" war aim.[126] Wilson's conversion to a position of support for equal franchise, a controversial move for the commander-in-chief, thus proved particularly crucial to national legislative victory after the military crisis. His endorsement not only influenced public attitudes toward woman suffrage but also helped to shape the perspectives of upper-class men—the Americans with the greatest political power.[127]

Many college students and alumni, uninterested in traditional war work or radical campaigns, or looking for additional ways to contribute to the equal-franchise cause, focused on other initiatives, such as civic-education work, to shape the ideal female voter. After 1917, once national woman suffrage seemed inevitable, CESL members became active in heightened political-literacy training designed to prepare women for future electoral duties. The citizenship-education programs launched during World War I gained widespread support from White women because suffragists framed them as a part of home-front mobilization. CESL members argued that the female sex must be prepared to take over men's roles, including responsibilities in the political and economic realms, while their husbands were fighting overseas. NAWSA representatives, including organizers from the CESL's remaining grassroots branches, maintained that any woman preparing to assume her husband's position in government required a basic understanding of how politics operated.[128]

Given their educational training and access to university resources like books, libraries, and classrooms, students and alumni spearheaded wartime political-literacy work. On campuses, particularly in places like New York and California, where state governments had already passed legislation granting full voting rights for women, some former student organizations had already shifted tactics from protesting for equal franchise to establishing civic study groups. In 1911, after the grassroots victory in California, the Equal Suffrage Study Club at Berkeley became the Civic Study Club. This group arranged presentations to teach young women about government. Members reviewed local, state, and national laws, political issues, and current candidates.[129] From 1917 to 1920, schools like Radcliffe developed college civics clubs, and members heard many presentations on female involvement in government, including a 1917 address by social reformer Marion Booth Kelley on "Women and Some Human Civic Problems." Kelley contended that expanding female duties to politics would uplift the sex by widening women's worldviews.[130] At other institutions, student supporters advocated for new political science classes as a progressive measure, both as extracurricular activities and as part of college programs, that would teach university women about government to better the nation.[131]

The remaining CESL alumni branches in urban centers added to this grassroots citizenship-education work on campuses by leading community activism developed to teach women more about politics. The Boston section, one of the CESL's last remaining branches, was crucial to political-literacy campaigns in Massachusetts. Members staged many informative public presentations about government, including a symposium on "How to Vote and How Not to Vote" in 1920. The Boston CESL also helped to fund the citizenship-education initiatives of the city's League of Women Voters (LWV) as the movement for suffrage concluded. The local CESL's final major contribution was the publication of a manual for Massachusetts electors dedicated to women's rights pioneer Lucy Stone; it was a popular handbook used across the United States. The first edition sold three thousand copies in fewer than four months.[132] The success of the publication allowed the Boston CESL to make a lasting mark on civic education long after the organization had formally disbanded and became a model for the LWV's campaign literature.

During World War I, the democratic and nationalistic wartime culture occasionally brought together the more moderate White and Black suffragists in these final political-literacy campaigns, as activists perceived them as acceptable civic endeavors for women of both races.[133] To deter college-educated African Americans from joining the NWP's radical campaigns, and to encourage activism to further the NAWSA's objectives, some Black activists went public with challenges to the controversial protests. The popular African American magazine *The Crisis* promoted the NAWSA's work by publishing favorable statements by White leaders like Carrie Chapman Catt that urged cross-racial cooperation in the woman-suffrage movement. The November 1917 issue of *The Crisis* attempted to improve African American attitudes toward the NAWSA by noting that White suffragists had declared that their national organization would "stand for" a "broad type of American democracy that knows no bias on the ground of race, color, creed, or sex."[134] During the war, the publication also relayed Catt's message that White and Black suffragists should put aside racial prejudice and unite around the common goal of female advancement in a male-dominated society. "Just as the world war is no white man's war but every man's war, so is the struggle for woman suffrage not white woman's struggle but every woman's struggle," she said.[135] The Black press further presented commentary from Catt that highlighted the NWP's racism to gain support for the NAWSA within the Black community. *The Crisis* noted that Catt had rebuked the NWP protesters for complaining about

their White picketers "being housed with Negro prisoners," and "not because they were prisoners" but "because they were black." She called this
"a strangely and cruelly undemocratic protest."[136] Promoting unity and
integration over separation in the woman-suffrage campaign marked a
change in strategy for many mainstream White and Black activists, who
had often upheld the racial divide.

For college-educated Black women in the NACWC and other grassroots organizations, supporting the NAWSA's political-literacy work was
not a tremendous stretch of their goals or principles. Civic-education
programs had become commonplace among African Americans by the
late 1910s because Black suffragists emphasized political study over direct action to maintain a less controversial public image. After 1917, on
and off campus, many college-educated African Americans stepped up
their current civic campaigns, fueled by new connections with NAWSA
representatives and increasingly perceiving education about government
as the most instrumental step toward winning woman suffrage because
of its potential benefits for the country's future.[137] Black equal-franchise
supporters in Harlem formed a nonpartisan organization in 1918 to
teach the community about civics, and the Equal Suffrage League of
Brooklyn held meetings on topics such as "the proper appreciation and
use of the ballot."[138] African American women in Manhattan attended
lectures on "preparation for citizenship" conducted at the local Young
Women's Christian Association, and the NACWC continued promoting
political literacy among Black women. One African American suffragist
remarked that in the campaigns for suffrage conducted by members of
her race, they had "not blown up any houses with dynamite" or "been
engaged in parading the streets in men's attire," mocking the work of the
more radical campaigners in the United States and overseas.[139] Instead,
African Americans had urged sustained "reading and studying" of politics as the best method to support the equal-franchise cause in the new
era.[140] The Crisis noted that if the Nineteenth Amendment passed, millions of Black women would have the right to vote. "Let them get ready,"
the publication recommended. In a call to action, supporters pressed
that, in the North and South, "Study clubs should be formed, with teachers and reading matter."[141]

Despite the NAWSA's moves to bridge the racial divide and emphasize certain parallel campaign goals, not all NACWC members,

college-educated African Americans, or others within the Black community changed positions to support White suffrage parties. Many African Americans, up to date on current political matters and familiar
with the nation's history of racial prejudice, viewed any appeals for
"sisterhood" as questionable. During spring 1916, Minnie B. Mosby,
secretary of the Columbus, Ohio, branch of the NAACP, represented
the sentiment held by many Black women, asserting, "We have nothing to say against equal suffrage. But," she went on, "before the colored women come out in favor of woman suffrage, we believe the
white women backing the movement should show their willingness
to help wipe out the discrimination against colored people on the part
of theatres, hotels, restaurants and soda fountains."[142] Some African
Americans argued that if the Nineteenth Amendment passed, White
citizens would ultimately try to disenfranchise Black female voters,
and that newly enfranchised White women would likely just contribute to the political power of the members of their race who upheld
White supremacy. Overall, *The Crisis* maintained a cooperative pro-
suffrage position on equal franchise in the late 1910s; however, some
articles revealed conflict within the Black community over whether to
view the looming federal legislation as positive or negative for African
Americans; one write-up in 1917 remarked, "Two wrongs never make
a right."[143] It continued, "We cannot punish the insolence of certain
classes of American white women or correct their ridiculous fears by
denying them their undoubted rights."[144] Black suffragists conceded,
"It goes without saying that the women's vote, particularly in the South,
will be cast almost unanimously, at first, for every reactionary Negro-
hating piece of legislation that is proposed."[145]

In 1919, the Susan B. Anthony Amendment lost more support among
upper-class and college-educated African Americans in organizations
such as the NAACP and the NACWC. This took place after White politicians made two controversial suggestions for alterations to the original legislation, and some White activists endorsed the changes. Late in
the campaign, A. A. Jones of New Mexico, chair of the Senate Suffrage
Committee, proposed the "Jones Amendment," and Senator Edward J.
Gay of Louisiana advocated the "Gay Resolution." Both alterations created loopholes in state enforcement of women's right to vote that stood
to keep Black female citizens disenfranchised. The Jones Amendment

would "permit women to vote in each state" but only to the same extent as men.[146] The law would leave in place any existing local exclusions from the franchise that restricted male citizens from casting ballots, extending those restrictions to the new female voters. The Gay Resolution would give the states, rather than the federal government, "exclusive authority to pass legislation for the enforcement" of the Nineteenth Amendment, thus providing another avenue to leave ultimate control over female voting rights in local hands. Sara Hunter Graham mentions the proposal of the Gay Resolution and other exclusionary options discussed at the time. She comments that NAWSA members also considered, for example, "an alternative amendment that would grant women the right to vote in congressional elections" only. Beyond this, another politician put forth a "substitute resolution" in order to bar "immigrant women" from the vote, "regardless of their husbands' citizenship." Graham points out that NAWSA did not back either proposition.[147]

Upon learning of attempts to alter the national legislation and allow more state power over the new electoral law, outraged NAACP members vowed that the group would not back the Nineteenth Amendment until White suffragists ensured equal voting rights for all women without limitations based on race or class.[148] Noted activists within the NACWC, including leader Nannie Burroughs, recommended that African Americans "kill woman suffrage" if the federal legislation seemed as though it would exclude Black women from the franchise.[149] To others of her race, she exclaimed that most mainstream suffragists were too "willing to throw" African Americans "overboard in order to get white women into the ship."[150] After hearing about the proposed changes to the woman-suffrage legislation, the Northeastern Federation of Women's Clubs, a regional body of the NACWC, took a particularly shrewd approach to challenging the prejudice they faced by seeking "cooperative membership" in the largely all-White NAWSA, a move that stood to affiliate six thousand Black women with the national organization.[151] The NACWC told NAWSA leaders that African Americans would only withdraw their application if the NAWSA formally opposed the Jones Amendment.[152] In doing so, the NACWC put pressure on White leaders, who feared a racial disaster if they added so many Black women to their organization's membership all at once.[153] Because of protests by Black and White suffragists, the Jones Amendment and other proposed changes to the equal-franchise legislation failed. The original version of the suffrage law passed through Congress. However, the memory of White attitudes, actions, and urgency to approve equal franchise by any means necessary, even at the expense of Black women, caused some African Americans to withdraw support from the mainstream women's movement and prompted renewed focus on racial equality in the period that followed.[154]

* * *

Despite racial tensions, all suffragists rejoiced after enough states ratified the Nineteenth Amendment on August 18, 1920, when Tennessee, the final state, endorsed the new legislation that granted American women the right to the franchise nationwide. In Washington, DC, suffragists, both White and Black, gathered in Poli's Theater to commemorate the event; Howard University even helped with the decorations. Jeanette Carter, an African American suffragist, later recalled the following: "The theatre was bedecked with flags and flowers and with a sea of faces in which those of women predominated, and the enthusiasm of the gathered host was so contagious none could escape infection of it. The women were rejoicing at the end of the long struggle, covering four generations, for the right to vote."[155] During the gathering, NAWSA leaders again tried to put aside divisions by giving patriotic speeches about how winning the ballot bettered the entire country's people. President Carrie Chapman Catt rejoiced, "It is not a Republican victory; not a Democratic victory; it is not a woman's victory nor a man's victory—but an American victory."[156] Ironically, despite this success, many African American voters, male and female, remained disenfranchised for decades, especially in the South, and would not taste true victory until much later.[157]

One positive effect of the Nineteenth Amendment's passage for all Americans, however, was the improvement in civic education that followed the woman-suffrage campaign. Catt appointed CESL cofounder Maud Wood Park as the first president of the national LWV, as she was particularly impressed by Park's work to engage university women in politics. Formed in 1920, the LWV trained female citizens for new electoral responsibilities, replacing the retiring NAWSA. Although it had been three years since the NCESL had formally disbanded, Park's early goals of promoting political literacy among the youth and recruiting more students and alumni to the equal-franchise cause had indelibly altered the women's rights movement and higher education.

The CESL's national and federal organizing for the amendment vote brought a new generation of university women to the forefront of female political activism, especially as leaders, for the first time. Although male voters and government officials had easily ignored marginal female citizens and their civic platforms, it was harder to dismiss the equal-franchise issue with a growing number of college-educated Americans from their own class rallying for their attention. During the early twentieth century, college recruits helped turn the woman-suffrage movement into a mainstream, accepted, and politically viable campaign. While the leaders of the NAWSA, its branches (such as the CESL), and the NWP were often at odds over tactics, their campaigns reinforced one another to bolster the movement for the ballot among the country's leaders. Without the ongoing educational tactics of more moderate groups like the CESL laying the groundwork by teaching the public about the equal-franchise issue, the activism of more contentious and dramatic organizations like the NWP might not have been as effective. Suffragists needed a combination of young blood, civic enlightenment, and political protest to win the vote for women in the national arena.

Conclusion

Following the Civil War, from the late nineteenth to the early twentieth century, opportunities for women in higher education increased
dramatically throughout the United States. By 1920, women made up
47 percent of all pupils at colleges and universities nationwide. Their
increased enrollment was a product of the need to fill seats because of
men's participation during the war and women's expanded participation
in the public sphere.[1] Though more women enrolled in higher education
than in prior eras, female students still faced considerable sex discrimination on campuses throughout much of the twentieth century. Over
time, some college women had sought the vote to help equalize perceptions of their status and role within society on and off campus. The vote
was a tool that they hoped would improve their plight and the plight
of others after them. After the national equal-franchise victory in 1920,
women's rights activism in higher education did not dissipate—the campus did not cease to be an important stage for the women's movement,
nor did the women's movement "gray" after the suffrage victory overall,
as some scholars have argued.[2] Many prominent female reform organizations continued campus activism to recruit and engage the youth to
achieve suffragists' goals of turning more women, particularly those of
the next generation, into active voters, promoting greater gender equity
in academia and society, and continuing the fight against political apathy among students, recognizing that much work remained following
the Nineteenth Amendment's passage.

Between what scholars have termed "first-" and "second-wave" feminism (activism for suffrage and activism for reproductive rights and
other issues in the 1960s and '70s), the League of Women Voters, the organization that members of the disbanded National American Woman
Suffrage Association formed in 1920, of which the College Equal Suffrage League was an affiliate, became a particularly prominent force in
turning young women into more engaged citizens and equal partners

in the public world.[3] In 1924 and 1925, the LWV started college campaigns to fulfill the legacy of the equal-franchise movement and to get women registered to vote and teach them about how the government worked and about the platforms of political parties.[4] One of the LWV's chief aims, on and off campus, was to ensure that newly enfranchised women—especially the younger generations who would become the nation's future leaders—were an informed and engaged voting bloc. The LWV promoted "active citizenship" as the new ideal for college women, and through this tactic, the organization aspired to combat what scholars called civic "slacking" among the younger generations.[5]

The group's campus activism, spearheaded by the LWV's first president and former CESL cofounder, Maud Wood Park, started with courses, schools, and institutes that cultivated discussion forums for female students to learn more about popular political issues directly from domestic and international civic leaders. This effort was designed to involve greater numbers of university women in government. LWV members motivated university women to sign up for these educational events by offering them initially as extracurricular options, which made the league's programs seem more entertaining, enriching, and supplemental than strictly scholarly. As citizenship courses became more publicly accepted and viewed as important to the nation, the LWV increasingly institutionalized its classes in schools, where participating pupils could sometimes receive university credit.[6] The LWV also encouraged female students to attend its courses through other tactics, such as issuing certificates of completion. The league's certificates could be professionally beneficial to graduates by serving as evidence of political proficiency on résumés, bolstering perceptions of female readiness for employment in the public sphere.[7] The LWV's campus events helped inspire more women to take political science classes and participate in college government.

After the equal-franchise victory in 1920, the National Woman's Party became another prominent force in encouraging university women to maintain interest in the government and exercise their citizenship rights. However, the NWP took a much more controversial approach to college campaigns. Instead of focusing on training civically minded young women for voting, which had been the LWV's chief goal, the NWP centered its activism on turning university women into political lobbyists for the Equal Rights Amendment. The NWP aspired to awaken students' civic consciousness using hands-on tactics that educated college women not only about casting ballots but also about female status and sex discrimination. Following the Nineteenth Amendment's passage, the group continued to motivate students to take up arms in very public ways in the fight for women's rights and female advancement in all aspects of society, an approach that clashed with the LWV's more subdued campaigns but had the effect of engaging students in women's rights activism after 1920 in the collegiate environment.

At the same time that the LWV was forming university branches in the 1920s, the NWP was expanding its newly created Students' Council, or university division, based on the precedent set by the CESL and designed to mobilize undergraduate women to take direct political action to support the parent organization's agenda.[8] NWP representatives advertised the Students' Council as a CESL replacement and the first "College Equal Rights League" for women to distinguish the group from more moderate civic study clubs within the academy, such as the LWV's campus sections.[9] During the 1920s and 1930s, the Students' Council attracted members from various East Coast institutions—including finishing schools, public schools, and the area's colleges—close to the NWP's primary headquarters in Washington, DC. NWP representatives campaigned in nearby locations, such as Maryland, Virginia, New York, Vermont, Massachusetts, Connecticut, and Pennsylvania.[10] The Students' Council set up early chapters at institutions of higher education, such as Yale Law School, the National University School of Law, and Goucher College.[11] By 1925, Students' Council members noted that the group included pupils from over forty establishments and had eight university sections to generate ERA backing among college women.[12]

Just as the former CESL founder, Park, was central to guiding the LWV's university campaigns, NWP veteran and Swarthmore College graduate Mabel Vernon was active in the NWP's campus work. Vernon's philosophy when campaigning among college women revolved around the NWP slogan "Education Helps Equal Rights."[13] She believed that students, teachers, and professors could be important allies in challenging the misconceptions about women that led to sex discrimination by using their academic influence to speak out against outdated perspectives on sex differences in classrooms. As with the CESL's early "obligation of opportunity" concept, employed to inspire female students to support woman suffrage by connecting the campaigns of older and newer generations of activists, Vernon insisted that current university women needed to repay prior organizers for securing the rights and freedoms that college women currently enjoyed by promoting the ERA. Vernon reminded female students that ideas about gender equality had been at the root of arguments for women's advancement in higher learning for centuries.[14]

The National Association of Colored Women's Clubs (NACWC—formerly the NACW)—an outlet for Black university women interested in politics and equality but barred from or discriminated against in many White organizations—similarly continued to garner a sizable following among middle- and upper-class African Americans, who aspired to advance their gender and race through new campaigns for civic engagement. As the NACWC expanded, the group developed fresh strategies for attracting younger generations, including planning an affiliate called the National Association of Colored Girls (NACG) in 1928. Officially founded in 1930, the NACG appointed Black activist Sallie W. Stewart, a teacher and former student at the University of Chicago and Indiana University, as its leader.[15] The NACG was not exclusively a college group; however, high school and university students comprised the majority of the members, who ranged in age from five to thirty-one.[16] Through the NACG, the NACWC set out to uplift African Americans' status and heighten involvement in government by turning more Black women into "community leaders" or young people who set a positive example for others of their race and gender through "proper" behavior, appearance, and political participation.

Black women have faced ongoing oppression based on factors such as racial and sex discrimination. They have responded to the injustices that they have confronted differently from both Black men and White women. Black women's activism interwove campaigns for racial uplift, social welfare, and civil rights.[17] Given this approach, like the LWV's African American branches, the NACG did not go to college campuses to garner support, at least not initially, and the group's organizing started first in Black communities to reach the broadest audiences.[18] In cities and neighborhoods, NACG members also promoted a unique kind of expanded citizenship common for generations among proponents of

African American social mobility. The NACG, like similar older Black women's organizations, was more concerned with members' morality and social conduct than strictly their political actions, which the organization viewed as central to molding a better populace. As in prior periods, one way in which upper- and middle-class African Americans had asserted their authority and status was through "proper" behavior, manners, dress, and decorum. The White community barred them at times from the economic opportunities and traditional avenues for advancement that Whites pursued. Because of this, Black civic activists focused more closely on these cultural elements in shaping their ideal for the modern woman.[19] For the NACG, reflecting a different experience for Black women, "good citizenship" meant more than just casting ballots or lobbying for greater rights. It also meant maintaining a respectable reputation.

After suffrage, women's rights advocates did not stop recruiting the younger generation and mobilizing them in the service of their organizations, but their ideologies and objectives kept them divided. The different visions for contemporary womanhood promoted to the youth by women's organizations such as the NACG, the NWP, and the LWV, in the post-suffrage period, are often unconsidered factors that fueled divisions among women's rights activists during what scholars have called the "interwave" years. Although some historians assume that the women's movement entered a second "doldrums" in the post-1920 period, female citizens did not abandon the women's rights cause following full enfranchisement, especially on the local level or on campus, and activism did not "gray" in the ways that many studies have contended. However, considering activism on and off campus provides more evidence for the argument that the female political agenda did become more fragmented. The campus campaigns of the LWV, NWP, and NACG did not always align, but the groups' activism kept the women's movement alive at colleges following the Nineteenth Amendment's passage. Scholarship that suggests that second-wave feminism on college campuses emerged solely because of civil rights demonstrations and anti–Vietnam War protests in the 1960s and 1970s has overlooked the longer tradition of women's organizing at universities that spanned the twentieth century.[20]

After 1920, groups such as the LWV, NWP, and NACWC continued to work to fulfill the legacy of suffragists by drawing more female students into political activism and interesting them in learning about how government operated in the larger society and on campus. Scholars have too long measured the success of these women's rights activists by the number of female citizens casting ballots or by the number of changes to the federal government that they helped establish. Although the Nineteenth Amendment's passage and the organizing that followed might not have resulted in as many women exercising their political voices in the ways that some campaigners had hoped, female civic activism in the twentieth century did alter the culture of higher education, forcing political science departments to hire more female faculty and accept more women students, leading to women's participation in college government, making curriculum more equitable between men and women, increasingly encouraging women to question other forms of sexism and their unequal status on campus, and fueling new gender ideals for contemporary womanhood. The political-literacy work of women's associations that started, because of the equal-franchise campaigns, before 1920 made civic education more accessible to Americans of all backgrounds and helped usher it into the central position within US society and education that it still holds. The amendment opened new doors for women in leadership roles and helped to create the societal change needed for their successful political careers today.

ACKNOWLEDGMENTS

This manuscript is the product of hard work, dedication, and overcoming many roadblocks. I have a multitude of people to thank for their commitment to my professional development and the project. I would like to foremost thank the faculty and staff at Binghamton University (SUNY) for their guidance while I was a PhD student. My advisor and committee—Diane Miller Sommerville, Thomas Dublin, Stephen Ortiz, and Adam Laats—all read numerous documents that I wrote, made detailed suggestions on my writing and arguments, and taught me the skills I needed to become a professional historian. I am grateful for everything I learned from them. Professors Dublin and Laats believed in my work on suffrage and women's education and offered essential professional and research-related advice that helped to make this book a reality.

At Binghamton, I would like to also express my appreciation to Professors Leigh Ann Wheeler, Wendy Wall, Nancy Appelbaum, Anne Bailey, Robert Parkinson, Elizabeth Casteen, Jean Quataert, Elisa Camiscioli, and Ashley Johnson Bavery for offering important mentoring at various moments during my time in New York. I would like to thank my former professors at the University of Massachusetts–Amherst for their assistance while I was a master's student. Heather Cox Richardson, Francis G. Couvares, José Angel Hernández, and Joyce Avrech Berkman all offered key support when I was beginning my career. Professor Richardson helped shape arguments for this project in its very early stages, and Professors Berkman and Couvares, at critical moments, helped me to find a path forward.

Key research and writing for the book was conducted as I became a new professor. I would like to thank Professors Katherine Hermes, Heather Munro Prescott, Mary Ann Mahony, Leah Glaser, Mark Jones, John Day Tully, and others in the History Department and women's studies program at Central Connecticut State University, where I was an undergraduate student and had my first full-time job as a visiting faculty member. I learned a lot at CCSU and gained experience that laid the foundation for the opportunities I currently have. I am especially grateful to David K. Thomson of Sacred Heart University for his professional guidance on how to navigate getting a book contract, as well as to David N. Luesink, Jennifer McLaughlin, John Roney, Bethany Wade, Kevin Gledhill, Jillian Plummer, and Gregory Viggiano, my SHU history colleagues, who keep me inspired and provide important community each semester. I would like to express my gratitude to my other friends throughout the university in different departments who keep every day full of laughter. Above all, I am particularly indebted to Charlotte Gradie, who pushed me hard to get my book underway and to submit a proposal to the press. Without her insistence, I am not sure I would have ever believed in myself enough to make this project a reality.

I am thankful to the many institutions that provided research grants and funding for this project. I would like to thank the Binghamton University History Department and graduate school, which offered assistantships, travel grants, and jobs until my degree was complete. I would like to thank the Schlesinger Library, the Sophia Smith Collection, and the Newcomb Archives for awarding me several grants to conduct research early in my project's development. At these institutions, Susan Tucker, Susan Landry, and Sarah Hutcheon, among others, were helpful with requests and vital in introducing sources that I would not have known about without their assistance.

For recent help with the development of the book and materials, I am grateful to several institutions. First, I am thankful to the team at New York University Press for giving me the opportunity to move forward with this project and to Clara Platter for advocating for my scholarship. They have made the process for a first book author clear, swift, and seamless. I was fortunate that they agreed to take a chance on me and my work. I thank my peer reviewers, Jennifer Frost and Thomas Dublin, who put hours into reading my drafts and writing detailed comments on them. I am also grateful to the many institutions that helped me acquire the images that I needed for the book: the Schlesinger Library, Harvard University, Columbia University, Barnard College, Howard University, the Library of Congress, Mount Holyoke College, Bryn Mawr College, and the Belmont-Paul Monument. At the Schlesinger, Diana Carey was a saint in dealing with my many emails, inquiries, and requests.

Also, regarding outside support, I would like to express my appreciation to Professors Sara Brooks Sundberg, Jessica Brannon-Wranosky, Rosalyn Terborg-Penn, Mary Kelley, and Beth Salerno, key faculty members at other institutions who offered advice while I worked on conference papers that would lead to later chapters of this book. Since then, others, such as Laura Prieto, Robert Chiles, Cathleen D. Cahill, Wendy L. Rouse, Allison K. Lange, Lauren C. Santangelo, and other Twitterstorians who post about suffrage on social media have been inspirational. The wonderful online community has kept me going and feeling less lonely as I have established my professional career.

Completing my project would have been impossible without the support of my friends and family. Particularly, I am indebted to Kevin Vrevich and Nidhi Shrivastava Farfaglia, my long-standing academic friends who have supported me during this process. They have offered advice on this book from the start over uncountable coffees and meals. I am grateful to my family—Debi, Michael, and Matthew Marino—for their patience as I have worked to establish a career. They endured many long trips back and forth from Connecticut to New York while I was in graduate school and fielded many long phone calls when I needed advice.

NOTES

INTRODUCTION

1 Ida Husted Harper, ed., *History of Woman Suffrage, 1900–1920*, vol. 5 (New York: National American Woman Suffrage Association, 1922), 663.

2 Harper, ed., *History of Woman Suffrage, 1900–1920*, vol. 5, 663.

3 "Mrs. Kelley's Lecture," *Barnard Bulletin*, April 29, 1908.

4 Ethel Puffer Howes, "The National College Equal Suffrage League," *Smith Alumnae Quarterly* 12, no. 1 (November 1920): 44.

5 Howes, "The National College Equal Suffrage League," 44.

6 Howes, "The National College Equal Suffrage League," 44.

7 These official figures do not account for the number of students that the association may have inspired to take up activism or form college clubs not affiliated with the league.

8 Harper, ed., *History of Woman Suffrage, 1900–1920*, vol. 5, 663.

9 Maud Wood Park, "College Equal Suffrage League Supplementary Notes," January 1943, reel 41, Subseries C. Suffrage and Women's Rights, Maud Wood Park Papers in the Woman's Rights Collection, 1870–1960 (microfilm edition), Schlesinger Library, Radcliffe Institute, Harvard University, Cambridge, MA (hereafter, Maud Wood Park Papers).

10 Katherine H. Adams and Michael L. Keene, *Alice Paul and the American Suffrage Campaign* (Urbana: University of Illinois Press, 2008); Margaret Mary Finnegan, *Selling Suffrage: Consumer Culture and Votes for Women* (New York: Columbia University Press, 1999); Inez Haynes Gillmore, *Up Hill with Banners Flying* (Penobscot, ME: Traversity Press, 1964); Christine A. Lunardini, *From Equal Suffrage to Equal Rights: Alice Paul and the National Woman's Party, 1910–1928* (Lincoln, NE: ToExcel Press, 1986); Doris Stevens, *Jailed for Freedom* (New York: Boni and Liveright, 1920).

11 Linda K. Kerber, *Women of the Republic: Intellect and Ideology in Revolutionary America* (Chapel Hill: University of North Carolina Press, 1997), 10, 185–232. For more information about women's education before the Civil War, see Mary Kelley, *Learning to Stand and Speak: Women, Education, and Public Life in America's Republic* (Chapel Hill: University of North Carolina Press, 2006); Lucia McMahon, *Mere Equals: The Paradox of Educated Women in the Early American Republic* (Ithaca, NY: Cornell University Press, 2012); Barbara Welter, "The Cult of True Womanhood," *American Quarterly* 18 (Summer 1966): 151–74; Rosemarie Zagarri, *Revolutionary Backlash: Women and Politics in the Early American Republic* (Philadelphia: University of Pennsylvania Press, 2007), 51–53.

12 Ellen Carol DuBois, *Harriot Stanton Blatch and the Winning of Woman Suffrage* (New Haven, CT: Yale University Press, 1997), 91; Finnegan, *Selling Suffrage*, 6; Jo Freeman, *A Room at a Time: How Women Entered Party Politics* (Lanham, MD: Rowman & Littlefield, 2000), 52.

13 Sara Hunter Graham, *Woman Suffrage and the New Democracy* (New Haven, CT: Yale University Press, 1996), 33–52.

14 For more information about the "Society Plan," see Nancy Cott, *The Grounding of Modern Feminism* (New Haven, CT: Yale University Press, 1987), 33; Graham, *Woman Suffrage and the New Democracy*, 33–52; Gayle Ann Gullett, *Becoming Citizens: The Emergence and Development of the California Women's Movement, 1880–1911* (Urbana: University of Illinois Press, 2000); 95, 100, 149, 184.

15 Nancy Nygard Pilon, "Women's Athletics at the University of Kansas during the Progressive Era, 1890–1920" (PhD diss., University of Kansas, 2008), 17.

16 For studies addressing college women's part in Progressive Era social reform and other political activism not related to suffrage, see Philip Altbach, *Student Politics in America: A Historical Analysis* (New York: McGraw-Hill, 1973), 21; Lewis S. Feuer, *The Conflict of Generations: The Character and Significance of Student Movements* (New York: Basic Books, 1969), 16; Helen Lefkowitz Horowitz, *Campus Life: Undergraduate Cultures from the End of the Eighteenth Century to the Present* (New York: Knopf, 1987), 11–22; Christine D. Myers, *University Coeducation in the Victorian Era: Inclusion in the United States and the United Kingdom* (New York: Palgrave Macmillan, 2010), 120–44; Margaret Nash, *Women's Education in the United States, 1780–1840* (New York: Palgrave Macmillan, 2005), 122, 125, 134, 137, 720; David P. Setran, *The College "Y": Student Religion in the Era of Secularization* (New York: Palgrave Macmillan, 2007), 33–35.

17 Horowitz, *Campus Life*, 195–200.

18 Barbara M. Solomon, *In the Company of Educated Women: A History of Women in Higher Education in America* (New Haven, CT: Yale University Press, 1985), 112.

19 Lynn D. Gordon, *Gender and Higher Education in the Progressive Era* (New Haven, CT: Yale University Press, 1990), 35, 194–95.

20 Helen Lefkowitz Horowitz, *Alma Mater: Design and Experience in the Women's Colleges from Their Nineteenth-Century Beginnings to the 1930s* (Amherst: University of Massachusetts Press, 1993), 286.

21 Anne M. Boylan, *The Origins of Women's Activism: New York and Boston, 1797–1840* (Chapel Hill: University of North Carolina Press, 2002), chap. 2, 55–73. For works that note the ages of women's rights activists across the twentieth century, see Nancy Cott, "Feminist Politics in the 1920s: The National Woman's Party," *Journal of American History* 71, no. 1 (June 1984): 43–68; Cott, *The Grounding of Modern Feminism*, 57, 151–52; Holly J. McCammon, "Stirring up Suffrage Sentiment: The Formation of the State Woman Suffrage Organizations, 1866–1914," *Social Forces* 80, no. 2 (December 2001): 449–80; Holly J. McCammon, Karen E. Campbell, Ellen M. Granberg, and Christine Mowery, "How Movements Win: Gendered Opportunity Structures and U.S. Women's Suffrage Movements, 1866

to 1919," *American Sociological Review* 66, no. 1 (February 2001): 49–70; Caryn E. Neumann, "The National Woman's Party and the Equal Rights Amendment, 1945–1977" (MA thesis, Florida Atlantic University, 1994), introduction.

22 Pilon, "Women's Athletics at the University of Kansas," 17.

23 Elna C. Green, *Southern Strategies: Southern Women and the Woman Suffrage Question* (Chapel Hill: University of North Carolina Press, 1997), xv, 25–26, 98–100, 153, 160, 175–76; Aileen S. Kraditor, *The Ideas of the Woman Suffrage Movement, 1890–1920* (New York: Columbia University Press, 1965), 49–55; Marjorie Spruill Wheeler, *New Women of the New South: The Leaders of the Woman Suffrage Movement in the Southern States* (New York: Oxford University Press, 1993), 102–13, 130–32, 135, 169.

24 Louise Michele Newman, *White Women's Rights: The Racial Origins of Feminism in the United States* (New York: Oxford University Press, 1999), chap. 2; Allison L. Sneider, *Suffragists in an Imperial Age: U.S. Expansion and the Woman Question, 1870–1929* (New York: Oxford University Press, 2008).

25 Until the suffrage centennial in the United States, there was little scholarship on Black women and suffrage. The topic often came up in other works about Black women's politics and social reform. See Ann D. Gordon and Bettye Collier-Thomas, eds., *African American Women and the Vote: 1837–1965* (Amherst: University of Massachusetts Press, 1997); Paula Giddings, *In Search of Sisterhood: Delta Sigma Theta and the Challenge of the Black Sorority Movement* (New York: Perennial, 2002), 57–62; Glenda Elizabeth Gilmore, *Gender and Jim Crow: Women and the Politics of White Supremacy in North Carolina, 1896–1920* (Chapel Hill: University of North Carolina Press, 1996); Rosalyn Terborg-Penn, *African American Women in the Struggle for the Vote, 1850–1920* (Bloomington: Indiana University Press, 1998); Deborah Gray White, *Too Heavy a Load: Black Women in Defense of Themselves, 1894–1994* (New York: Norton, 1999).

Since 2020, several scholars have written key monograph-length studies of women of color and suffrage, arguing for their central (rather than marginal) place in the campaign and recovering their contributions to state and national campaigns. For example, see Cathleen D. Cahill, *Recasting the Vote: How Women of Color Transformed the Suffrage Movement* (Chapel Hill: University of North Carolina Press, 2020); Martha S. Jones, *Vanguard: How Black Women Broke Barriers, Won the Vote, and Insisted on Equality for All* (New York: Basic Books, 2020).

26 Tamara L. Brown, Gregory S. Parks, and Clarenda M. Phillips, *African American Fraternities and Sororities: The Legacy and the Vision* (Lexington: University Press of Kentucky, 2012), 172, 193–94; Jessica Harris, "Women of Vision, Catalyst for Change: The Founders of Delta Sigma Theta Sorority," in *Black Greek-Letter Organizations in the Twenty-First Century: Our Fight Has Just Begun*, ed. Gregory Parks (Lexington: University Press of Kentucky, 2008); Giddings, *In Search of Sisterhood*, 57–62; Terborg-Penn, *African American Women in the Struggle for the Vote*, 105, 123.

27 Kristi Andersen, *After Suffrage: Women in Partisan and Electoral Politics before the New Deal* (Chicago: University of Chicago Press, 1996), 447–48, 456. Also, see articles from the period, such as William F. Ogburn and Inez Goltra, "How Women Vote," *Political Science Quarterly* 34 (September 1919): 413–33; Stuart D. Rice and Malcolm M. Willey, "American Women's Ineffective Use of the Vote," *Current History* 20 (1924): 641–47. In addition, see early studies of women's rights, such as William Henry Chafe, *The American Woman: Her Changing Social, Economic, and Political Roles, 1920–1970* (New York: Oxford University Press, 1972); Kraditor, *The Ideas of the Woman Suffrage Movement*; William L. O'Neill, *Everyone Was Brave: The Rise and Fall of Feminism in America* (Chicago: Quadrangle Books, 1969).

28 See Andersen, *After Suffrage*, 2, 4, 6–8; Paula Baker, "The Domestication of Politics: Women and American Political Society, 1780–1920," *American Historical Review* 89 (June 1984): 620–47; Cott, *The Grounding of Modern Feminism*; Elisabeth S. Clemens, "Organizational Repertoires and Institutional Change: Women's Groups and the Transformation of U.S. Politics, 1890–1920," *American Journal of Sociology* 98 (January 1992): 755–98; Jo Freeman, *A Room at a Time*; J. Stanley Lemons, *The Woman Citizen: Social Feminism in the 1920s* (Urbana: University of Illinois Press, 1973); Liette P. Gidlow, *The Big Vote: Gender, Consumer Culture, and the Politics of Exclusion, 1890s-1920s* (Baltimore, MD: Johns Hopkins University Press, 2004), esp. 80–109; Michael E. McGerr, "Political Style and Women's Power, 1830–1930," *Journal of American History* 77 (December 1990): 864–85; Robyn Muncy, *Creating a Female Dominion in American Reform, 1890–1935* (New York: Oxford University Press, 1994), esp. 125–28; Lorraine Gates Schuyler, *The Weight of Their Votes: Southern Women and Political Leverage in the 1920s* (Chapel Hill: University of North Carolina Press, 2006), esp. introduction; Kathryn Kish Sklar, "Historical Foundations of Women's Power in the Creation of the American Welfare State, 1830–1930," in *Mothers of a New World: Maternalist Politics and the Origins of Welfare States*, eds. Seth Koven and Sonya Michel (New York: Routledge, 1993), 43–93; Susan Ware, *Beyond Suffrage: Women in the New Deal* (Cambridge, MA: Harvard University Press, 1981); Jan Doolittle Wilson, *The Women's Joint Congressional Committee and the Politics of Maternalism, 1920–30* (Urbana: University of Illinois Press, 2007).

29 Ellen Carol DuBois, *Feminism and Suffrage: The Emergence of an Independent Women's Movement in America, 1848–1869* (Ithaca, NY: Cornell University Press, 1978), introduction, 17–18.

30 Jana Nidiffer, "The National College Equal Suffrage League," in *The Educational Work of Women's Organizations, 1890–1960*, eds. Anne Meis Knupfer and Christine Woyshner (New York: Palgrave Macmillan, 2008), 82, 95–96; Nidiffer, "Corrective Lenses: Suffrage, Feminist Poststructural Analysis, and the History of Higher Education," in *Reconstructing Policy in Higher Education: Feminist Poststructural Perspectives*, eds. Elizabeth J. Allan, Susan Van Deventer Iverson, and Rebecca Ropers-Huilman (New York: Routledge, 2010), 52–55.

31 Nidiffer, "The National College Equal Suffrage League," 82.

32 Altbach, *Student Politics in America*, 20; Robert Cohen, *When the Old Left Was Young: Student Radicals and America's First Mass Student Movement, 1929–1941* (New York: Oxford University Press, 1993); Feuer, *The Conflict of Generations*; Seymour Martin Lipset, *Rebellion in the University: A History of Student Activism in America* (London: Routledge & Kegan Paul, 1972); Jeffery A. Turner, *Sitting In and Speaking Out: Student Movements in the American South, 1960–1970* (Athens: University of Georgia Press, 2010); David L. Westby, *The Clouded Vision: The Student Movement in the United States in the 1960s* (Lewisburg, PA: Bucknell University Press, 1976).

33 Jacquelyn Dowd Hall, "The Long Civil Rights Movement and the Political Uses of the Past," *Journal of American History* 91, no. 4 (March 2005): 1233–63.

34 Linda Eisenmann, *Higher Education for Women in Postwar America, 1945–1965* (Baltimore, MD: Johns Hopkins University Press, 2006). See also Gordon, *Gender and Higher Education*, 1, 33–34, 38, 50–51, 156–59. Similar scholarship mentions the CESL with little detail in overviews of extracurricular activities during the Progressive Era. Myers, *University Coeducation in the Victorian Era*, 137; Horowitz, *Alma Mater*, 193–94, 222, 255, 286; Solomon, *In the Company of Educated Women*, 111–14, 125–26.

35 Kraditor, *The Ideas of the Woman Suffrage Movement*, 49–55.

36 For more information about the hostile attitudes toward women's higher education from the late nineteenth to the early twentieth century, see Roger L. Geiger, *To Advance Knowledge: The Growth of American Research Universities, 1900–1940* (Abingdon, UK: Routledge, 2004), 53–56; Gordon, *Gender and Higher Education*, 189; Christopher J. Lucas, *American Higher Education: A History* (New York: St. Martin's, 1994), 155–58, 205; Frederick Rudolph and John R. Thelin, *The American College and University: A History* (New York: Knopf, 1990), 316; John R. Thelin, *A History of American Higher Education* (Baltimore, MD: Johns Hopkins University Press, 2011), 55–56, 83–84, 186.

CHAPTER 1. ADDING "INTELLECTUAL PRESTIGE"

1 Susan B. Anthony and Ida Husted Harper, eds., *History of Woman Suffrage*, vol. 4 (Indianapolis, IN: Hollenbeck, 1902), 349–50, 387–88, 400–401; "Report of the National Women Suffrage Convention held at Washington," *Geneva Advertiser & Gazette*, Geneva, New York, Newspaper Clipping, Scrapbook 3 1897–1904 in Miller NAWSA Suffrage Scrapbooks, 1897–1911, Rare Book and Special Collections Division, Library of Congress, Washington, DC.

2 Anthony and Harper, eds., *History of Woman Suffrage*, vol. 4, 385–86.

3 Anthony and Harper, eds., *History of Woman Suffrage*, vol. 4, 385–86.

4 Park's accounts in the conference's immediate aftermath shape this positive interpretation of her experience. Following the gathering, she noted how the suffrage pioneers inspired her and how she, like her friend Inez Haynes Irwin, believed that the younger generation had a debt to pay to earlier women's rights activists. Other scholars have offered a negative depiction of Park's time at the convention.

See Sharon Hartman Strom, "Leadership and Tactics in the American Woman Suffrage Movement: A New Perspective from Massachusetts," *Journal of American History* 62 (September 1975): 296–315.

A late remembrance written by Park in January 1943 informs these accounts. She was almost seventy-two years old when she drafted it, just twelve years before her death in 1955. Park recalls little beyond a silly story about a bear fight and a southern activist's accent. She suggests that even prominent organizer Carrie Chapman Catt, whom she earlier had recognized as an "incomparable leader," "made only a minor impression" on her. Examining this document holistically reveals a pessimistic slant uncharacteristic of Park in her younger years. Near the end of her life, she could have been frustrated with the suffrage movement's results, as some former women's rights activists were, and disappointed with the League of Women Voters' progress. Regardless, Park's admiration for Susan B. Anthony is apparent in all of her writings. See Maud Wood Park, "College Equal Suffrage League Supplementary Notes," January 1943, reel 30, Subseries A. Personal and Biographical, Maud Wood Park Papers.

5 "Address of Mrs. Maud May Wood Park," Program of the College Evening, Thirty-Eighth Annual Convention of the National American Woman Suffrage Association, February 8, 1906, Records of the National American Woman Suffrage Association, 1839–1961, microfilm edition (Washington, DC: Library of Congress Photoduplication Service, 1981) (hereafter, NAWSA Records), Reel 32, Frame 000259.

6 For Park and Irwin's biographies, see Catherine I. Hackett, "The Lady Who Made Lobbying Respectable," *Woman's Journal* 8, no. 24 (1924): 12–13; Inez Haynes Irwin, "The Making of a Militant," in *These Modern Women: Autobiographical Essays from the Twenties*, ed. Elaine Showalter (New York: Feminist Press, City University of New York, 1989), 33–39; Showalter, "Inez Leonore Haynes Gillmore Irwin," in *Notable American Women: The Modern Period*, eds. Barbara Sicherman and Carol Hurd Green (Cambridge, MA: Belknap Press of Harvard University Press, 1993), 368–69; Sharon Hartman Strom, "Maud May Wood Park," in *Notable American Women: The Modern Period*, eds. Barbara Sicherman and Carol Hurd Green (Cambridge, MA: Belknap Press of Harvard University Press, 1993), 519–21.

7 "Address of Mrs. Maud May Wood Park," box 47, reel 32, Subject File, 1851–1953, NAWSA Records.

8 Historian Ellen Carol DuBois has written the most extensive scholarship on working-class and professional women in the equal-franchise movement. She challenges traditional depictions of the suffrage campaign as a "middle-class" reform effort, and she suggests that the equal-franchise victory was in part a result of the influence of trade unionists. Despite extensive coverage of Harriot Stanton Blatch's activities and the campaigns of the Equality League of Self-Supporting Women (ELSSW), DuBois's texts do not provide an in-depth look at the activism of the CESL, which also helped to form connections among women of different backgrounds. DuBois argues that compared to the ELSSW, the CESL was much

more conservative in its methods, which urged some dissatisfied members to join the Equality League's ranks. Ellen Carol DuBois, *Harriet Stanton Blatch and the Winning of Woman Suffrage* (New Haven, CT: Yale University Press, 1997), 96, 99–100, 130, 161; DuBois, "Working Women, Class Relations, and Suffrage Militance: Harriot Stanton Blatch and the New York Woman Suffrage Movement, 1894–1909," *Journal of American History* 74 (June 1987): 35–36.

In addition, for more studies that emphasize the significance of suffragists' use of public protest in the twentieth century, see Gullett, *Becoming Citizens*; Margaret Mary Finnegan, *Selling Suffrage: Consumer Culture and Votes for Women* (New York: Columbia University Press, 1999); Rebecca J. Mead, *How the Vote Was Won: Woman Suffrage in the Western United States, 1868–1914* (New York: New York University Press, 2004); Jessica Sewell, "Sidewalks and Store Windows as Political Landscapes," *Perspectives in Vernacular Architecture* 9 (2003): 85–98; Sewell, *Women and the Everyday City: Public Space in San Francisco, 1890–1915* (Minneapolis: University of Minnesota Press, 2011).

9 Barbara Berenson, *Massachusetts in the Woman Suffrage Movement: Revolutionary Reformers* (Charleston, SC: History Press, 2018). Berenson's book discusses many of the challenges that Massachusetts's activists faced throughout the campaign in broadening their state coalitions and overcoming the opposition.

10 Eleanor Flexner and Ellen FitzPatrick, *Century of Struggle: The Woman's Rights Movement in the United States* (Cambridge, MA: Belknap Press of Harvard University Press, 1996), 139–41.

11 Elizabeth Cady Stanton, Susan B. Anthony, and Matilda Joslyn Gage, eds., *History of Woman Suffrage*, vol. 2 (New York: Fowler & Wells, 1882), 382.

12 Stanton, Anthony, and Gage, eds., *History of Woman Suffrage*, vol. 2, 382.

13 Despite these harsh comments, in his speech Douglass recognized the contributions of women's rights activists like Stanton to the antislavery campaign. He also told audiences, for example, "Let me tell you that when there were few houses in which the black man could have put his head, this wooly head of mine found a refuge in the house of Mrs. Elizabeth Cady Stanton, and if I had been blacker than sixteen mid-nights, without a single star, it would have been the same." Susan B. Anthony helped in the abolition cause also through political statements, relentless campaigning, and other important actions such as hiding runaway slaves in her home. See Melba Joyce Boyd, *Discarded Legacy: Politics and Poetics in the Life of Frances E. W. Harper, 1825–1911* (Detroit, MI: Wayne State University Press, 1994), 127–29; Flexner and FitzPatrick, *Century of Struggle*, 137–38; and Louise Michele Newman, *White Women's Rights: The Racial Origins of Feminism in the United States* (New York: Oxford University Press, 1999).

14 Stanton, Anthony, and Gage, eds., *History of Woman Suffrage*, vol. 2, 383.

15 *Proceedings of the First Anniversary of the American Equal Rights Association Held at the Church of the Puritans, New York, May 9–10, 1867* (New York: Robert J. Johnston, 1867), 55.

16 *Proceedings of the First Anniversary of the American Equal Rights Association*, 55.

17 *Proceedings of the First Anniversary of the American Equal Rights Association*, 55.

18 Stanton, Anthony, and Gage, eds., *History of Woman Suffrage*, vol. 2, 383–84.

19 Stanton, Anthony, and Gage, eds., *History of Woman Suffrage*, vol. 2, 383–84.

20 Boyd, *Discarded Legacy*, 129.

21 Jacqueline Van Voris, *Carrie Chapman Catt: A Public Life* (New York: Feminist Press, 1996), 18.

22 Harriet Sigerman, "Laborers for Liberty: 1860–1890," in *No Small Courage: A History of Women in the United States*, ed. Nancy F. Cott (New York: Oxford University Press, 2007), 307; and Voris, *Carrie Chapman Catt*, 18.

23 Sigerman, "Laborers for Liberty: 1860–1890," 307.

24 Letter with Enclosure, Lucy Stone to Susan B. Anthony, Office of the American Woman Suffrage Association, Boston, November 7, 1887, in *The Selected Papers of Elizabeth Cady Stanton and Susan B. Anthony: Their Place inside the Body-Politic, 1887 to 1895*, vol. 5, ed. Ann D. Gordon (New Brunswick, NJ: Rutgers University Press, 2009), xxv, 52–53.

25 I refer to Inez as Inez Haynes "Irwin" instead of "Gillmore" because she went by that last name for most of her life after she divorced her first husband in 1913 to remarry and eventually take the new last name "Irwin" in 1916. Showalter, "Inez Leonore Haynes Gillmore Irwin," 368–70.

26 Irwin, "The Making of a Militant," 35; and Showalter, "Inez Leonore Haynes Gillmore Irwin," 368–370.

27 Hackett, "The Lady Who Made Lobbying Respectable," 12–13.

28 Hackett, "The Lady Who Made Lobbying Respectable," 12–13.

29 For more about William Croswell Doane see chapter 4 on antisuffragists, and "The 'New Woman' Denounced," *New York Times*, June 7, 1895.

30 Irwin, "The Making of a Militant," 39; Showalter, "Inez Leonore Haynes Gillmore Irwin," 368–70.

31 Irwin's parents' ages differed by twenty-four years. Her mother was younger than her father and was his second wife. The number of children in the household created strains. Irwin recalled later that her mother gave up all of the activities that she enjoyed in her youth, like horseback riding, to invest herself in domestic duties. Financial upkeep to care for so many became a significant difficulty for the family. She notes, however, that her father supported women's rights and that her parents' relationship remained strong despite these circumstances. As a testament to their bond, Irwin's mother committed suicide not long after her father died. "Introduction to 'The Making of a Militant,'" in *These Modern Women: Autobiographical Essays from the Twenties*, ed. Elaine Showalter (New York: Feminist Press, City University of New York, 1989), 33, 38.

32 Irwin, "The Making of a Militant," 38–39.

33 Showalter, "Inez Leonore Haynes Gillmore Irwin," 368–70.

34 Park's and Irwin's husbands assisted in supporting their activism. Both women's spouses respected their ambitions and encouraged them to use their talents to their full potential. Maud married first husband Charles Edward Park in 1897,

while still a student at Radcliffe. Charles Park worked as an architect, and he endorsed the suffrage cause. Unfortunately, he died prematurely in 1904. Inez's first husband, Rufus Hamilton Gillmore, also encouraged her intellectual development and participation in women's rights campaigns. He worked as a newspaper reporter, but the relationship ended in divorce by the early 1910s. Both women later remarried. Showalter, "Inez Leonore Haynes Gillmore Irwin," 368–70; Strom, "Maud May Wood Park," 519–22.

35 Allan Odden and Carolyn Kelley, *Paying Teachers for What They Know and Do: New and Smarter Compensation Strategies to Improve Schools* (Thousand Oaks, CA: Corwin Press, 2002), 29–30.

36 Odden and Kelley, *Paying Teachers for What They Know and Do*, 32.

37 Showalter, "Inez Leonore Haynes Gillmore Irwin," 368–70; and Strom, "Maud May Wood Park," 519–22.

38 Park's first public stand in favor of woman suffrage occurred amid her coursework when her professor asked her to write about the "votes for women" issue in an assignment. She recalled later, "My paper was very short, and I was quite proud of it when it was read to the class." She continued, "I still think that I have never better expressed my credo." Park inquired why so many in contemporary societies found it reasonable to permit men to select women's political stances and then assert them through casting a ballot. She compared this absurdity to such other illogical actions as men picking out hats for women and then proceeding to wear them around. Park cited this essay as her "first open revolt" in favor of women's right to vote and argued that from that point on her colleagues "marked" her "as a suffragist" on campus. She remarked that while she believed firmly in women's equality by this time, the idea of campaigning for the cause remained obscure to her. Park wrote, "It never occurred to me that there was anything to do; I was too busy making use of the opportunities that Miss [Susan B.] Anthony and her co-workers had supplied to think that I had to do anything to get further opportunities for other women." See Draft "Address of Mrs. Park of Radcliffe College," undated, NAWSA Records, Reel 32, Frame 000266.

39 Stella Scott Gillman and her husband, Arthur, helped to found Radcliffe by proposing the initial idea for the college in late 1878. Bainbridge Bunting, *Harvard: An Architectural History* (Cambridge, MA: Harvard University Press, 1998), 128–29.

40 Draft "Address of Mrs. Maud May Wood Park"; Hackett, "The Lady Who Made Lobbying Respectable," 12–13; and "Prominent Graduate," *Radcliffe Magazine*, February 11, 1911, 91–92.

41 Hackett, "The Lady Who Made Lobbying Respectable," 12–13.

42 Hackett, "The Lady Who Made Lobbying Respectable," 12–13.

43 Draft "Address of Mrs. Park of Radcliffe College."

44 Patricia Marzzacco, "'The Obligation of Opportunity': Maud Wood Park, the College Equal Suffrage League, and the Response of Women Students in Massachusetts Colleges, 1900–1920" (PhD diss., Harvard University, 2003), 26.

45 Marzzacco, "'The Obligation of Opportunity,'" 31.

46 Rheta Childe Dorr, *Susan B. Anthony: The Woman Who Changed the Mind of a Nation* (New York: F.A. Stokes, 1928), 3; Carol Lasser and Marlene Merrill, *Friends and Sisters: Letters between Lucy Stone and Antoinette Brown Blackwell, 1846–93* (Urbana: University of Illinois Press, 1987), 234; Judith Wellman, *The Road to Seneca Falls: Elizabeth Cady Stanton and the First Woman's Rights Convention* (Urbana: University of Illinois Press, 2004), 229.

47 Suffrage Map, Austin Woman Suffrage Association, Erminia Thompson Folsom Papers, Archives and Information Services Division, Texas State Library and Archives Commission, Austin, TX.

48 Many scholars have termed the period from 1896 to 1910 the suffrage "doldrums" or downturn. For more about the "doldrums" argument, see DuBois, *Harriot Stanton Blatch and the Winning of Woman Suffrage*, 91; Rebecca Edwards, *Angels in the Machinery: Gender in American Party Politics from the Civil War to the Progressive Era* (New York: Oxford University Press, 1997), 63–64; Finnegan, *Selling Suffrage*, 6; Freeman, *A Room at a Time*, 52.

49 Carolyn Summers Vacca, *A Reform against Nature: Woman Suffrage and the Rethinking of American Citizenship, 1840–1920* (New York: Peter Lang, 2004), 97.

50 Harriot Stanton Blatch renamed her Equality League of Self-Supporting Women, formed in 1907, as the Women's Political Union in 1910. See DuBois, *Harriot Stanton Blatch and the Winning of Woman Suffrage*, 94, 119. For more on the San Francisco Wage Earners' Suffrage League see Susan Englander, *Class Conflict and Coalition in the California Woman Suffrage Movement, 1907–1912: The San Francisco Wage Earners' Suffrage League* (San Francisco: Mellen Research University Press, 1992), and Gullett, *Becoming Citizens*, 177.

51 Ida Husted Harper, ed., *History of Woman Suffrage*, vol. 6 (New York: National American Woman Suffrage Association, 1922), 484–85.

52 Historian Sara Hunter Graham refers to this period as a time of "suffrage renaissance," countering the "doldrums" interpretation. She stresses its importance as a time for morale and membership building. Graham mentions the CESL briefly in her book; however, the bulk of her discussion emphasizes the importance of Carrie Chapman Catt's "Society Plan" more broadly. Graham, *Woman Suffrage and the New Democracy*, 33–52.

53 "Suffragettes Not Shrieking Sisters," *San Francisco Call*, February 14, 1909, 22.

54 "Suffragettes Not Shrieking Sisters," 22.

55 Cofounder Maud Wood Park commented later in life that the CESL "brought to the movement a kind of intellectual prestige that was needed at the moment, somewhat as women of acknowledged social position in some of the big cities gave, a little later, a new and helpful impetus." Park, "College Equal Suffrage League Supplementary Notes."

56 "Famous Woman Writer Tells Why She Joined Feminist Cause," *The Sun*, August 10, 1913, 4.

57 Lauren C. Santangelo, *Suffrage and the City: New York Women Battle for the Ballot* (New York: Oxford University Press, 2019), 61.

58 Berenson, *Massachusetts in the Woman Suffrage Movement*, chap. 7.

59 College Equal Suffrage League (Boston), Flyer, undated, box 11, folder 12, Series I. United States, Suffrage Collection, 1851–2009, Sophia Smith Collection, Smith College, Northampton, Massachusetts (hereafter, Sophia Smith Suffrage Collection); College Equal Suffrage League, Minutes of the Second Annual Meeting of the Council, Seattle, July 1909, box 4, folder 6, Sophia Smith Suffrage Collection

60 Berenson, *Massachusetts in the Woman Suffrage Movement*, chap. 7.

61 For more about Progressive Era nativism and fear of "race suicide," see Thomas G. Dyer, *Theodore Roosevelt and the Idea of Race* (Baton Rouge: Louisiana State University Press, 1992); Linda Gordon, *The Moral Property of Women: A History of Birth Control Politics in America* (Urbana: University of Illinois Press, 2002), chap. 3; John Higham, *Strangers in the Land: Patterns of American Nativism, 1860–1925* (New Brunswick, NJ: Rutgers University Press, 2002).

62 Marion McB. Schlesinger, Mary A. E. M. Buckminster, and Mary Leavens, "Arguments in Favor of Woman Suffrage," pamphlet, 1905, box 4, folder 6, Sophia Smith Suffrage Collection.

63 College Equal Suffrage League (Boston), CESL Advertisement, undated, College Equal Suffrage League, Minutes of the Second Annual Meeting of the Council, Seattle, July 1909, box 4, folder 6, Sophia Smith Suffrage Collection; Schlesinger, Buckminster, and Leavens, "Arguments in Favor of Woman Suffrage"; The College Equal Suffrage League (Boston), Flyer, undated.

64 College Equal Suffrage League (Boston), Flyer, undated.

65 The immigration statistics from 1902 to 1903 are cited here: Schlesinger, Buckminster, and Leavens, "Arguments in Favor of Woman Suffrage." Then, again here: College Equal Suffrage League (Boston), Flyer, undated; College Equal Suffrage League, Minutes of the Second Annual Meeting of the Council.

66 Schlesinger, Buckminster, and Leavens, "Arguments in Favor of Woman Suffrage."

67 College Equal Suffrage League (Boston), CESL Advertisement, undated; Schlesinger, Buckminster, and Leavens, "Arguments in Favor of Woman Suffrage."

68 College Equal Suffrage League (Boston), CESL Advertisement, undated; Schlesinger, Buckminster, and Leavens, "Arguments in Favor of Woman Suffrage."

69 "Woman Suffrage before 1920," Gilder Lehrman Institute of American History, accessed September 5, 2015, www.gilderlehrman.org/.

70 "Dispute Woodrow Wilson," *New York Times*, March 15, 1908, 6.

71 Schlesinger, Buckminster, and Leavens, "Arguments in Favor of Woman Suffrage"; College Equal Suffrage League of Boston, Flyer, undated. For more information on suffrage and progressive reform, see Maureen A. Flanagan, *America Reformed: Progressives and Progressivisms, 1890s–1920s* (New York: Oxford University Press, 2007); Glenda Elizabeth Gilmore, *Gender and Jim Crow: Women and the Politics of White Supremacy in North Carolina, 1896–1920* (Chapel Hill: University of North Carolina Press, 1996); Gullett, *Becoming Citizens*; Wheeler, *New Women of the New South*.

72 College Equal Suffrage League, Flyer, undated.

73 College Equal Suffrage League, Flyer, undated.

74 College Equal Suffrage League of Massachusetts, Pamphlet, March 1912, box 11, folder 12, Sophia Smith Suffrage Collection.

75 College Equal Suffrage League of Massachusetts, Pamphlet, March 1912.

76 "By Talented Girls," *Boston Sunday Globe*, November 30, 1902, 20; "Presented Two Plays," *Boston Daily Globe*, April 26, 1900, 10.

77 "All Women of Talent," *Boston Daily Globe*, December 3, 1902, 5; "Two Comedies Played," *Boston Daily Globe*, January 29, 1904, 7; "Three Plays Presented," *Boston Daily Globe*, February 1, 1905, 8; "With Skill and Art," *Boston Daily Globe*, March 6, 1906, 4.

78 The date of the New York CESL's founding is unclear. Dates range from 1904 to 1906. See "Caroline Lexow Babcock" and "Collegiate Equal Suffrage League of New York," *Encyclopedia of Women in American Politics*, 1st ed. (London: Bloomsbury Academic, 1999), p. 17.

79 Santangelo, *Suffrage and the City*, 82.

80 Berenson, *Massachusetts in the Woman Suffrage Movement*, chap. 7.

81 "Collegiate Equal Suffrage League of New York."

82 Francis Fenton, Review of Helen Sumner, "Equal Suffrage: The Results of an Investigation in Colorado for the Collegiate Equal Suffrage League of New York State," *American Journal of Sociology* 15, no. 6 (May 1910): 843–46.

83 Earl Barnes, *Woman in Modern Society* (New York: B.W. Huebsch, 1912), 195–98.

84 Santangelo, *Suffrage and the City*, 61.

85 Santangelo, *Suffrage and the City*, 82.

86 Gullett, *Becoming Citizens*, 185.

87 Santangelo, *Suffrage and the City*, 55.

88 Santangelo, *Suffrage and the City*, 55; "Cornell Girl in Political Fight," *Ithaca Daily News*, December 6, 1909, 8.

89 Ellen Carol DuBois, *Woman Suffrage and Women's Rights* (New York: New York University Press, 1998), 192; "Mrs. Blatch to 'Raise Cain,'" *Geneva Daily Times*, December 8, 1909, 2.

90 "Mrs. Pankhurst Given Welcome," *Duluth News-Tribune*, October 26, 1909, 1.

91 "Our Girl in English Jail," *The Sun*, November 30, 1909, 5.

92 "Change in Suffrage Tactics," *New York Evening Post*, May 25, 1910, 10.

93 "Look to Oyster Bay for Aid," *New York Times*, June 24, 1910, 7.

94 "The Girl Who Threw Stones," *The Sun*, November 24, 1909, 2; "The World of Women," *Utica Herald-Dispatch*, December 16, 1909, 3.

95 "News of Women's Clubs," *New York Evening Post*, December 8, 1909, 6; "Girls to Free Suffragette," *Morning Oregonian*, November 25, 1909, 2.

96 "Suffragists' Plans for Turnout," *New York Daily People*, May 14, 1910.

97 "1,200 Suffragists March in Parade," *New York Herald*, May 22, 1910, 3.

98 Thomas Wirth, Biographical Sketch of Jessie Ashley, Biographical Database of NAWSA Suffragists, 1890–1920, Women and Social Movements in the

United States, 1600–2000 (Alexandria, VA: Alexander Street, 2020), Record ID 1010596324. https://documents.alexanderstreet.com/.

99 "Adopt New Tactics," *New York Daily People*, May 26, 1910, 4.

100 "Adopt New Tactics," 4.

101 For more information on the Triangle Factory Fire, see Jo Ann E. Argersinger, *The Triangle Fire: A Brief History with Documents* (Boston: Bedford/St. Martins, 2009); David Von Drehle, *Triangle: The Fire That Changed America* (New York: Grove Press, 2003); Annelise Orleck, *Common Sense and a Little Fire: Women and Working-Class Politics in the United States, 1900–1965* (Chapel Hill: University of North Carolina Press, 1995), parts 2–3.

102 "Mrs. Shaw Hits Nail," *New York Daily People*, April 2, 1911.

103 "Mrs. Shaw Hits Nail."

104 "Women Talk on the Fire," *The Sun*, April 1, 1911, 6.

105 Frances Diodato Bzowski, "Spectacular Suffrage; or, How Women Came out of the Home and into the Streets and Theaters of New York City to Win the Vote," *New York History* 76 (January 1995): 74.

106 Bzowski, "Spectacular Suffrage," 74.

107 Jonathan Gill, *Harlem: The Four-Hundred-Year History from Dutch Village to Capital of Black America*, 1st ed. (New York: Grove Press, 2011).

108 See, more recent work on suffrage such as Cathleen D. Cahill, *Recasting the Vote: How Women of Color Transformed the Suffrage Movement* (Chapel Hill: University of North Carolina Press, 2020); Martha S. Jones, *Vanguard: How Black Women Broke Barriers, Won the Vote, and Insisted on Equality for All* (New York: Basic Books, 2020); as well as the study, Newman, *White Women's Rights*.

109 For more about the NAWSA's early position on race, see Newman, *White Women's Rights*; Deborah Gray White, *Too Heavy a Load: Black Women in Defense of Themselves, 1894–1994* (New York: Norton, 1999), 103.

110 Berenson, *Massachusetts in the Woman Suffrage Movement*, chap. 7.

111 Only two references to CESL campaigners potentially addressing Black audiences in New York and California came up in my research. In 1910, Mary Donnelly of the Collegiate Equal Suffrage League of New York City spoke at a meeting of the Harlem branch of Alva Belmont's Political Equality Association. See "Suffrage Class to Close," *New York Herald*, May 29, 1910, 6. In 1911, Gail Laughlin of Denver, a visiting guest lecturer commissioned by the CESL of Northern California, also gave a presentation at the Third Baptist Church in San Francisco alongside other suffragists from the city. See "Encouraging Reports Sent In by Workers," *San Francisco Call*, August 22, 1911, 7; "Woman Quits Law Practice to Aid Cause," *San Francisco Call*, August 23, 1911, 7. The CESL, however, was not responsible for either of these events, and it is unclear whether these speakers were representing the organization in each case or whether Black women were in attendance. In California, Black women did participate in the CESL's poll-watching activities in 1911. African American

women asked White suffragists if they could take part, and they only campaigned in areas with high populations of Black voters. College Equal Suffrage
League of Northern California, *Winning Equal Suffrage in California: Reports
of the Committees of the College Equal Suffrage League of Northern California in
the Campaign of 1911* (San Francisco: National College Equal Suffrage League,
1913), 105.

112 Jean Gould Bryant, "From the Margins to the Center: Southern Women's Activism, 1820–1970," *Florida Historical Quarterly* 77 (Spring 1999): 417; Gilmore,
Gender and Jim Crow, chaps. 4–5.

113 Cahill, *Recasting the Vote*; Jones, *Vanguard*; Rosalyn Terborg-Penn, *African
American Women in the Struggle for the Vote: 1850–1920* (Bloomington: Indiana
University Press, 1998).

114 Angela Y. Davis, *Women, Race, and Class* (New York: Vintage Books, 2011), 131–47.
For more about Mary Church Terrell, also see Mary Church Terrell, *A Colored
Woman in a White World* (Salem, NH: Ayer Co., 1986).

115 Wendy B. Sharer, *Vote and Voice: Women's Organizations and Political Literacy,
1915–1930* (Carbondale: Southern Illinois University Press, 2007), 20. For more
about the NACWC's founding and history, see Floris Barnett Cash, *African
American Women and Social Action: The Clubwomen and Volunteerism from Jim
Crow to the New Deal, 1896–1936* (Westport, CT: Greenwood, 2001); Elizabeth
Lindsay Davis and Sieglinde Lemke, *Lifting as They Climb* (New York: G.K. Hall,
1996); Martha S. Jones, *All Bound Up Together: The Woman Question in African
American Public Culture, 1830–1900* (Chapel Hill: University of North Carolina
Press, 2007), chaps. 5–6; White, *Too Heavy a Load*, chaps. 1–2.

116 Deborah Gray White comments that Black clubwomen believed that the keys to
uplifting the race were social service and self-help work. Deborah Gray White,
"The Cost of Club Work, the Price of Black Feminism," in *Visible Women: New
Essays on American Activism*, ed. Nancy A. Hewitt (Urbana: University of Illinois
Press, 1993), 248.

117 Bryant, "From the Margins to the Center," 415.

118 Berenson, *Massachusetts in the Woman Suffrage Movement*, chap. 7.

119 "Josephine St. Pierre Ruffin," National Park Service, November 4, 2021, www.nps
.gov/. For more about Josephine St. Pierre Ruffin, see Rodger Streitmatter, *Raising
Her Voice: African-American Women Journalists Who Changed History* (Lexington: University Press of Kentucky, 1994), chap. 5.

120 Terborg-Penn, *African American Women in the Struggle for the Vote*, 87.

121 Ella Wagner, "Sarah J. Garnet," National Park Service, March 11, 2021, www.nps
.gov/; Julie A. Gallagher, *Black Women and Politics in New York City* (Urbana:
University of Illinois Press, 2012), 22.

122 "Aids Colored Suffragettes," *New York Times*, September 28, 1910, 6; "15,000
Colored Women to Vote in the Harlem District: Suffragists Are Organizing,"
New York Age, November 22, 1917, 1; "Garnet Memorial Services," *New York
Age*, November 2, 1911, 7; "Manhattan and the Bronx," *New York Age*, July 26,

1917, 8; "Negro Women Form a Suffrage Club," *New York Times*, February 24, 1910, 6; "Negro Women for Suffrage," *New-York Daily Tribune*, February 6, 1910, 4; "Suffrage for Negresses," *New York Times*, January 19, 1910, 5.

123 Anne Razey Gowdy, "Alice Dunbar-Nelson," in *The History of Southern Women's Literature*, eds. Carolyn Perry and Mary Weaks-Baxter (Baton Rouge: Louisiana State University Press, 2002), 225; "Josephine St. Pierre Ruffin," in *Great African-American Women*, 3rd ed., eds. Darryl Lyman and Michael Russell (Middle Village, NY: Jonathan David Co., 2005), 196–97; "Phyllis Wheatley Club," *Times-Picayune*, December 29, 1907, 27; "The Phyllis Wheatley Club Sends an Open Letter to Parents," *Times-Picayune*, September 25, 1902, 10; Sylvanie F. Williams, "The Phyllis Wheatley Club," *Woman's Era* 2 (November 1895), in Emory Women Writers Resource Project, Women's Advocacy Collection, accessed May 11, 2014, http://pid.emory.edu/; "Sylvanie Francoz Williams," Voices of Progress, Historic New Orleans Collection, accessed May 18, 2022, www.hnoc.org/.

124 Anthony and Harper, eds., *History of Woman Suffrage, 1883–1900*, vol. 4, 498–501; "Colored Suffragists," *San Francisco Call*, August 6, 1896, 5; "Friends of Suffrage," *San Francisco Call*, July 30, 1896, 7; "Naomi Bowman Talbert Anderson," Archives of Women's Political Communication, Iowa State University, accessed May 18, 2022, https://awpc.cattcenter.iastate.edu/; Lawrence B. de Graaf, "Race, Sex, and Region: Black Women in the American West, 1850–1920," in *The Gendered West: The American West*, eds. Gordon Morris Bakken and Brenda Farrington (New York: Routledge, 2013), 97–98; "Suffrage Campaign in Yolo," *San Francisco Call*, September 15, 1896, 5.

125 "Colored Suffragist Rally Will Be Held," *San Francisco Call*, October 9, 1911, 3; "Gold Contest Leaders Running Close Race," *San Francisco Call*, March 13, 1907, 9; Phyllis Gale, "Myra Simmons, Black Suffragist, 1881–1865," *Newsletter of Berkeley Historical Society* 37, no. 1 (Winter 2019): 11, www.berkeleyhistorical society.org/.

126 Linda J. Lumsden, *Rampant Women: Suffragists and the Right of Assembly* (Knoxville: University of Tennessee Press, 1997), 161. For more about Ida B. Wells, see Paula Giddings, *Ida: A Sword among Lions; Ida B. Wells and the Campaign against Lynching* (New York: Amistad, 2008); Ashawnta Jackson, "The Alpha Suffrage Club and Black Women's Fight for the Vote," JSTOR Daily, September 8, 2020, https://daily.jstor.org/; Patricia Ann Schechter, *Ida B. Wells-Barnett and American Reform, 1880–1930* (Chapel Hill: University of North Carolina Press, 2001); James West Davidson, *They Say: Ida B. Wells and the Reconstruction of Race* (Oxford: Oxford University Press, 2007).

127 For more about the positive relationship between Black women's activism and churches during the early twentieth century, see Nancy A. Hewitt, *Southern Discomfort: Women's Activism in Tampa, Florida, 1880s–1920s* (Urbana: University of Illinois Press, 2001); Evelyn Brooks Higginbotham, *Righteous Discontent: The Women's Movement in the Black Baptist Church, 1880–1920* (Cambridge, MA: Harvard University Press, 1997); Martha S. Jones, *All Bound Up Together: The Woman*

Question in African American Public Culture, 1830–1900 (Chapel Hill: University of North Carolina Press, 2007), 175–76.

Deborah Gray White has offered a more critical interpretation of the Black church and modern women's activism. She argues that NACWC leaders were skeptical of African American religious figures because they believed that Black ministers and preachers allegedly were "corrupt" and "ignorant." White, "The Cost of Club Work, the Price of Black Feminism," 262. Despite the historical debate, suffrage sources still reveal that many African American woman-suffrage events hosted by members of both races occurred in churches because they were important community centers.

128 "City News in Brief," *San Francisco Call*, July 30, 1896, 7; "Colored Suffragist Rally Will Be Held," *San Francisco Call*, October 9, 1911, 3.

129 "Female Suffrage Notes," *New York Age*, September 27, 1917.

130 Gallagher, *Black Women and Politics in New York City*, 22; "Negro Women for Suffrage," 4. For more about Alva Belmont, see Sylvia D. Hoffert, *Alva Vanderbilt Belmont: Unlikely Champion of Women's Rights* (Bloomington: Indiana University Press, 2012).

CHAPTER 2. SUCCESSES IN THE WEST, STRUGGLES IN THE SOUTH, AND WIDESPREAD EFFECTS

1 Barbara F. Berenson, *Massachusetts in the Woman Suffrage Movement: Revolutionary Reformers* (Charleston, SC: History Press, 2018); excerpt from *Massachusetts in the Woman Suffrage Movement: Revolutionary Reformers*, *Western Law Review* 42, no. 3 (2020): 367; Doris Weatherford, "Maud Wood Park," in *Women in American Politics: History and Milestones*, vol. 1 (Newbury Park, CA: Sage, 2012), 421.

2 International Woman Suffrage Alliance Pamphlet, 1925, box 57, reel 40, Subject File, 1851–1953, NAWSA Records; Laura A. Cauble, "About Mrs. Park," *Dairymen's League News*, November 2, 1923, 8; Joan C. Tonn, *Mary P. Follett: Creating Democracy, Transforming Management* (New Haven, CT: Yale University Press, 2008), 172.

3 Sharon Hartman Strom, "Leadership and Tactics in the American Woman Suffrage Movement: A New Perspective from Massachusetts," *Journal of American History* 62 (September 1975): 303.

4 Mary K. Trigg, *Feminism as Life's Work: Four Modern American Women through Two World Wars* (New Brunswick, NJ: Rutgers University Press, 2014).

5 Berenson, *Massachusetts in the Woman Suffrage Movement*; excerpt from *Massachusetts in the Woman Suffrage Movement*, 367.

6 Gullett, *Becoming Citizens*, 184, 257; "Suffragettes Not Shrieking Sisters," *San Francisco Call*, February 14, 1909, 22.

7 Elizabeth Cady Stanton, Susan B. Anthony, Matilda Joslyn Gage, and Ida Husted Harper, eds., *History of Woman Suffrage, 1900–1920*, vol. 6 (New York: J.J. Little & Ives, 1922), 662. For more about Charlotte Anita Whitney, see Haig A. Bosmajian, *Anita Whitney, Louis Brandeis, and the First Amendment* (Madison, NJ:

Fairleigh Dickinson University Press, 2010); Beth Slutsky, *Gendering Radicalism: Women and Communism in Twentieth-Century California* (Lincoln: University of Nebraska Press, 2015), chap. 2.

8 Maud Wood Park, "Supplementary Notes," January 1943, reel 30, Subseries A. Personal and Biographical, Maud Wood Park Papers.

9 Gullett, *Becoming Citizens*, 8.

10 Santangelo, *Suffrage and the City*, 63.

11 The primary study that addresses suffragists' shift from "justice" to "expediency" arguments is Kraditor's *Ideas of the Woman Suffrage Movement*, 49–55. Other scholars have since challenged Kraditor on her thesis and suggested that the transition in campaign rhetoric was more complicated. In particular, see Steven M. Buechler, *Women's Movements in the United States: Woman Suffrage, Equal Rights, and Beyond* (New Brunswick, NJ: Rutgers University Press, 1990).

12 Gullett, *Becoming Citizens*, 1.

13 Gullett, *Becoming Citizens*, 2, 12, 107.

14 Gullett, *Becoming Citizens*, 2.

15 Gullett, *Becoming Citizens*, 2.

16 Gullett, *Becoming Citizens*, 12.

17 Gullett, *Becoming Citizens*, 2.

18 Gullett, *Becoming Citizens*, 12, 108.

19 Gullett, *Becoming Citizens*, 107.

20 Gullett, *Becoming Citizens*, 107.

21 Gullett, *Becoming Citizens*, 187.

22 "Mothers with Franchise Right Will Develop Better Citizens," *San Francisco Call*, August 7, 1911, 5.

23 "Mothers with Franchise Right Will Develop Better Citizens," 5.

24 "Mothers with Franchise Right Will Develop Better Citizens," 5.

25 "Mothers with Franchise Right Will Develop Better Citizens," 5.

26 "Mothers with Franchise Right Will Develop Better Citizens," 5.

27 "Men Join in Urging Votes for Fair Sex," *San Francisco Call*, June 7, 1911, 1.

28 "Women Closing Campaign with Whirl," *San Francisco Call*, October 5, 1911, 4.

29 Frances Kaplan, "Women's Suffrage in California: What One Document Reveals," California Historical Society, September 24, 2021, https://californiahistoricalsociety.org/.

30 Bosmajian, *Anita Whitney, Louis Brandeis, and the First Amendment*, 45–46; Molly Silvestrini, "Biographical Sketch of Charlotte Anita Whitney," Biographical Database of NAWSA Suffragists, 1890–1920, Women and Social Movements in the United States, 1600–2000 (Alexandria, VA: Alexander Street, 2020), Record ID 1010111765. https://documents.alexanderstreet.com/.

31 "Suffragettes Not Shrieking Sisters."

32 "Suffragettes Not Shrieking Sisters."

33 Jackie M. Blount, *Destined to Rule the Schools: Women and the Superintendency, 1873–1995* (Albany: State University of New York Press, 1998), 37, 61, 66. For

more about teachers and suffrage, see Patricia Anne Carter, *"Everybody's Paid but the Teacher": The Teaching Profession and the Women's Movement* (New York: Teachers College, 2002), chap. 4; Kate Rousmaniere, *Citizen Teacher: The Life and Leadership of Margaret Haley* (Albany: State University of New York Press, 2005), 127–28.

34 Anita Whitney, "Appeal Is Made to the Teachers," *Santa Ana Daily Register*, August 21, 1911.

35 Jackie M. Blount, *Fit to Teach: Same-Sex Desire, Gender, and School Work in the Twentieth Century* (Albany: State University of New York Press, 2006), 55.

36 Rousmaniere, *Citizen Teacher*, 127–28.

37 Rosalind Rosenberg, *Changing the Subject: How the Women of Columbia Shaped the Way We Think about Sex and Politics* (New York: Columbia University Press, 2004), 63.

38 Blount, *Destined to Rule the Schools*, 37, 61, 66; Carter, *"Everybody's Paid but the Teacher,"* chap. 4; Rousmaniere, *Citizen Teacher*, 127–28.

39 Dora T. Israel, "Report on Presenting Equal Suffrage to School Teachers," in *Winning Equal Suffrage in California: Reports of Committees of the College Equal Suffrage League of Northern California*, 1913, 73, Folder: California: 1895, 1907–17, n.d., Sophia Smith Suffrage Collection,

40 "High School Teacher to Address Meeting," *San Francisco Call*, June 7, 1911, 5; "Votes for Women Have Many Champions Here," *Oakland Tribune*, June 16, 1911.

41 "Suffrage League Will Hold Open Meeting," *Oakland Tribune*, July 10, 1911.

42 Whitney, "Appeal Is Made to the Teachers."

43 "Business Equality Man's Reason for Giving Woman Vote," *San Francisco Call*, September 7, 1911, 7; "Girls' High School Teachers to Organize," *San Francisco Call*, August 17, 1911, 5; "Suffrage Orators Address Teachers and Club Members," *San Francisco Call*, August 10, 1911, 7; "Wage Earners' League to Hold Rally in the Mission," *San Francisco Call*, August 31, 1911, 5; "Women Dance for Suffrage and Delight," *San Francisco Call*, August 27, 1911, 31.

44 "Woman Attorney to Speak on Suffrage," *Oakland Tribune*, September 19, 1911, 3.

45 Blount, *Destined to Rule the Schools*, 37, 61, 66; Carter, *"Everybody's Paid but the Teacher,"* chap. 4; Rousmaniere, *Citizen Teacher*, 127–28.

46 Amanda Ritter-Maggio, "Biographical Sketch of Fannie Williams McLean," Biographical Database of NAWSA Suffragists, 1890–1920, Women and Social Movements in the United States, 1600–2000 (Alexandria, VA: Alexander Street, 2020), Record ID 1011147509, https://documents.alexanderstreet.com/.

47 "High School Teacher to Address Meeting," *San Francisco Call*, June 7, 1911, 5.

48 "Our School System Plea for Suffrage Is Woman's Argument," *San Francisco Call*, August 29, 1911, 7.

49 "Our School System Plea for Suffrage Is Woman's Argument."

50 Livia Gershon, "The 19th-Century Activist Who Tried to Transform Teaching," *JSTOR Daily*, August 7, 2017.

51 Gershon, "The 19th-Century Activist Who Tried to Transform Teaching."

52 Gershon, "The 19th-Century Activist Who Tried to Transform Teaching."

53 "Battle for Woman Suffrage Now Has Board of Strategy," *San Francisco Call*, August 7, 1911, 5.

54 "Margaret Haley on Trip to Help Suffragists," *San Francisco Call*, August 17, 1911, 5.

55 Gullett, *Becoming Citizens*, 2.

56 Gullett, *Becoming Citizens*, 34.

57 Gullett, *Becoming Citizens*, 12.

58 Gullett, *Becoming Citizens*, 178.

59 Gullett, *Becoming Citizens*, 178.

60 Gullett, *Becoming Citizens*, 178.

61 Gullett, *Becoming Citizens*, 178.

62 Gullett, *Becoming Citizens*, 179.

63 "Duncan McKinlay Will Be Heard on Votes for Women," *Oakland Tribune*, June 13, 1911, 1; "Votes for Women Have Many Champions Here," 16.

64 "Votes for Women Have Many Champions Here," 16.

65 "Duncan McKinlay Will Be Heard on Votes for Women."

66 "Battle for Woman Suffrage Now Has Board of Strategy," 5.

67 "American Biscuit Girls Form a Club," *San Francisco Call*, August 17, 1911, 5.

68 Gullett, *Becoming Citizens*, chaps. 3–4; Mead, *How the Vote Was Won*, chaps. 6–7.

69 Sewell, *Women and the Everyday City*, 131.

70 Santangelo, *Suffrage and the City*, 84.

71 "Suffragists Have Aid of Editor in Plans for Meeting," *San Francisco Call*, September 10, 1911, 29.

72 "Battle for Woman Suffrage Now Has Board of Strategy," 5.

73 "Battle for Woman Suffrage Now Has Board of Strategy."

74 Sewell, *Women and the Everyday City*, 143–44.

75 Sewell, *Women and the Everyday City*.

76 "Banners and Flags to Fly for Suffrage," *San Francisco Call*, August 17, 1911, 5.

77 "Suffragists to Serve on Central Committee for State Campaign," *San Francisco Call*, August 28, 1911, 5.

78 Mead, *How the Vote Was Won*, 141.

79 Santangelo, *Suffrage and the City*, 92.

80 Karen Lynne Skahill, "'A Higher Ambition': Bay Area Women Fight for Suffrage in California" (MA thesis, San Jose State University, 2004), 67.

81 "Women Closing Campaign with a Whirl," 4.

82 Robert P. J. Cooney Jr., "A Brief Summary of the 1911 Campaign," California Women's Suffrage Centennial, California Secretary of State, accessed December 27, 2022, www.sos.ca.gov/.

83 "Happenings around S.F. Bay," *Santa Cruz Sentinel*, October 5, 1911, 7.

84 "Women Are Wanted for Picket Duty at the Polls," *San Francisco Call*, October 5, 1911; "Vote on Proposed Amendments Light in Many Sections of State, Due to Indifference," *Oakland Tribune*, October 10, 1911.

85 "Vote on Proposed Amendments Light in Many Sections of State, Due to Indiffer-
    ence."

86 Santangelo, *Suffrage and the City*, 116.

87 "California Women's Suffrage: Overview of the October 10, 1911 Election," See
    California, accessed December 27, 2022, www.seecalifornia.com/; Cooney Jr.,
    "A Brief Summary of the 1911 Campaign."

88 CESL of Northern California, *Winning Equal Suffrage in California*.

89 Gullett, *Becoming Citizens*, 2.

90 Excerpt from *Massachusetts in the Woman Suffrage Movement*, 382.

91 Gullett, *Becoming Citizens*, 1.

92 Caroline Lexow, "List of Branches, Sections, and Chapters of the College Equal
    Suffrage League," in Minutes of the Second Annual Meeting of the Council,
    Seattle, Washington, July 1909, 5–12, carton 8, folder 41, McLean Family Papers,
    1850–1950, Bancroft Library, University of California, Berkeley, CA.

93 Newspapers publicized Park's visit widely. See "A Woman's Reasons for Wanting
    Vote," *Times-Picayune*, January 24, 1909, 6; "College Suffragists," *Times-Picayune*,
    January 26, 1909, 11; "Mrs. Maud Wood Park," *Times-Picayune*, January 17, 1909,
    22; "Mrs. Park Will Address Era Club," *New Orleans Item*, January 22, 1909, 7;
    "Noted Suffragist Coming Saturday," *New Orleans Item*, January 17, 1909; "Suffrage
    at Newcomb," *Times-Picayune*, January 28, 1909, 7. Aside from longer write-ups,
    the local newspapers included shorter announcements of her scheduled talks in
    the city and on campus. Articles comment that Park also was trying to arrange a
    visit to Louisiana State University, but it is unclear whether the plans to speak at
    the school materialized.

94 Joan Marie Johnson, *Southern Women at the Seven Sisters Colleges: Feminist Val-
    ues and Social Activism, 1875–1915* (Athens: University of Georgia Press, 2010), 162.

95 Lexow, "List of Branches, Sections, and Chapters of the College Equal Suffrage
    League," 5–12.

96 Anne Firor Scott, "After Suffrage: Southern Women in the Twenties," in *Myth and
    Southern History*, eds. Patrick Gerster and Nicholas Cords (Urbana: University of
    Illinois Press, 1989), 83–84.

97 Evelyn A. Kirkley, "'This Work Is God's Cause': Religion in the Southern Woman
    Suffrage Movement, 1880–1920," *Church History* 59 (December 1990): 508–9.

98 "Caroline E. Merrick (1825–1908)," Voices of Progress, Historic New Orleans Col-
    lection, accessed December 27, 2022, www.hnoc.org/; "Kate Gordon (1861–1932),"
    Voices of Progress, Historic New Orleans Collection, accessed December 27, 2022,
    www.hnoc.org/; "Kate M. Gordon," in *Notable American Women: The Modern
    Period*, eds. Edward T. James, Janet Wilson James, Paul S. Boyer (Cambridge,
    MA: Belknap Press of Harvard University Press, 1971), 66–68; Beth Willinger
    and Susan Tucker, eds., *Newcomb College, 1886–2006: Higher Education for
    Women in New Orleans* (Baton Rouge: Louisiana State University Press, 2012);
    "The Era Club," Louisiana Women's Collection: A History of Political Activism,

Howard-Tilton Memorial Library Online Exhibits, Tulane University, accessed December 27, 2002, https://exhibits.tulane.edu/.

99 "Caroline E. Merrick (1825–1908)"; "Kate Gordon (1861–1932)"; letter from Kate M. Gordon to Roberta Wellford (January 11, 1916), Primary Document, Virginia Humanities, Encyclopedia of Viriginia, accessed December 27, 2022, https://encyclopediavirginia.org/; "Kate M. Gordon," in *Notable American Women*; Leslie Gale Parr, *A Will of Her Own: Sarah Towles Reed and the Pursuit of Democracy in Southern Public Education* (Athens: University of Georgia Press, 2010), 18–19; "The Era Club," Louisiana Women's Collection; Willinger and Tucker, eds., *Newcomb College, 1886–2006*.

100 Parr, *A Will of Her Own*, 17.

101 Bryant, "From the Margins to the Center," 418–19.

102 Eric Seiferth, "What Role Did Louisianans Play in the Women's Suffrage Movement?" Historic New Orleans Collection, March 20, 2020, www.hnoc.org/.

103 *Historical Dictionary of Women's Education in the United States*, 1st ed. (London: Bloomsbury Academic, 1998), s.v. "National College Equal Suffrage League," 295–97.

104 Excerpt from *Massachusetts in the Woman Suffrage Movement*, 383.

105 Excerpt from *Massachusetts in the Woman Suffrage Movement*, 366; Berenson, *Massachusetts in the Woman Suffrage Movement*, 381.

106 Excerpt from *Massachusetts in the Woman Suffrage Movement*, 374; Berenson, *Massachusetts in the Woman Suffrage Movement*.

107 "Massachusetts Sees End of Long Fight," *Evening Post*, New York, February 25, 1915, 14.

108 Eleanor Piper, CESL of Boston, 1914–1915, Report of the Executive Board, May 19, 1915, reel 41, Subseries C. Suffrage and Women's Rights, Maud Wood Park Papers.

109 "Massachusetts Sees End of Long Fight."

110 Excerpt from *Massachusetts in the Woman Suffrage Movement*, 381. A "newsie" is a girl who sells papers on streetcorners.

111 Eleanor Piper, Report of the Secretary, College Equal Suffrage League of Boston, 1913–14, May 28, 1914, box 47, reel 32, Subject File, 1851–1953, NAWSA Records.

112 Eleanor Piper, CESL of Boston, 1915–1916, Report of the Secretary, reel 41, Subseries C. Suffrage and Women's Rights, Maud Wood Park Papers.

113 Excerpt from *Massachusetts in the Woman Suffrage Movement*; Berenson, *Massachusetts in the Woman Suffrage Movement*, 380.

114 "All Are Ready for Winning Campaign," *Evening Post*, New York, February 25, 1915.

115 "Faculties Favor Suffrage," *New York Herald*, April 21, 1914.

116 Chelsea Gibson, "Biographical Sketch of Katrina Brandes Ely Tiffany," Biographical Database of NAWSA Suffragists, 1890–1920 (Alexandria, VA: Alexander Street, 2020), Record ID 1010596289, https://documents.alexanderstreet.com/.

117 "All Are Ready for Winning Campaign."

118 The ESCC was comprised of the New York City Woman Suffrage Party, CESL, Equal Franchise Society, Men's League for Woman Suffrage, and the New York State Suffrage Association. Carrie Chapman Catt was the chair. Linda J. Lumsden, *Rampant Women: Suffragists and the Right of Assembly* (Knoxville: University of Tennessee Press, 1997), 161.

119 Santangelo, *Suffrage and the City*, 59.

120 Santangelo, *Suffrage and the City*, 61.

121 Santangelo, *Suffrage and the City*, 70.

122 Santangelo, *Suffrage and the City*, 70.

123 Santangelo, *Suffrage and the City*, 105.

124 Santangelo, *Suffrage and the City*, 73.

125 "Name Schools for Women," *New York Times*, January 10, 1915; "Suffragettes Pick the 'Immortals' of Their Own Sex," *Evening World*, January 9, 1915.

126 "A Million Women: Appeal to the Voters of New York State for Justice," *Holley Standard*, October 28, 1915, 2; "'Suffs' in Silent Protest," *Brooklyn Daily Eagle*, June 9, 1915, 9; "30 Suffragists 'Protest Silently' When Aliens Become U.S. Citizens," *Washington Post*, June 13, 1915, 12; "Women Speechless to Aid Suffrage," *New York Times*, June 8, 1915, 5.

127 "Mute Women See Aliens Get Votes," *New York Times*, June 9, 1915, 13.

128 "Their Declaration of Independence," *Geneva Daily Times*, July 3, 1915, 12.

129 "Their Declaration of Independence," 12.

130 "Their Declaration of Independence," 12.

131 "Early Suffrage Protests," *New York Times*, July 11, 1915.

132 "Women Report Good Treatment," *Syracuse Herald*, November 2, 1915.

133 "Women Report Good Treatment."

134 Santangelo, *Suffrage and the City*, 121.

135 Doris Daniels, "Building a Winning Coalition: The Suffrage Fight in New York State," *New York History* 60 (January 1979): 77–78.

136 Santangelo, *Suffrage and the City*, 78, 101.

137 Santangelo, *Suffrage and the City*, 122.

138 "Massachusetts Woman Suffrage Victory Parade: Instructions for Marchers," Boston, 1915, Broadsheet, Collections Online, Massachusetts Historical Society, www.masshist.org/.

139 Strom, "Leadership and Tactics in the American Woman Suffrage Movement," 314–15.

140 Strom, "Leadership and Tactics in the American Woman Suffrage Movement," 296.

141 Strom, "Leadership and Tactics in the American Woman Suffrage Movement," 315.

142 "Massachusetts Woman Suffrage Victory Parade: Instructions for Marchers."

143 Rev. Francis J. Grimke, "The Logic of Woman Suffrage," in "Votes for Women: A Symposium by Leading Thinkers of Colored America," *The Crisis*, August 1915, 178–79.

144 "Francis J. Grimke" Short Biography, Gallery, *Blackbird Archive: An Online Journal of Literature and the Arts*, accessed May 18, 2022, https://blackbird.vcu.edu/.

145 "Expressions of Woman's Rights," *New York Age*, October 14, 1915, 1.

146 "Suffragists Hold Large Mass Meeting," *Baltimore Afro-American*, December 26, 1914, 4.

147 Garth E. Pauley, "W. E. B. Du Bois on Woman Suffrage: A Critical Analysis of His Crisis Writings," *Journal of Black Studies* 30 (January 2000): 397.

148 Equal Suffrage League (U.S.), Petition from the Equal Suffrage League, March 17, 1908, W. E. B. Du Bois Papers, Special Collections and University Archives, University of Massachusetts, Amherst Libraries, Amherst, MA. The only description found of the bill was on page 4 of the April 11, 1908, edition of the *Brooklyn Daily Eagle*. Untitled, *Brooklyn Daily Eagle*, April 11, 1908, 4.

149 Hon. Robert H. Terrell, "Our Debt to Suffragists," in "Votes for Women: A Symposium by Leading Thinkers of Colored America," *The Crisis*, August 1915, 181.

150 "Expressions of Woman's Rights," *New York Age*, October 14, 1915; Gilmore, *Gender and Jim Crow*, chap. 8.

151 Pauley, "W. E. B. Du Bois on Woman Suffrage," 400.

152 Pauley, "W. E. B. Du Bois on Woman Suffrage," 400.

153 Pauley, "W. E. B. Du Bois on Woman Suffrage," 396.

154 Pauley, "W. E. B. Du Bois on Woman Suffrage," 396.

155 W. E. B. Du Bois, "Votes for Women," *The Crisis*, November 1917, 8.

156 "Views and Reviews," *New York Age*, October 21, 1915.

157 Pauley, "W. E. B. Du Bois on Woman Suffrage," 401, 406. For more about the "Talented Tenth" concept related to women, see Gilmore, *Gender and Jim Crow*, chaps. 4–5; Evelyn Brooks Higginbotham, *Righteous Discontent: The Women's Movement in the Black Baptist Church, 1880–1920* (Cambridge, MA: Harvard University Press, 1997), 28.

158 Gilmore, *Gender and Jim Crow*, chap. 8; Higginbotham, *Righteous Discontent*; Mary B. Talbert, "Women and Colored Women," in "Votes for Women: A Symposium by Leading Thinkers of Colored America," *The Crisis*, August 1915, 184.

159 Deborah Gray White, "The Cost of Club Work, the Price of Black Feminism," in *Visible Women: New Essays on American Activism*, ed. Nancy A. Hewitt (Urbana: University of Illinois Press, 1993), 248, 254, 256.

160 White, "The Cost of Club Work, the Price of Black Feminism," 254, 258–59.

161 N. H. Burroughs, "Black Women and Reform," in "Votes for Women: A Symposium by Leading Thinkers of Colored America," *The Crisis*, August 1915, 187.

162 Burroughs, "Black Women and Reform," 187. For more information on Black women's struggle to gain respect in the political system and the courts during the early twentieth century, see Hannah Rosen, *Terror in the Heart of Freedom: Citizenship, Sexual Violence, and the Meaning of Race in the Postemancipation South* (Chapel Hill: University of North Carolina Press, 2009), chaps. 5–6.

163 Coralie Franklin Cook, "Votes for Mothers," in "Votes for Women: A Symposium by Leading Thinkers of Colored America," *The Crisis*, August 1915, 184.

164 Burroughs, "Black Women and Reform," 187.

165 Gilmore, *Gender and Jim Crow*, chap. 8; Kris Schumacher, "Black Women's Struggle for the Suffrage," *Womanspeak* 6, no. 4 (April 1985): 8.

166 Du Bois, "Votes for Women," 8.

167 Santangelo, *Suffrage and the City*, 125.

168 "New Campaign for Suffrage," *Boston Sunday Globe*, February 20, 1916, 46.

169 "New Campaign for Suffrage."

170 "Suffragists Busy, Conferences Arranged for Boston and Other Cities," *Boston Globe*, February 14, 1916, 16.

171 "College Equal Suffrage League Meets," *Boston Sunday Globe*, October 22, 1916, 8.

172 Daniels, "Building a Winning Coalition," 76–80.

173 Daniels, "Building a Winning Coalition," 76–80; Santangelo, *Suffrage and the City*, 125.

174 Santangelo, *Suffrage and the City*, 124.

175 Any cursory search through small-scale and local New York state newspapers brings up dozens of hits on work outside the city. See, for example, "Coming and Going," *Buffalo Evening News*, April 20, 1917, 11; "Lecture at the Court House," *Angelica Advocate*, October 7, 1915, 1; "Make Plans for 1917 Suffrage Campaign," *Buffalo Courier*, November 17, 1916; "Mohawk," *Utica Herald-Dispatch*, June 8, 1917; "Suffrage Leaders See Victory Ahead," *Utica Herald-Dispatch*, September 18, 1917, 3.

176 Daniels, "Building a Winning Coalition," 76–80.

CHAPTER 3. "THE OBLIGATION OF OPPORTUNITY"

1 "Address by Miss Points," *Barnard Bulletin*, December 8, 1912, 1.

2 "Columbia Men Want Woman Suffrage," *Columbia Spectator*, November 24, 1909, 6.

3 Juliet Stuart Poyntz, "Suffragism and Feminism at Barnard," *Barnard Bear* 9, no. 7 (1914): 1–2.

4 Nidiffer, "The National College Equal Suffrage League," 82, 95–96; Nidiffer, "Corrective Lenses," 52–55.

5 John T. Bethell, Richard M. Hunt, and Robert Shenton, eds., *Harvard A to Z* (Cambridge, MA: Harvard University Press, 2004), 25; Robert A. McCaughey, *Stand, Columbia: A History of Columbia University in the City of New York, 1754–2004* (New York: Columbia University Press, 2003), 89; Clarence L. Mohr and Joseph E. Gordon, *Tulane: The Emergence of a Modern University, 1945–1980* (Baton Rouge: Louisiana State University Press, 2001), xxi; Samuel Eliot Morison, *The Founding of Harvard College* (Cambridge, MA: Harvard University Press, 1995); Verne A. Stadtman, *The University of California, 1868–1968: A Centennial Publication of the University of California* (New York: McGraw-Hill, 1970), 35; Susan Tucker and Beth Ann Willinger, eds., *Newcomb College, 1886–2006: Higher Education for Women in New Orleans* (Baton Rouge: Louisiana State University Press, 2012).

Recent scholarship on woman suffrage emphasizes how the use of nontraditional public spaces in the twentieth century was central to the success of campaigns. Ellen Carol DuBois, *Harriot Stanton Blatch and the Winning of Woman Suffrage* (New Haven, CT: Yale University Press, 1997); Margaret Finnegan, *Selling Suffrage: Consumer Culture and Votes for Women* (New York: Columbia University Press, 1999); Sara Hunter Graham, *Woman Suffrage and the New Democracy* (New Haven, CT: Yale University Press, 1996); Sewell, *Women and the Everyday City*; Sewell, "Sidewalks and Store Windows as Political Landscapes," *Perspectives in Vernacular Architecture* 9 (2003): 85–98. For works on the National Woman's Party stressing the ways in which suffragists confronted male politicians, see Katherine H. Adams and Michael L. Keene, *Alice Paul and the American Suffrage Campaign* (Urbana: University of Illinois Press, 2008); Christine A. Lunardini, *From Equal Suffrage to Equal Rights: Alice Paul and the National Woman's Party, 1910-1928* (Lincoln, NE: ToExcel Press, 1986).

6 "Suffragists Invoke Lincoln, 1910," History Resources, Gilder Lehrman Collection, accessed January 3, 2023, www.gilderlehrman.org/; "Woman Suffrage Meeting," Clipping, *Boston Evening Globe*, page 3, January 24, 1912, DG095, Folder: Harvard Men's League for Woman Suffrage, 1911–1912: correspondence, Allen S. Olmsted II Papers, Swarthmore College Peace Collection, Swarthmore College, Swarthmore, PA.

7 Carol Berklin, *Revolutionary Mothers: Women in the Struggle for America's Independence* (New York: Knopf, 2005); Linda K. Kerber, *Women of the Republic: Intellect and Ideology in Revolutionary America* (Chapel Hill: University of North Carolina Press, 2000); Mary Beth Norton, *Founding Mothers and Fathers: Gendered Power and the Forming of American Society* (New York: Vintage, 1997).

8 The rules varied based on community (towns in the Northeast, such as places in Massachusetts, in particular, were more progressive), with few options available in most areas except to the upper classes, who might have resources for a private tutor. Prospects in the North were better than in the South and the West, given the number of urban areas with educated European transplants and women's rights activists. In the colonial era, some young women and men were educated in "dame schools" run by older women, often from a neighborhood home, which taught basic reading, writing, and arithmetic for a fee. Donald Hugh Parkerson and Jo Ann Parkerson, *Transitions in American Education: A Social History of Teaching* (London: Routledge, 2014), 66–69.

9 Casey Rekowski, "Horace Mann's Vision in Action: Bridgewater Normal School's Female Teachers," Bridgewater State University *Undergraduate Review* 4, no. 1 (2008): 3–8.

10 Flexner and FitzPatrick, *Century of Struggle*, 22; Gordon, *Gender and Higher Education in the Progressive Era*, 15.

11 Anthony and Harper, eds., *History of Woman Suffrage*, vol. 4, 354–56.

12 Flexner and FitzPatrick, *Century of Struggle*, 28–29.

13 Christie Farnham, *The Education of the Southern Belle: Higher Education and Student Socialization in the Antebellum South* (New York: New York University Press, 1994), 11, 25.

14 Anthony and Harper, eds., *History of Woman Suffrage*, vol. 4, 354.

15 Margaret Nash, *Women's Education in the United States, 1780–1840* New York: Palgrave Macmillan, 2016), chap. 4.

16 Kabria Baumgartner, *In Pursuit of Knowledge: Black Women and Educational Activism in Antebellum America* (New York: New York University Press, 2019), chaps. 1–2.

17 Erik F. Brooks and Glenn L. Starks, *Historically Black Colleges and Universities: An Encyclopedia* (Santa Barbara, CA: Greenwood, 2011), 39–42, 87–91; Barbara Winslow, "Education Reform in Antebellum America," Gilder Lehrman Institute of American History, accessed May 28, 2022, http://ap.gilderlehrman.org/.

18 Flexner and FitzPatrick, *Century of Struggle*, 28; Gordon, *Gender and Higher Education in the Progressive Era*, 17.

19 Flexner and FitzPatrick, *Century of Struggle*, 116; Gordon, *Gender and Higher Education in the Progressive Era*, 17.

20 Flexner and FitzPatrick, *Century of Struggle*, 117; Gordon, *Gender and Higher Education in the Progressive Era*, 17, 52.

21 Gordon, *Gender and Higher Education in the Progressive Era*, 21; Andrea G. Radke-Moss, *Bright Epoch: Women and Coeducation in the American West* (Lincoln: University of Nebraska Press, 2008).

22 International influences also played a role in the development of private women's colleges. Historian Helen Lefkowitz Horowitz notes that a group of men and women who advocated greater equality in higher education pushed university administrators to allow female students to take the Cambridge Local Exam in 1865. Not long after, a British woman named Emily Davies who assisted in this early endeavor helped to begin a separate college for women undergraduates that followed the same standards as the men's institutions in the local area in 1869. Davies recruited prominent allies among the city's elite to contribute to the institution's development, acquired a home for holding the various classes, and began her school, which grew rapidly from a few eager pupils to many attendees. The small school expanded to transform into Girton College for women, which affiliated with the larger Cambridge University for men. The college accepted American students, who traveled overseas to attend the institution and returned home to describe their experiences. This academy set an example for the creation of the coordinate institutes in the United States. Horowitz, *Alma Mater*, 98.

23 Gordon, *Gender and Higher Education in the Progressive Era*, 26.

24 Gordon, *Gender and Higher Education in the Progressive Era*, 26.

25 Horowitz, *Alma Mater*, 102.

26 Horowitz, *Alma Mater*, 134–35.

27 Horowitz, *Alma Mater*, 137.

28 Gordon, *Gender and Higher Education in the Progressive Era*, 166–68, 172.

29 Gordon, *Gender and Higher Education in the Progressive Era*, 4–6, 35, 194–95; Horowitz, *Alma Mater*, 286; Horowitz, *Campus Life*, 195, 201; Christine D. Myers, *University Coeducation in the Victorian Era: Inclusion in the United States and the United Kingdom* (New York: Palgrave Macmillan, 2010), 137; Solomon, *In the Company of Educated Women*, 112.

30 Gordon, *Gender and Higher Education in the Progressive Era*, 4–6, 35, 194–95; Horowitz, *Alma Mater*, 286; Horowitz, *Campus Life*, 195, 201; Myers, *University Coeducation in the Victorian Era*, 137; Solomon, *In the Company of Educated Women*, 112.

31 Gordon, *Gender and Higher Education in the Progressive Era*, 4–6, 35, 194–95; Horowitz, *Alma Mater*, 286; Horowitz, *Campus Life*, 195, 201; Myers, *University Coeducation in the Victorian Era*, 137; Solomon, *In the Company of Educated Women*, 112.

32 Horowitz, *Alma Mater*, 286.

33 Chapter 4 discusses these negative perspectives on women's education in more depth. Also see Edward Hammond Clarke, *Sex in Education: or, A Fair Chance for Girls* (Boston: James R. Osgood, 1874), 22; Gordon, *Gender and Higher Education in the Progressive Era*, 31; Cynthia Eagle Russett, *Sexual Science: The Victorian Construction of Womanhood* (Cambridge, MA: Harvard University Press, 1991).

34 Patricia Marzzacco, "'The Obligation of Opportunity': Maud Wood Park, the College Equal Suffrage League, and the Response of Women Students in Massachusetts Colleges, 1900–1920" (PhD diss., Harvard University, 2003), 45; "Speech—Maud Wood Park," extract from Speech at the College Evening, February 8, 1906, box 47, reel 32, "Subject File, 1851–1953," NAWSA Records.

35 "Speech—Maud Wood Park."

36 "National College Equal Suffrage League: Suggested Work for College Chapters, City Leagues, and the Executive Secretary," pamphlet, undated, box 2, folder 5.24: "Woman Suffrage—Vassar College," Woman Suffrage and Women's Rights Collection, Archives and Special Collections Library, Vassar College, Poughkeepsie, NY.

37 Stella Bloch, "Barnard's Suffrage Club," *New York Times*, December 29, 1910, 8.

38 Bloch, "Barnard's Suffrage Club," 8.

39 "Suffrage Club Meeting," *Barnard Bulletin*, March 2, 1914, 3.

40 "Equal Suffrage League," *Tulane Weekly*, February 12, 1914, 5.

41 "Equal Suffrage League," 5.

42 There are conflicting reports about when the club started: 1909, 1910, or 1911. "Women to Study Equal Suffrage," *San Francisco Call*, February 18, 1910, 9; "New Club Will Study Equal Suffrage Question," *Daily Californian*, August, 28, 1911, 7. "Women Studies from Equal Suffrage League," *Daily Californian*, October 6, 1909, 8.

43 "Equal Suffrage Society to Meet Friday Afternoon," *Daily Californian*, February 8, 1910, 2.

44 "National College Equal Suffrage League."

45 "New Club Will Study Equal Suffrage Question," *Daily Californian*, August, 28, 1911, 7.

46 "Who Said 'Votes for Women'?" *Tulane Weekly*, April 9, 1914, 4.

47 "Prize Competition," *Radcliffe Magazine*, June 1902, 142–43.

48 Untitled, *Radcliffe Magazine*, February 1910, 105.

49 "Civics Club," *Radcliffe News*, February 1917, 4.

50 "California Wins from Stanford," *San Jose Evening News*, April 16, 1910, 8; "Stanford to Argue for Woman Suffrage," *Daily Californian*, March 7, 1910, 1.

51 "Other Colleges," *Barnard Bulletin*, April 8, 1914, 3.

52 "Civics Club," 4; "Newcomb Notes," *Times-Picayune*, November 28, 1907, 4; "Yale Victor over Harvard," *New York Times*, March 28, 1914, 6.

53 "National College Equal Suffrage League."

54 "Yale Victor over Harvard," 6.

55 Gullett, *Becoming Citizens*, 151–201; Wheeler, *New Women of the New South*, xiii, 24, 102, 127.

56 "A Woman's Reasons for Wanting Vote," *Times-Picayune*, January 24, 1909, 6.

57 John R. Thelin, *A History of American Higher Education* (Baltimore, MD: Johns Hopkins University Press, 2011), 55–56, 83–84,186; Roger L. Geiger, *To Advance Knowledge: The Growth of American Research Universities, 1900–1940* (New Brunswick, NJ: Taylor & Francis, 2004), 53–56; Gordon, *Gender and Higher Education in the Progressive Era*, 189; Christopher J. Lucas, *American Higher Education: A History* (New York: St. Martin's Press, 1994), 155–58, 205; Frederick Rudolph and John R. Thelin, *The American College and University: A History* (New York: Knopf, 1990), 316.

58 "Mrs. Maud Wood Park to Speak Here on Her Way around the World," *Times-Picayune*, January 17, 1909, 22.

59 Untitled, *Barnard Bulletin*, November 3, 1909, 2.

60 For a detailed look at Florence Luscomb's life and activism, see Sharon Hartman Strom and Florence Luscomb, *Political Woman: Florence Luscomb and the Legacy of Radical Reform* (Philadelphia: Temple University Press, 2001).

61 Maud Wood Park helped to found BESAGG in 1901. The group worked for social and civic change. BESAGG had a favorable standing among college-educated Americans, in part because of its Americanization programs to prepare immigrants for US citizenship. Marzzacco, "'The Obligation of Opportunity,'" 104.

62 "Florence Luscomb," National Park Service, last modified March 8, 2022, www .nps.gov/.

63 Ann Clifford, "Florence Hope Luscomb (1887–1985)," Stonehurst National Historic Landmark, accessed May 28, 2022, http://stonehurstwaltham.org/.

64 Clipping, "Mr. Olmsted Explains," Unidentified Newspaper, April 30, 1912, box 3, folder: Harvard Men's League for Woman Suffrage, 1911–1912: Miscellaneous, Allen S. Olmsted II Papers, Swarthmore College Peace Collection, Swarthmore College, Swarthmore, PA (hereafter, Allen Olmsted Papers.)

65 For more information about NAWSA leaders Anna Howard Shaw and Madeline McDowell Breckinridge, see Emily Newell Blair and Virginia Jeans Laas, *Bridging Two Eras: The Autobiography of Emily Newell Blair, 1877–1951* (Columbia: Univer-

sity of Missouri Press, 1999), 164, 168; Sophonsiba Preston Breckinridge, *Madeline McDowell Breckinridge: A Leader in the New South* (Chicago: University of Chicago Press, 1921), 15; Trisha Franzen, *Anna Howard Shaw: The Work of Woman Suffrage* (Urbana: University of Illinois Press, 2014); Wil A. Linkugel, Martha Watson, and Anna Howard Shaw, *Anna Howard Shaw: Suffrage Orator and Social Reformer* (New York: Greenwood Press, 1991); Wheeler, *New Women of the New South*, xviii; "Suffragists Plan Busy Program," *Harvard Crimson*, December 9, 1914.

66 See, for example, the Harvard Club's rejection of the elderly lawyer Charles R. Saunders as a guest speaker. Agnes E. Ryan to Allen S. Olmsted, March 28, 1912, box 3, folder: Harvard Men's League for Woman Suffrage, 1911–1912: correspondence, Allen Olmsted Papers; Mary B. Strong to Allen S. Olmsted, March 30, 1912, box 3, folder: Harvard Men's League for Woman Suffrage, 1911–1912: correspondence, Allen Olmsted Papers; Mary B. Strong to Allen S. Olmsted, April 29, 1912, box 3, folder: Harvard Men's League for Woman Suffrage, 1911–1912: correspondence, Allen Olmsted Papers.

67 Lillian Leslie Tower, "A Radcliffe Woman, She Moved to Ward 7," *Boston Daily Globe*, March 12, 1911, 40.

68 Tower, "A Radcliffe Woman, She Moved to Ward 7."

69 "Mrs. Snowden's Lecture," *Barnard Bulletin*, November 4, 1908.

70 Equal Suffrage Club, *Radcliffe Magazine*, April 1910, 161.

71 "Equal Suffrage League," *Tulane Weekly*, February 26, 1914, 5.

72 The stories of the Pankhursts' campaigns are covered in works such as Estelle Sylvia Pankhurst, *The Suffragette Movement: An Intimate Account of Persons and Ideals* (London: Lovat Dickson & Thompson, 1935); Linda Ford, "Alice Paul and the Politics of Nonviolent Protest," in *Votes for Women: The Struggle for Suffrage Revisited*, ed. Jean H. Baker (New York: Oxford University Press, 2002), 174–88.

73 Elizabeth Crawford, *The Women's Suffrage Movement: A Reference Guide, 1866–1928* (London: University College London Press, 1999), 94.

74 Jennifer Holmes, *A Working Woman: The Remarkable Life of Ray Strachey* (Leicester, UK: Matador, 2019).

75 "Barring Hunger Strike and Window-Smashing, Newcomb Girls United to Get Votes," *New Orleans Item*, February 5, 1914, 4; "Suffragist Lectures," *Barnard Bulletin*, March 10, 1909, 1.

76 Maroula Joannou and June Purvis, "Introduction," in *The Women's Suffrage Movement: New Feminist Perspectives*, ed. Maroula Joannou and June Purvis (Manchester, UK: Manchester University Press, 1998), 3.

77 "Suffragist Lectures," 1.

78 "Barring Hunger Strike and Window-Smashing, Newcomb Girls United to Get Votes," 4; "President Anna Shaw, and Miss Costelloe of England, Give the Latest Phases of Woman's War," *Times-Picayune*, May 3, 1910, 13; "Suffragist Lectures," 1.

79 "President Anna Shaw, and Miss Costelloe of England, Give the Latest Phases of Woman's War," 13.

80 Rachel Costelloe married Oliver Strachey in 1911 to become Rachel Strachey. Friends nicknamed her "Ray" and Frances Elinor Rendel, "Ellie." These names often appear in primary and secondary sources instead of their full names. Both women grew up together, attended the same schools, and became involved in parallel suffrage circles. They studied abroad at Bryn Mawr College in Pennsylvania in 1909 in part because the institution's leader, M. Carey Thomas, was Ray's second cousin. For more biographical information about Costelloe and Rendel, see Barbara Caine, "Strachey, Rachel Pearsall Conn [Ray] (1887–1940)," *Oxford Dictionary of National Biography*, Oxford University Press, 2004, online ed., May 2011, accessed July 2, 2023, www.oxforddnb.com; Kathryn Dood, "Ray Strachey, 1887–1940," in *Modern Feminisms: Political, Literary, Cultural*, ed. Maggie Humm (New York: Columbia University Press, 1992), 35–37.

81 "Suffragist Lectures," 1.

82 Elizabeth Paschal O'Connor (Mrs. T. P. O'Connor), an American woman who married an Irish politician and lived in London, defined the difference between a "suffragist" and a "suffragette." O'Connor, a journalist, reiterated to New York newspapers that one of the Pankhursts had argued that a "suffragist is a persuader and a suffragette is a soldier." She commented, "I believe in using persuasion first and then becoming a soldier. But in England, we have tried persuasion. Well-meaning women worked for years with gentle methods and no attention was paid to them. This is a vulgar age, but it is better to be a vulgar and successful woman than an unsuccessful lady." "Mrs. T. P. O'Connor and the Suffragette," *Hartford Courant*, January 10, 1910, 1; "Mrs. T. P. O'Connor Dies of Pneumonia," *New York Times*, September 2, 1931, 21.

83 Pankhurst, *The Suffragette Movement*, 221; Ford, "Alice Paul and the Politics of Nonviolent Protest," 176; "President Anna Shaw, and Miss Costelloe of England, Give the Latest Phases of Woman's War," 13.

84 Pankhurst, *The Suffragette Movement*, 221.

85 For more information about Harriot Stanton Blatch's suffrage activism in New York, see Ellen Carol DuBois, *Harriot Stanton Blatch*; "Barnard Girls Test Wireless 'Phones,'" *New York Times*, February 26, 1909, 7.

86 "Barnard Girls Test Wireless 'Phones,'" 7.

87 "Equal Suffrage Society Formed by College Women," *Daily Californian*, October 1, 1909, 2.

88 "Who Said 'Votes for Women'?"

89 A Suffragist and Anti-Suffragist, "Woman's Ignorance of Woman," *Barnard Bulletin*, January 17, 1912, 3; "Summer Normal Lectures," *Times-Picayune*, July 26, 1911, 15; Juliet Poyntz, "Suffragism and Feminism at Barnard," 1–2.

90 "Address by Miss Points," 1, 3.

91 Joyce Antler, "'After College, What?': New Graduates and the Family Claim," *American Quarterly* 32, no. 4 (1980): 409, https://doi.org/10.2307/2712460.

92 "Mrs. Maud Wood Park Lectures to the Student Body at Weekly Assembly," *Tulane Weekly*, February 11, 1909, 2.

93 "Mrs. Maud Wood Park to Speak Here on Her Way around the World," 22.

94 "Mrs. Maud Wood Park Lectures to the Student Body at Weekly Assembly."

95 For more information about Lucy Stone's life, see Alice Stone Blackwell, *Lucy Stone: Pioneer of Woman's Rights* (Charlottesville: University Press of Virginia, 2001); Andrea Moore Kerr, *Lucy Stone: Speaking Out for Equality* (New Brunswick, NJ: Rutgers University Press, 1992); "Suffrage Class at Newcomb," *Times-Picayune*, May 4, 1910, 5.

96 Oberlin College's history is explored in John Barnard, *From Evangelicalism to Progressivism at Oberlin College, 1866–1917* (Columbus: Ohio State University Press, 1969); Roland M. Baumann, *Constructing Black Education at Oberlin College: A Documentary History* (Athens: Ohio University Press, 2010); J. Brent Morris, *Oberlin, Hotbed of Abolitionism: College, Community, and the Fight for Freedom and Equality in Antebellum America* (Chapel Hill: University of North Carolina Press, 2014); E. H. Fairchild, *Historical Sketch of Oberlin College* (Springfield, MO: Republic Printing Company, 1868); Robert Samuel Fletcher, *A History of Oberlin College: From Its Foundation through the Civil War* (New York: Arno, 1971).

97 "A Woman's Reasons for Wanting Vote," 6.

98 Anthony and Harper, eds., *History of Woman Suffrage*, vol. 4, 355.

99 "College Suffragists," *Times-Picayune*, January 26, 1909, 11.

100 For more information about the history of women in medicine, see Judith Bellafaire and Mercedes Graf, *Women Doctors in War* (College Station: Texas A&M University Press, 2009); Patricia D'Antonio, *American Nursing: A History of Knowledge, Authority, and the Meaning of Work* (Baltimore, MD: Johns Hopkins University Press, 2010); Darlene Clark Hine, *Black Women in White: Racial Conflict and Cooperation in the Nursing Profession, 1890–1950* (Bloomington: Indiana University Press, 1989); Judith Walzer Leavitt, *Women and Health in America: Historical Readings* (Madison: University of Wisconsin Press, 1999); Charissa J. Threat, *Nursing Civil Rights: Gender and Race in the Army Nurse Corps* (Urbana: University of Illinois Press, 2015).

101 A Suffragist and Anti-Suffragist, "Woman's Ignorance of Woman."

102 "Approved List of Colleges and Universities," in Constitution of the National College Equal Suffrage League, c. 1911, box 47, reel 32, "Subject File, 1851–1953," NAWSA Records.

103 For more about the "politics of respectability," see Martha Biondi, *Black Revolution on Campus* (Berkeley: University of California Press, 2014), 33–34; Angela Boswell and Judith N. MacArthur, *Women Shaping the South: Creating and Confronting Change* (Columbia: University of Missouri Press, 2006), 152; Kevin K. Gaines, *Uplifting the Race: Black Leadership, Politics, and Culture in the Twentieth Century* (Chapel Hill: University of North Carolina Press, 1996), 45–46, 57, 76–83; Gilmore, *Gender and Jim Crow*, chaps. 6–7; Kali N. Gross, *Hannah Mary Tabbs and the Disembodied Torso: A Tale of Race, Sex, and Violence in America* (New York: Oxford University Press, 2016), 158; Georgina Hickey, *Hope and Danger in*

the New South City (Athens: University of Georgia Press, 2003); Evelyn Brooks Higginbotham, *Righteous Discontent: The Women's Movement in the Black Baptist Church, 1880–1920* (Cambridge, MA: Harvard University Press, 1994), 14–15, 100, 145; Tera Hunter, *To 'Joy My Freedom: Black Women's Lives and Labors in the South after the Civil War* (Cambridge, MA: Harvard University Press, 1997); E. Frances White, *Dark Continent of Our Bodies: Black Feminism and the Politics of Respectability* (Philadelphia: Temple University Press, 2001), 36–39, 122–23; Deborah Gray White, *Too Heavy a Load: Black Women in Defense of Themselves, 1894–1940* (New York: Norton, 1999).

104 Adele Logan Alexander, "Adella Hunt Logan, the Tuskegee Woman's Club, and African Americans in the Suffrage Movement," in *Votes for Women! The Woman Suffrage Movement in Tennessee, the South, and the Nation*, ed. Marjorie Spruill Wheeler (Knoxville: University of Tennessee Press, 1995), 89; "Miss Anthony South," *Colored American*, undated, c. 1903, 2.

105 "Joint Discussion of Politics," *Evening Star*, November 1, 1912, 2.

106 The most significant work on Black sororities and suffrage is Paula Giddings, *In Search of Sisterhood: Delta Sigma Theta and the Challenge of the Black Sorority Movement* (New York: Morrow, 1988), 17–18, 29, 41–49; Terborg-Penn, *African American Women in the Struggle for the Vote*, 105, 123. Other studies mention Delta Sigma Theta and Alpha Kappa Alpha's work for the campaign. See Caryn E. Neumann, "Black Feminist Thought in Black Sororities," in *Black Greek-Letter Organizations in the Twenty-First Century: Our Fight Has Just Begun*, ed. Gregory Parks (Lexington: University Press of Kentucky, 2008), 169–87; Michael H. Washington and Cheryl L. Nunez, "Education, Racial Uplift, and the Rise of the Greek-Letter Tradition: The African American Quest for Status in the Early Twentieth Century," in *African American Fraternities and Sororities: The Legacy and the Vision*, eds. Tamara L. Brown, Gregory S. Parks, and Clarenda M. Phillips (Lexington: University Press of Kentucky, 2012) 137–80; Deborah Elizabeth Whaley, *Disciplining Women: Alpha Kappa Alpha, Black Counterpublics, and the Cultural Politics of Black Sororities* (Albany: State University of New York Press, 2010), 35–36, 43–43, 52.

Some primary sources suggest that White sororities were involved in woman-suffrage activism but not to the same extent as Black college groups. White sororities were often less political and more devoted to charity work and social reform. References to White sorority activism for the ballot are rare. See this short note from a Florida Greek leader to a politician in Washington, DC, supporting the suffrage amendment in 1918: Mrs. Frank Brown to Hon. Frank Clark, January 7, 1918, "Hearings before the Committee on Woman Suffrage, House of Representatives, Sixty-Fifth Congress, Second Session on H.J. Res. 200" (Washington: Government Printing Office, 1918), 321.

107 For more information about Mary Church Terrell, see Nikki L. M. Brown, *Private Politics and Public Voices: Black Women's Activism from World War I to the New Deal* (Bloomington: Indiana University Press, 2006), 32–33, 56–65, 105, 115–16,

133, 143, 151–58; Stephanie J. Shaw, *What a Woman Ought to Be and to Do: Black Professional Women Workers during the Jim Crow Era* (Chicago: University of Chicago Press, 1996), 8, 14, 22, 35–39, 47, 60–61, 112–31, 138–40, 209, 221.

108 "Mrs. Dunbar Speaks on Woman Suffrage," *Washington Bee*, February 12, 1916, 1.

109 Euell A. Nielsen, "Alice Ruth Moore Dunbar-Nelson," BlackPast.org, May 19, 2007, www.blackpast.org/.

110 An overview of Jeanette Rankin's life and political work can be found in Norma Smith, *Jeannette Rankin: America's Conscience* (Helena: Montana Historical Society Press, 2002); "Miss Rankin Favors Universal Suffrage," *New York Age*, May 10, 1917, 1. A short PBS episode on Rankin notes that she made racist comments to Mississippi senator John Sharp Williams. After he commented, "If we pass your amendment, then Negro women could vote," she responded, "But couldn't you keep them from voting the same way you keep the Negro man from voting?" "Jennette Rankin: The Woman Member of Congress," *American Masters*, PBS.org, August 12, 2020, www.pbs.org/.

111 Eola Adeline Evans, "Activity of Black Women in the Woman Suffrage Movement, 1900–1920" (MA thesis, Lamar University, 1987), 40; Margaret Murray Washington, "Club Work among Negro Women," 1895, in Chelsea Kuzma and Kathryn Kish Sklar, "How Did the Views of Booker T. Washington and W. E. B. Du Bois toward Woman Suffrage Change, 1900–1915?" in Kathryn Kish Sklar and Thomas Dublin, eds., *Women and Social Movements in the United States, 1600–2000*, accessed through Bartle Library, Binghamton University, May 9, 2014, www.binghamton.edu/; "The Tenth Annual Report of the Tuskegee Woman's Club," 1905, in Kuzma and Sklar, "How Did the Views of Booker T. Washington and W. E. B. Du Bois toward Woman Suffrage Change?"

112 Terborg-Penn, *African American Women in the Struggle for the Vote*, 104–5.

113 Adele Logan Alexander, "Adella Hunt Logan: Brief Life of a Rebellious Black Suffragist: 1863–1915," *Harvard Magazine*, September–October 2019, www.harvard magazine.com/.

114 Alexander, "Adella Hunt Logan, the Tuskegee Woman's Club, and African Americans in the Suffrage Movement," 84.

115 Nell Irvin Painter, *Sojourner Truth: A Life, a Symbol* (New York: Norton, 1997).

116 Linda M. Perkins, "Lucy Diggs Slowe: Champion of the Self-Determination of African American Women in Higher Education," *Journal of Negro History* 81, no. 1–4 (1996): 89; Kris Schumacher, "Black Women's Struggle for the Suffrage," *Womanspeak* 6, no. 4 (April 1985): 1, 8, 10.

117 "Columbia Must Get $2,000,000 in 6 Days," *New York Times*, November 15, 1915, 5.

118 "La Follette Would Use Greek Theater," *San Francisco Call*, April 29, 1912, 1.

119 Beth L. Bailey, *Sex in the Heartland* (Cambridge, MA: Harvard University Press, 1999), xx, xxi, 66–92, 205, 236–40; Kathleen A. Bogle, *Hooking Up: Sex, Dating, and Relationships on Campus* (New York: New York University Press, 2008), 22; David A. Hoekema, *Campus Rules and Moral Community: In Place of Loco Parentis* (Lanham, MD: Rowman & Littlefield, 1993).

120 "Columbia Must Get $2,000,000 in 6 Days," 5.

121 Before the Pankhurst lecture, Harvard administrators permitted some female lecturers on campus; for example, Florence Kelley gave a presentation at the university. However, Kelley was an acceptable orator because, beyond suffrage, she was involved in other reform activities deemed socially appropriate for female citizens, like efforts to curb child labor. By the Progressive Era, since she was an authority among women activists and nationally esteemed for social work in college-educated circles, school leaders allowed her talk, as long as her presentation took place outside Harvard Yard in another building. "Eliot Keeps Up Suffrage Fight," *Boston American*, December 1, 1911, box 3, folder: Harvard Men's League for Woman Suffrage, 1911–1912: controversy with Board of Overseers re: allowing woman suffragists to speak on campus, Allen Olmsted Papers; Walter Lippman, "Free Speech at Harvard," undated clipping, c. 1911, box 3, folder: Harvard Men's League for Woman Suffrage, 1911–1912: controversy with Board of Overseers re: allowing woman suffragists to speak on campus, Allen Olmsted Papers. For more information about Florence Kelley's life and her political activism, see Kathryn Kish Sklar, *Florence Kelley and the Nation's Work: The Rise of Women's Political Culture, 1830–1900* (New Haven, CT: Yale University Press, 1995).

122 "Mrs. Pankhurst's Lecture," *Harvard Crimson*, December 6, 1911.

123 "Disorder at Harvard," *New York Times*, December 5, 1911, 12.

124 Untitled clipping, *Woman's Journal*, November 11, 1911, box 3, folder: Harvard Men's League for Woman Suffrage, 1911–1912: controversy with Board of Overseers re: allowing woman suffragists to speak on campus, Allen Olmsted Papers.

125 Allen S. Olmsted, Memories of the Conversation between Major H. S. Higginson, a member of the Harvard Corporation, and A. S. Olmsted, November 2, 1911, box 3, folder: Harvard Men's League for Woman Suffrage, 1911–1912: controversy with Board of Overseers re: allowing woman suffragists to speak on campus, Allen Olmsted Papers; Henry L. Higginson to John B. Olmsted, December 6, 1911, box 3, folder: Harvard Men's League for Woman Suffrage, 1911–1912: controversy with Board of Overseers re: allowing woman suffragists to speak on campus, Allen Olmsted Papers.

126 Olmsted, Memories of the Conversation between Major H. S. Higginson and A. S. Olmsted.

127 Henry L. Higginson to John B. Olmsted.

128 Untitled clipping, *Life*, January 18, 1912, 173, 182, box 3, folder: Harvard Men's League for Woman Suffrage, 1911–1912: controversy with Board of Overseers re: allowing woman suffragists to speak on campus, Allen Olmsted Papers; "Samuel A. Eliot of the Suffrage Club, Grandson of President Emeritus Charles W. Eliot of Harvard," clipping, ca. 1911/1912, box 3, folder: Harvard Men's League for Woman Suffrage, 1911–1912: controversy with Board of Overseers re: allowing woman suffragists to speak on campus, Allen Olmsted Papers.

129 Untitled clipping, *Life*.
130 "Turn Down Suffragist at Harvard," *Boston Post*, December 29, 1911, box 3, folder: Harvard Men's League for Woman Suffrage, 1911–1912: controversy with Board of Overseers re: allowing woman suffragists to speak on campus, Allen Olmsted Papers.
131 "Free Speech at Harvard," *New York Post*, March 16, c. 1911/1912, box 3, folder: Harvard Men's League for Woman Suffrage, 1911–1912: controversy with Board of Overseers re: allowing woman suffragists to speak on campus, Allen Olmsted Papers.
132 "Free Speech at Harvard."
133 "Harvard Petition Started," *Evening Record*, November 29, 1911, box 3, folder: Harvard Men's League for Woman Suffrage, 1911–1912: controversy with Board of Overseers re: allowing woman suffragists to speak on campus, Allen Olmsted Papers.
134 "Harvard Men Hire Hall for Mrs. Pankhurst," *Boston Herald*, November 30, 1911, box 3, folder: Harvard Men's League for Woman Suffrage, 1911–1912: controversy with Board of Overseers re: allowing woman suffragists to speak on campus, Allen Olmsted Papers.
135 "Suffragists Are Attacked," *Boston American*, c. 1911, box 3, folder: Harvard Men's League for Woman Suffrage, 1911–1912: controversy with Board of Overseers re: allowing woman suffragists to speak on campus, Allen Olmsted Papers.
136 John B. Olmsted to Henry L. Higginson, c. Nov. or Dec. 1911, box 3, folder: Harvard Men's League for Woman Suffrage, 1911–1912: controversy with Board of Overseers re: allowing woman suffragists to speak on campus, Allen Olmsted Papers.
137 Lippman, "Free Speech at Harvard."
138 "Under Harvard's Ban, Suffragists Get Hall Nearby," *Boston Journal*, November 30, 1911, box 3, folder: Harvard Men's League for Woman Suffrage, 1911–1912: controversy with Board of Overseers re: allowing woman suffragists to speak on campus, Allen Olmsted Papers.
139 "Jeers for Mrs. Pankhurst," *New York Times*, December 7, 1911, 8.
140 G. Peabody Gardine [*sic*], Report, Meeting of the President and Fellows of Harvard College in Boston, January 8, 1912, box 3, folder: Harvard Men's League for Woman Suffrage, 1911–1912: controversy with Board of Overseers re: allowing woman suffragists to speak on campus, Allen Olmsted Papers.
141 Winthrop H. Wade, Report, Meeting of the Board of Overseers of Harvard College in Boston, February 28, 1912, box 3, folder: Harvard Men's League for Woman Suffrage, 1911–1912: controversy with Board of Overseers re: allowing woman suffragists to speak on campus, Allen Olmsted Papers.
142 Gillian Hines, Biographical Sketch of Jessie Ashley, Biographical Database of NAWSA Suffragists, 1890–1920, Women and Social Movements in the United States, 1600–2000 (Alexandria, VA: Alexander Street, 2020), Record ID 1011002029, https://documents.alexanderstreet.com/d/1011002029; "Suffrage

Breaks into Harvard," *New York Times*, November 19, 1913, 2; "Suffrage Talk in Emerson," *Harvard Crimson*, November 18, 1913.

143 "Co-eds to Fight Disfranchisement," *San Francisco Call*, January 21, 1908, 10; "Shall We Disfranchise the Women?" *Daily Californian*, January 22, 1908.

144 "Co-eds to Fight Disfranchisement," 10.

145 Gordon, *Gender and Higher Education in the Progressive Era*, 78–79; "Co-eds to Fight Disfranchisement," 10.

146 "Cry for Suffrage Raised at Columbia," *New York Times*, April 28, 1912, 14.

147 "M.K., in Favor of Freshmen," *Barnard Bulletin*, April 24, 1912, 6.

148 Untitled in "Letter Box" Column, *Radcliffe News*, September 29, 1917, 2.

149 "Barnard Delegates Attend Columbia Convention," *Barnard Bulletin*, April 17, 1912, 3; "Mock Convention Names Roosevelt," *New York Times*, April 4, 1912, 10.

150 "Politics at Barnard: The Campaign," *Barnard Bulletin*, November 6, 1912, 1.

151 "Straw Vote Shows Suffrage Majority," *Columbia Spectator*, November 1, 1915, 1; "Wilson Now Has 300 Lead over Hughes," *Columbia Spectator*, August 12, 1916, 1.

152 "Ivins, Jr., Suffragist Hero," *New York Times*, February 28, 1910, 9.

153 "Militants Daub College Walls," *New York Herald*, May 12, 1913, 20; "Sign on Hamilton Statue," *New York Times*, May 9, 1913, 1.

154 Gladys Slade, president of the school's suffrage organization, stated, "I think that some of the boys are responsible for both signs. They probably did it just for a lark and are trying to lay the blame on us." Rosemary Wise, the secretary of the club, asserted that she "did not believe it possible for any of the Barnard girls to play such pranks." Investigators asked the young supporters, "Are there any militant suffragettes in Barnard College?" But students continued to deny their association. "Militants Daub College Walls," 20.

155 "Woman Suffrage Campaign in Louisiana," *Times-Picayune*, July 5, 1910, 4.

156 "Teachers to Carry Suffrage Doctrine," *New Orleans Item*, July 7, 1915.

157 Clara Bertagnolli, "I Found It in the Archives: Women's Suffrage," Library, Information, and Technology Services Blog, Mount Holyoke College, accessed December 6, 2013, http://pub.mtholyoke.edu; untitled, *Barnard Bulletin*, November 2, 1915, 1.

158 "Civics Club," *Radcliffe News*, February 1917, 4; "Suffrage Speakers' Class," *Radcliffe News*, January 1917, 6.

159 For more about the suffrage schools, see Henrietta W. Livermore, *The "Blue Book" Suffrage School: Founded on Woman Suffrage; History, Arguments, and Results* (New York: National Woman Suffrage Publishing Co., 1916). Also, see popular NAWSA publications during the 1910s, such as *History of Woman Suffrage*, *The Suffragist*, the *Woman Citizen*, and the *Woman Patriot*.

160 Tuskegee Institute, Onyx Gazette Yearbook 1914 (Tuskegee, AL: Graduating Class of 1914), 11, Tuskegee University Archives, Tuskegee University, Tuskegee, AL.

161 Lincoln University of Missouri Yearbook, 1915 (Jefferson City, MO: Graduating Class of 1915), 2, University Archives, Page Library, Lincoln University, Jefferson City, MO.

162 "Miss Rankin Favors Universal Suffrage," *New York Age*, May 10, 1917, 1.

CHAPTER 4. "NEW" WOMANHOOD DENOUNCED

1 Horowitz, *Alma Mater*, 134–35.

2 "Annie Nathan Meyer," *New York Times*, September 25, 1951; Linda K. Kerber, "Annie Nathan Meyer," in *Notable American Women: The Modern Period*, ed. Barbara Sicherman and Carol Hurd Green (Cambridge, MA: Belknap Press of Harvard University Press, 1993), 473–74; "Mrs. Meyer Dead: Barnard Trustee," *New York Times*, September 24, 1951; Stephen Birmingham, *The Grandees: America's Sephardic Elite* (Syracuse, NY: Syracuse University Press, 1997), 317–19.

3 Welter, "The Cult of True Womanhood: 1820–1860," 151–74.

4 For more on how the equal-franchise question was entangled in debates about and changes in popular conceptions of gender, see Michael E. McGerr, *A Fierce Discontent: The Rise and Fall of the Progressive Movement in America, 1870–1920* (New York: Free Press, 2003) and Anne Firor Scott and Andrew MacKay Scott, *One Half the People: The Fight for Woman Suffrage* (Urbana: University of Illinois Press, 1982).

5 Over time, the scholarship on antisuffragists has transitioned from diminishing to legitimizing opponents' efforts. From 1960 to the 1990s, historians of women who placed more weight on the victors wrote early suffrage studies that included only brief discussions of antisuffrage activism. These works were frequently biased and downplayed opponents' campaigns. Feminist scholars viewed writing women's history as part of organizing and fostering a common culture in their movement. The studies mentioned antisuffrage movements to emphasize the valor of women's rights activists. See Kraditor, *The Ideas of the Woman Suffrage Movement*, 14; Flexner and FitzPatrick, *Century of Struggle*, 290. Even Anne Myra Goodman Benjamin's book on antisuffragists does not seem to take opponents' organizing seriously. Benjamin portrays suffrage challengers as ineffective and unsophisticated. Anne Myra Goodman Benjamin, *A History of the Anti-Suffrage Movement in the United States from 1895 to 1920: Women against Equality* (Lewiston, NY: Edwin Mellen Press, 1991), 19–20.

During the 1990s and 2000s, a rise in conservatism and the decline of a strong, organized women's rights front led more scholars to pay attention to antisuffrage activism as a factor in the prolonged battle for the vote. New studies have focused on debunking the myths created by earlier historians, giving opponents more agency and placing them on equal footing with their counterparts. Now antisuffragists were skilled female politicians too, who supported their own version of women's rights. Jane Jerome Camhi, *Women against Women: American Anti-Suffragism, 1880–1920* (Brooklyn, NY: Carlson Publishing, 1994), 1; Nancy F. Cott, *The Grounding of Modern Feminism* (New Haven, CT: Yale University Press, 1987), 44; Susan Goodier, *No Votes for Women: The New York State Anti-Suffrage Movement* (Urbana: University of Illinois Press, 2013); Elna C. Green, *Southern Strategies: Southern Women and the Woman Suffrage Question* (Chapel Hill: University of North Carolina Press, 1997), 32; Thomas J. Jablonsky, *The Home, Heaven, and Mother Party: Female Anti-Suffragists in the United States, 1868–1920* (Brooklyn, NY: Carlson Publishing, 1994), xxv; Susan E. Marshall, *Splinted Sisterhood: Gender and Class in the Campaign against Woman Suffrage* (Madison: University of Wisconsin Press, 1997), 180; Elizabeth Gillespie McRae, "Caretakers of Southern Civilization: Georgia Women and the Anti-Suffrage Campaign, 1914–1920," *Georgia Historical Quarterly* 82 (Winter 1998): 802–3; Anastasia Sims, "Beyond the Ballot: The Radical Vision of the Antisuffragists," in *Votes for Women! The Woman Suffrage Movement in Tennessee, the South, and the Nation*, ed. Marjorie Spruill Wheeler (Knoxville: University of Tennessee Press, 1995), 105.

6 Annie Nathan Meyer, "Suffrage at Barnard," *New York Times*, December 24, 1910, 8.

7 Mrs. Thomas Allen, "The College Anti-Suffrage League," *Woman's Protest* 10 (1916): 13.

8 Although men served as important supporters in on- and off-campus groups, women constituted the leadership of most college antisuffrage organizations. However, early scholars—like Eleanor Flexner, Ellen Frances FitzPatrick, and Aileen Kraditor—too often positioned men as the principal antisuffrage leaders because they claimed that men from big business, such as the liquor industry, played the greatest role in fueling the campaign against female voting rights. Kraditor, *The Ideas of the Woman Suffrage Movement*; Flexner and FitzPatrick, *Century of Struggle*, 290.

Many of the first works to discuss opposition to suffrage framed the struggle for and against the vote as a contest between men and women over extending female influence into the male-dominated public sphere. In the 1990s, Jane Jerome Camhi's antisuffrage study became one of the earliest texts to depict women as leaders of the resistance. She argued that female antisuffragists were "a silent majority" who had been "ignored" too long by scholars who stressed male opposition to the ballot. Camhi, *Women against Women*, 1.

9 Mrs. Arthur M. Dodge, "Case against Votes for Women," *New York Times*, March 7, 1915, SM15.

10 Charles William Eliot, 1834–1926 [*Sacramento Daily Record-Union*], "Leaflet: Was Unjustly Quoted: President Eliot of Harvard University Writes a Letter," October 14, 1896, Ann Lewis Women's Suffrage Collection, accessed December 27, 2022, https://lewissuffragecollection.omeka.net/; Marzzacco, "'The Obligation of Opportunity,'" 86; excerpt from *Massachusetts in the Woman Suffrage Movement*, 359–84.

11 Benjamin Ide Wheeler, "Opposed to Suffrage," *Jose Mercury News*, April 2, 1916, 17.

12 Lee Anne Titangos and Alison Wannamaker, "A Centennial Celebration, California Women and the Vote, Room Three, The Opposition," Bancroft Library, University of California–Berkeley, last modified August 15, 2011, accessed September 24, 2015, http://bancroft.berkeley.edu/.

13 Booker T. Washington to Charles Monroe Lincoln, Tuskegee, Alabama, December 14, 1908, in Kuzma and Sklar, "How Did the Views of Booker T. Washington and W. E. B. Du Bois toward Woman Suffrage Change, 1900–1915?"

14 Booker T. Washington to Charles Monroe Lincoln.

15 Washington, "Club Work among Negro Women," 1895.

16 Washington, "Club Work among Negro Women," 1895.

17 Washington, "Club Work among Negro Women," 1895.

18 Giddings, *In Search of Sisterhood*, 45, 59–60.

19 Four years before, in 1909, the Howard University debate team won an oratory competition on woman suffrage. The team took the side of the opposition and beat pro-suffrage supporters from Lincoln University. "And Howard Won," *Baltimore Afro-American*, May 1, 1909; "Anti-Suffragists Plan for Active Campaign," *Washington, D.C. Evening Star*, May 30, 1913, 10.

20 Joan N. Burstyn, *Victorian Education and the Ideal of Womanhood* (London: Croom Helm, 1980), chap. 5; Clarke, *Sex in Education*; Edward H. Clarke, *The Building of a Brain* (Boston: J.R. Osgood, 1874); Ornella Moscucci, *The Science of Woman: Gynecology and Gender in England, 1800–1929* (Cambridge: Cambridge University Press, 1990), 16; Cynthia E. Russett, *Sexual Science: The Victorian Construction of Womanhood* (Cambridge, MA: Harvard University Press, 1989), 11; Carroll Smith-Rosenberg and Charles Rosenberg, "The Female Animal: Medical and Biological Views of Woman and Her Role in Nineteenth-Century America," in *No Other Gods: On Science and American Social Thought*, ed. Charles Rosenberg (Baltimore, MD: Johns Hopkins University Press, 1976), 55; Londa Schiebinger, *The Mind Has No Sex? Women in the Origins of the Modern Science* (Cambridge, MA: Harvard University Press, 1989), chaps. 7–8.

21 "Mrs. Meyer Resents Suffrage Hysteria," *New York Times*, March 27, 1910, 8.

22 Annie Nathan Meyer, "Suffrage and College Women," *New York Times*, March 7, 1909, 11.

23 "Suffrage Invades Barnard," *The Sun*, September 29, 1911, 8.

24 "The 'Antis' Have Their Say," *The Sun*, November 2, 1909, 3.

25 Annie Nathan Meyer, "Suffrage at Barnard," *New York Times*, December 24, 1910, 8; Annie Nathan Meyer, "A Communication," *Barnard Bulletin* October 26, 1910, 1.

26 "Suffragism and Colleges," *New York Times*, December 27, 1910, 8.

27 "Suffragism and Colleges," 8.

28 "Colleges as Sponsors of Cults," *New York Times*, January 5, 1911, 8.

29 Meyer, "Suffrage at Barnard," 8.

30 "Suffragism and Colleges," 8.

31 "Colleges as Sponsors of Cults," 8.

32 E.K.R., "College Suffragettes," *New York Times*, January 3, 1911, 8.
33 Annie Nathan Meyer, "Academic Costumes and Suffrage," *New York Times*, May 24, 1910, 8.
34 Virginia Gildersleeve, *Many a Good Crusade: Memoirs of Virginia Cocheron Gildersleeve* (New York: Macmillan, 1954), 71; Rosalind Rosenberg, "The Legacy of Dean Gildersleeve," *Barnard Magazine* 84 (Summer 1995): 17–21.
35 Margaret C. Robinson to LeBaron Russell Briggs, April 22, 1914, box 8, folder 79, Series I., Incoming Correspondence, 1912/1913–1913/1914, Rand-Russell, LeBaron Russell Briggs, Records of the President of Radcliffe College, 1903–1925, Radcliffe College Archives, Schlesinger Library, Radcliffe Institute, Harvard University, Cambridge, MA (hereafter, LeBaron Russell Briggs records).
36 Mrs. Charles Bullock to LeBaron Russell Briggs, April 23, 1914, box 8, folder 67, Series I., Incoming Correspondence, 1912/1913/1914, Boody-Byerly, 1913/1914, LeBaron Russell Briggs records.
37 Meyer, "A Communication," 1.
38 Annie Nathan Meyer, "Barnard Girls and Suffrage," *New York Times*, December 18, 1910.
39 A Barnard Graduate, "Barnard Girls and Suffrage," *New York Times*, December 21, 1910, 10.
40 Meyer, "A Communication," 1.
41 "Columbia Cold to Suffrage," *New York Times*, December 11, 1909, 2.
42 Meyer, "Barnard Girls and Suffrage."
43 Letter to the Editor, Helen K. Stevens, *Barnard Bulletin*, November 9, 1915, 2.
44 Socialist Club, "To the Editors of the Barnard Bulletin," *Barnard Bulletin*, February 9, 1910, 3.
45 "Clues on Woman Suffrage," *Utica Herald-Dispatch*, November 20, 1909, 6.
46 "Will Debate Eras," *Times-Picayune*, March 18, 1913, 16.
47 Poyntz, "Suffragism and Feminism at Barnard," 1–2.
48 Poyntz, "Suffragism and Feminism at Barnard," 1–2.
49 Cott, *The Grounding of Modern Feminism*, 44.
50 E.K.R., "College Suffragettes," 8.
51 E.K.R., "College Suffragettes," 8.
52 Barnard Graduate, "Men Are Afraid," *New York Times*, September 1, 1915, 8.
53 Barnard Graduate, "Men Are Afraid," 8; Cindy Sondik Aron, *Ladies and Gentlemen of the Civil Service: Middle-Class Workers in Victorian America* (New York: Oxford University Press, 1987), 115; Jessie Bernard, *The Future of Marriage* (New Haven, CT: Yale University Press, 1982), 118.
54 Aron, *Ladies and Gentlemen of the Civil Service*, 115.
55 Barnard Graduate, "Men Are Afraid," 8; Aron, *Ladies and Gentlemen of the Civil Service*, 115. Society expected men to be strong protectors and providers, in essence, the "sturdy oaks." Many people viewed challenges to these ideals as "deviant" and "unnatural." Bernard, *The Future of Marriage*, 118.

56 For more on the cultural image and construction of the college man during the early twentieth century, see Daniel A. Clark, *Creating the College Man: American Mass Magazines and Middle-Class Manhood, 1890–1915* (Madison: University of Wisconsin Press, 2010).

57 Flexner and FitzPatrick, *Century of Struggle*, 290, 293; Green, *Southern Strategies*, 32; Laura McKee Hickman, "Thou Shalt Not Vote: Anti-Suffrage in Nebraska, 1914–1920," *Nebraska History* 80 (Summer 1999): 55.

58 "Suffrage Army Out on Parade," *New York Times*, May 5, 1912, 1.

59 Green, *Southern Strategies*, 99. For more information on violence against African Americans from the late nineteenth to the early twentieth century, see Giddings, *Ida: A Sword among Lions*; Gilmore, *Gender and Jim Crow*, chap. 8; Rosen, *Terror in the Heart of Freedom*.

60 "Late Literary News," *Baltimore Afro-American*, December 26, 1914, 4.

61 Michele Wallace and Jamilah Lemieux, *Black Macho and the Myth of the Superwoman* (London: Verso, 2015), introduction.

62 "Votes for Women," *The Crisis*, November 1917, 8.

63 "Late Literary News," 4.

64 Kraditor, *The Ideas of the Woman Suffrage Movement*, 17–18.

65 "Womanhood in Peril Dr. Schlapp Says," *New York Times*, March 10, 1909, 14.

66 "Activity of Modern Woman a Racial Problem," *New York Times*, August 13, 1911, 6.

67 JD Thomas, "Desiring Suffrage as a Neurological Disorder," blog entry, Accessible Archives, July 8, 2018, www.accessible-archives.com/.

68 "Womanhood in Peril Dr. Schlapp Says," 14.

69 "Womanhood in Peril Dr. Schlapp Says," 14.

70 Mrs. Arthur M. Dodge, "Case against Votes for Women," *New York Times*, March 7, 1915, 15.

71 Cott, *Grounding of Modern Feminism*, 44; Camhi, *Women against Women*, 6; Susan Goodier, "The Other Woman's Movement: Anti-Suffrage Activism in New York State, 1865–1932" (PhD diss., State University of New York–Albany, 2007); Goodier, *No Votes for Women*, 79, 115, 19–120, 136, 142.

72 "Mrs. White at the Civics Club," *Radcliffe News*, December 1914, 7.

73 "Mrs. Meyers Attacks Suffrage Leaders," *New York Times*, November 15, 1909, 7.

74 "Churchill Attacked by Male Suffragette," *Hartford Courant*, November 28, 1910, 12; "Pay Suffragettes in Their Own Coin," *Hartford Courant*, March 5, 1912, 1.

75 "Crank Emulates Miss Davison's Feat," *Hartford Courant*, June 20, 1913, 16. For more information on Emily Davison's actions, see "Derby Suffragette Not Expected to Live," *Hartford Courant*, June 7, 1913, 1; "Suffragette Grabs King's Derby Horse," *Hartford Courant*, June 5, 1913, 1; "Suffragette Hurt by King's Horse May Live," *Hartford Courant*, June 6, 1913, 15.

76 Report of the Education and Organization Committee, May 21, 1913, 4, carton 2, folder: Education and Organization Committee 1913, Massachusetts Association

Opposed to the Further Extension of Suffrage to Women Records, 1895–1920, Massachusetts Historical Society, Boston, MA (hereafter, MAOFESW records).

77 Mrs. Thomas Allen, "The College Anti-Suffrage League," *Woman's Protest* 10, no. 2 (1916): 13.

78 Meyer, "Suffrage and College Women," 11.

79 Meyer, "Suffrage and College Women," 11.

80 Meyer, "Suffrage and College Women," 11.

81 Annie Nathan Meyer, "Corrects Rev. Anna Shaw," *New York Times*, February 9, 1909, 6.

82 Meyer, "Corrects Rev. Anna Shaw," 6.

83 Meyer, "Corrects Rev. Anna Shaw," 6.

84 Annie Nathan Meyer, Letter to the Editor, *Barnard Bulletin*, November 2, 1915.

85 Camhi, *Women against Women*, 1; Hickman, "Thou Shalt Not Vote," 55; Jablonsky, *The Home, Heaven, and Mother Party*, xxv.

86 Marshall, *Splinted Sisterhood*, 138–39.

87 "Mice to Daunt Suffragists," *New York Times*, February 2, 1913, 1; "Rats and Mice: American Students and the Suffragettes," *Liverpool Echo*, February 3, 1913.

88 "Stampede Parade with Many Rats," *Lewiston Saturday Journal*, February 1, 1913.

89 "Will Debate Eras," *Times-Picayune*, March 18, 1913, 16.

90 "Eves Reverse Eden: Newcomb College Girls Join the Anti-Suffrage Ranks," *Times-Picayune*, March 13, 1913, 9.

91 "Tulane Suffragists 'Fakes,' Say Antis, Issuing Defy to Era Club," *New Orleans Item*, March 14, 1913, 3.

92 "Vengeance on Era Club Fills Tulane," *New Orleans Item*, April 13, 1913, 18.

93 "Suffrage at Tulane," *Times-Picayune*, March 12, 1913.

94 "Suffrage at Tulane."

95 "Barring Hunger Strike and Window-Smashing, Newcomb Girls Unite to Get Votes."

96 "Newcomb Girls Join Tulane Youth as Anti-Suffragists," *New Orleans Item*, March 12, 1913.

97 "Newcomb Girls Join Tulane Youth as Anti-Suffragists."

98 Green, *Southern Strategies*, 32; Sims, "Beyond the Ballot," 108–9.

99 Green, *Southern Strategies*, 88.

100 Sims, "Beyond the Ballot," 108–9; Lorraine Gates Schuyler, *The Weight of Their Votes: Southern Women and Political Leverage in the 1920s* (Chapel Hill: University of North Carolina Press, 2006), 14–15.

101 Schuyler, *The Weight of Their Votes*, 14; McRae, "Caretakers of Southern Civilization," 818–19.

102 Sims, "Beyond the Ballot," 105, 108–9, 116.

103 For more on the charivari, see Natalie Z. Davis, *Society and Culture in Early Modern France: Eight Essays* (Stanford, CA: Stanford University Press, 1975), 101–23; Emma Dillon, *The Sense of Sound: Musical Meaning in France, 1260–1330* (Oxford: Oxford University Press, 2011), chap. 3; Edward Muir, *Ritual in Early Modern*

Europe (Cambridge: Cambridge University Press, 2005), 108–9; Julius R. Ruff, *Violence in Early Modern Europe, 1500–1800* (Cambridge: Cambridge University Press, 2001) 161–62; E. P. Thompson, *Customs in Common* (New York: New Press, 1993), 467–531.

104 "Mock Suffragists Startle Broadway," *New York Times*, May 16, 1913, 11.

105 "Mock Suffragists Startle Broadway," 11.

106 "Mock Suffragists Startle Broadway," 11.

107 "Mock Suffragists Startle Broadway," 11.

108 "Mock Suffragists Startle Broadway," 11.

109 "Mock Suffragists Startle Broadway," 11.

110 The pioneering work on the transition from "justice" to "expediency" arguments in the equal-franchise campaign is Aileen S. Kraditor's *Ideas of the Woman Suffrage Movement*.

111 "Mrs. Deland Flays Women's Foibles," *New York Times*, December 11, 1909, 2.

112 Annie Nathan Meyer, "Sex Superiority," *New York Times*, May 30, 1909, 7.

113 Annie Nathan Meyer, "Women Legislators," *New York Times*, September 12, 1909, 8.

114 Meyer, "Women Legislators," 8.

115 "Clues on Woman Suffrage," *Utica Herald-Dispatch*, November 20, 1909, 6.

116 Annie Nathan Meyer, untitled article, *New York Times*, May 5, 1911, 10.

117 Annie Nathan Meyer, Letter to the Editor, *Barnard Bulletin*, February 23, 1910.

118 Mrs. Gilbert E. Jones, "The Position of the Anti-Suffragists," *Annals of the American Academy of Political and Social Science* 35, Supplement (May 1910): 18–19.

119 Meyer, "Letter to the Editor," *Barnard Bulletin*, February 23, 1910, 1.

120 "Women's Suffrage a Failure, He Says," *New York Times*, January 17, 1909.

121 "Colorado and Suffrage," *New York Times*, January 21, 1911, 12.

122 Jones, "The Position of the Anti-Suffragists," 20.

123 David Farrell et al., "Women at Cal: When California Passed the Woman Suffrage Amendment, 1910–1915, Room Six, A Vote of Their Own," Bancroft Library, University of California–Berkeley, last modified October 19, 2011, accessed September 24, 2015, http://bancroft.berkeley.edu/.

124 Farrell et al., "Women at Cal."

125 Benjamin, *A History of the Anti-Suffrage Movement*, 59.

126 "The Difficult Question," *Radcliffe Magazine*, April 1911, 113.

127 Goodier, "The Other Woman's Movement," 2.

128 "Anti-Suffragist Denounces Ballot," *San Francisco Call*, February 15, 1911, 9.

129 Annie Nathan Meyer, "Spreadhenism's Spirit," *New York Times*, March 20, 1911, 8.

130 "Miss Dorman of the Wage Earners Anti-Suffrage League Discusses Votes for Women," *Radcliffe News*, November 24, 1916, 2; "The Civics Club," *Radcliffe News*, October 30, 1914, 2.

131 Meyer "Spreadhenism's Spirit," 8.

132 "Mrs. Catt Takes Issue with Mrs. Meyer's Buffalo Speech," *New York Times*, March 15, 1908, 11.

133 "Anti-Suffragist Denounces Ballot," *San Francisco Call*, February 15, 1911, 9.

134 Green, *Southern Strategies*, 100; Gilmore, *Gender and Jim Crow*, chaps. 6–7; Wallace and Lemieux, introduction, *Black Macho and the Myth of the Superwoman*.

135 See the scholarship on the history of the Black family and gender roles during slavery. For example, Elizabeth Fox-Genovese, *Within the Plantation Household: Black and White Women of the Old South* (Chapel Hill: University of North Carolina Press, 1988); Gilmore, *Gender and Jim Crow*, chap. 1; Herbert G. Gutman, *The Black Family in Slavery and Freedom, 1750–1925* (Oxford: Basil Blackwell, 1976); Jacqueline Jones, *Labor of Love, Labor of Sorrow: Black Women, Work, and the Family, from Slavery to the Present* (New York: Perseus Books Group, 2009); Deborah Gray White, *Ar'n't I a Woman? Female Slaves in the Plantation South* (New York: Norton, 1999).

136 "Woman Suffrage," *The Crisis*, November 1915, 29.

137 May Martel, "Votes versus Mothers," *New York Age*, September 5, 1912, 5.

138 Gilmore, *Gender and Jim Crow*, chaps. 2, 6–7; Green, *Southern Strategies*, 100.

139 "Some Anti-Suffrage Sentiments," *Times-Picayune*, July 12, 1912, 9; "Women Opposed to Woman Suffrage Are Leaders in Manifold Activities," *New York Herald*, June 14, 1914, 4.

140 "Case against Votes for Women, Mrs. Arthur M. Dodge," *New York Times*, March 7, 1915, SM15.

141 History: MAOFESW, 4–5, carton 2, folder: History: MAOFESW, MAOFESW records; "Women Opposed to Woman Suffrage Are Leaders in Manifold Activities," 4.

142 "Professor Jordan No Suffragist," *New York Times*, March 22, 1910, 4.

143 "Progressive Women Who Are Opposed to the Ballot," *Boston Sunday Herald*, October 12, 1913.

144 Annie Nathan Meyer, Letter to the Editor, *Barnard Bulletin*, November 2, 1915, 2.

145 "Some Anti-Suffrage Sentiments," *Times-Picayune*, July 12, 1912, 9.

146 "Progressive Women Who Are Opposed to the Ballot," 3.

147 "Miss Arnold Decries Militant Suffrage," *New York Times*, January 4, 1910, 6. For more information on Junior League branches developing in different locations in later periods, see "Junior Anti-Suffrage League Is Organized, Johnstown," *New York Morning Herald*, February 9, 1917, 1.

148 Report of the Education and Organization Committee, January 5, 1910, 1, carton 2, folder: Education and Organization Committee, 1909–1910, MAOFESW records.

149 "Anti-Suffrage Assoc. Plans Busy Season," *Boston Sunday Herald*, October 12, 1913, 3.

150 Report of the Education and Organization Committee, January 19, 1916, 1, carton 2, folder: Education and Organization Committee, 1916, MAOFESW records.

151 "Antis Invite Walsh and Curley to Rally," *Boston Herald*, October 29, 1914, 10.

152 "Aviation and the Army," *Outlook*, April 5, 1916; "Fashion Pageant at Plaza," *New York Times*, March 2, 1916, 11; "Junior Anti-Suffrage League Raises $800 for Training Aviators," *Flying* 5 (April 1916): 126.

153 "Junior Anti-Suffrage League Fete," *New York Times*, January 28, 1917, 3.
154 "Junior Anti-Suffrage Fete Feb. 7," *New York Times*, January 14, 1917, 18; "Junior Anti-Suffrage League Fete," 3; "Pose as Posters at Vanity Fete," *New York Times*, February 8, 1917, 12.
155 Annie Nathan Meyer, "Test of Women's Votes," *New York Times*, November 12, 1917, 12.
156 Libby Jean Cavanaugh, "Opposition to Female Enfranchisement: The Iowa Anti-Suffrage Movement" (MA thesis, Iowa State University, 2007), 5, 35, 43, 89–91.
157 Camhi, *Women against Women*, 119.

CHAPTER 5. "HOW THE VOTE WAS WON"
 1 "College Evening," October 15–21, 1908, Enclosure: 40th Annual Convention of the National American Woman Suffrage Association, 10, Miller NAWSA Suffrage Scrapbooks, 1897–1911, Library of Congress, American Memory, accessed May 18, 2014, http://hdl.loc.gov/; Mary Whitall Worthington, "The College Equal Suffrage Chapter," *Tipyn O'Bob*, 1908–1909, 52–53.
 2 Lisa Marie Baumgartner, "Alice Paul, The National Woman's Party, and a Rhetoric of Mobilization" (PhD diss., University of Minnesota, 1994), 7; Sara Hunter Graham, *Woman Suffrage and the New Democracy* (New Haven, CT: Yale University Press, 1996), 88–90, 151, 164; "Carrie Chapman Catt," American Memory, "Votes for Women," Selections from the National American Woman Suffrage Association Collection, 1848–1921, last modified October 19, 1998, accessed September 3, 2015, http://memory.loc.gov/.
 3 Graham, *Woman Suffrage and the New Democracy*, 21–25, 110, 149, 151, 164.
 4 For works that discuss suffrage demographics and the age of women's rights activists, see Anne M. Boylan, *The Origins of Women's Activism: New York and Boston, 1797–1840* (Chapel Hill: University of North Carolina Press, 2002), chap. 2, 55–73; Nancy Cott, "Feminist Politics in the 1920s: The National Woman's Party," *Journal of American History* 71, no. 1 (June 1984): 43–68; Cott, *The Grounding of Modern Feminism* (New Haven, CT: Yale University Press, 1987), chap. 5, 57–58; Holly J. McCammon, "Stirring up Suffrage Sentiment: The Formation of the State Woman Suffrage Organizations, 1866–1914," *Social Forces* 80, no. 2 (December 2001): 449–80; Holly J. McCammon, Karen E. Campbell, Ellen M. Granberg, and Christine Mowery, "How Movements Win: Gendered Opportunity Structures and U.S. Women's Suffrage Movement, 1866 to 1919," *American Sociological Review* 66, no. 1 (February 2001): 49–70; Caryn E. Neumann, "The National Woman's Party and the Equal Rights Amendment, 1945–1977" (MA thesis, Florida Atlantic University, 1994), 18–20.
 5 See Barbara J. Bank, *Gender and Higher Education* (Baltimore, MD: Johns Hopkins University Press, 2011); Miriam E. David, *Feminism, Gender, and Universities: Politics, Passion, and Pedagogies* (Burlington, VT: Ashgate, 2014); Linda Eisenmann, *Higher Education for Women in Postwar America, 1945–1965* (Baltimore, MD: Johns Hopkins University Press, 2006); Ruth Rosen, *The World*

Split Open: How the Modern Women's Movement Changed America (New York: Viking, 2000); Benita Roth, *Separate Roads to Feminism: Black, Chicana, and White Feminist Movements in America's Second Wave* (Cambridge: Cambridge University Press, 2004); Deborah Siegel, *Sisterhood, Interrupted: From Radical Women to Girls Gone Wild* (Basingstoke, UK: Palgrave Macmillan, 2007).

6 Tim Warren, "She Was a Woman Ahead of Her Time: M. Carey Thomas, the Power and Passion," *Baltimore Sun*, September 4, 1994, ww.baltimoresun.com/; Helen Lefkowitz Horowitz, *The Power and Passion of M. Carey Thomas* (Champaign: University of Illinois Press, 1999).

7 Warren, "She Was a Woman Ahead of Her Time"; Horowitz, *The Power and Passion of M. Carey Thomas.*

8 Warren, "She Was a Woman Ahead of Her Time."

9 Horowitz, *The Power and Passion of M. Carey Thomas.*

10 Suzanne Gould, "AAUW's Long Road to Women's Suffrage," August 23, 2013, American Association of University Women, accessed March 24, 2014, www.aauw.org/; Ethel Puffer Howes, "Report of the National College Equal Suffrage League to August 1, 1916," 206–8 in *Handbook of the National American Woman Suffrage Association and Proceedings of the Forty-Eighth Annual Convention, Atlantic City, NJ, September 4–10, 1916*, ed. Hannah J. Patterson (New York: National Woman Suffrage Publishing); College Equal Suffrage League, National Headquarters of League, Miss Caroline Lexow, Minutes of the Second Annual Meeting of the Council, Seattle, July 1909, Sophia Smith Suffrage Collection, Series I. United States, Folder: Organizations, College Equal Suffrage League, 1905–1914, page 30, Plan of Work for the Executive Committee.

11 Howes, "Report of the National College Equal Suffrage League," 206–8.

12 Lexow, "Minutes of the Second Annual Meeting."

13 Howes, "Report of the National College Equal Suffrage League," 206–8.

14 National College Equal Suffrage League, "Suggested Work for College Chapters, City Leagues, and the Executive Secretary," pamphlet, undated, box 5, folder 23: Series II. Woman Suffrage—Vassar College, Woman Suffrage and Women's Rights Collection, Archives and Special Collections Library, Vassar College Libraries, Poughkeepsie, NY (hereafter, Vassar Woman Suffrage and Women's Rights Collection).

15 Lexow, "Minutes of the Second Annual Meeting."

16 Howes, "Report of the National College Equal Suffrage League," 206–8.

17 Howes, "Report of the National College Equal Suffrage League," 206–8; Lexow, "Minutes of the Second Annual Meeting"; NCESL, "Suggested Work for College Chapters, City Leagues, and the Executive Secretary."

18 "College Equal Suffrage League to Meet with 'Suffs,'" *Columbus Daily Enquirer*, November 7, 1915, 16.

19 "Suffragists Going Abroad," *New York Times*, March 23, 1911, 6.

20 "College Equal Suffrage League to Meet with 'Suffs,'" 16.

21 "To Meet under Ten-Starred Flag," *Greensboro Record*, November 20, 1912, 1.

22 "'ABC' of Suffrage," *Washington Post*, December 14, 1913, 10.

23 "Seek Suffrage Leader," *Washington Post*, December 14, 1915, 4; "Young Suffragists to Greet Visitors," *Washington Herald*, October 25, 1915, 9. "Planning New Work for Suffrage," *Boston Sunday Globe*, November 7, 1915, 59; "Plan Week's Session for Suffrage," *Duluth News-Tribune*, October 31, 1915, 5.

24 "Speeches to Be Made on How to Win Suffrage by Making Friends Instead of Enemies," *Evening Star* (Washington, DC), December 17, 1915, 2.

25 "Cleaning-Up War Begun," *Washington Post*, March 2, 1910, 12; "Trash under Cover," *Washington Herald*, March 2, 1910, 12.

26 "Cleaning-Up War Begun," 12; "Trash under Cover," 12.

27 "City Briefs," *Washington Post*, April 22, 1916, 14; "Police News Notes," *Washington Post*, April 23, 1916, A19.

28 "Miss Lathrop Suffrage Guest," *Washington Post*, February 4, 1917, 16; "Speeches to Be Made," *Evening Star*, December 17, 1915, 2.

29 The results noted above are from the suffragists' report after studying the textbook used in Washington, DC, schools in 1914. Upon examining an edition of the textbook, however, a few discrepancies appear, possibly due to an error, different editions, or an attempt to exaggerate the suffragists' positions. First, I could find no references to Clara Barton. However, the book does include brief mentions of Martha Washington, Mary Ball Washington, Virginia Dare, Catharine Littlefield Greene, Elizabeth Hutchinson Jackson, and Nancy Hanks Lincoln. See Winifred Mallon, "The Forgotten Women of History," *The Suffragist* 2, no. 31 (1914): 7–8; and the textbook, David Henry Montgomery, *The Beginner's American History* (Boston: Ginn & Company, 1893), www.gutenberg.org/, accessed May 10, 2014.

30 Mallon, "The Forgotten Women of History," 7–8.

31 Mallon, "The Forgotten Women of History," 7–8.

32 Scholar Ellen Carol DuBois also points out that women were challenging social inequality, including their unequal partnerships with men in marriage. Ellen Carol DuBois, *Woman Suffrage and Women's Rights* (New York: New York University Press, 1998), introduction.

33 "Suffragists Organizing Fight for Married Women Teachers," *Washington Times*, December 17, 1914, 5; "Upholds Married Teachers," *Washington Post*, January 27, 1915, 4.

34 "Suffragists Organizing Fight for Married Women Teachers," 5.

35 "Women Will Persist," *Washington Post*, March 29, 1913, 14.

36 "Suffragists Plead Again," *Washington Post*, February 17, 1914, 4.

37 "Politics," *The Crisis*, April 1913, 267.

38 "Politics," 267.

39 "Politics," 267.

40 "Huge Suffrage Parade in Washington: Over 7,000 in 'Votes for Women,'" *New York Daily People*, March 4, 1913, 1. As many scholars have argued, White northern suffragists who headed national suffrage organizations consistently worried about losing southern support over the race issue. See Green, *Southern Strategies*,

26; Kraditor, *The Ideas of the Woman Suffrage Movement, 1890–1920*, chaps. 7–8; Wheeler, *New Women of the New South*, chap. 4.

41 May Martel, "Colored Women in Demonstration," *New York Age*, March 13, 1913.

42 "Huge Suffrage Parade in Washington," 1; "Suffrage Paraders," *The Crisis*, April 1913, 296.

43 "Social Uplift," *The Crisis*, July 1914, 113.

44 Eleanor Piper, CESL of Boston, 1915–1916, Report of the Secretary, reel 41, Subseries C. Suffrage and Women's Rights, Maud Wood Park Papers.

45 "Women to Parade for Federal Amendment," *New Orleans Item*, October 1, 1916, 16.

46 For more information, see B. H. Gilley, "Kate Gordon and Louisiana Woman Suffrage," *Louisiana History* 24 (Summer 1983): 289–306; Janet G. Hudson, *Entangled by White Supremacy: Reform in World War I–Era South Carolina* (Lexington: University Press of Kentucky, 2009), chap. 8; Kathryn W. Kemp, "Jean and Kate Gordon: New Orleans Social Reformers, 1898–1933," *Louisiana History: The Journal of the Louisiana Historical Association* 24 (Autumn 1983): 389–401; Green, *Southern Strategies*, chap. 4; Wheeler, *New Women of the New South*, chaps. 4–5.

47 "Suffrage Advocates Spurred to Activity," *Times-Picayune*, October 7, 1916, 25.

48 "Suffrage Advocates Spurred to Activity," 25.

49 Maud Wood Park, *Front Door Lobby* (Boston: Beacon, 1960).

50 See Baumgartner, "Alice Paul, the National Woman's Party, and a Rhetoric of Mobilization," 12; Kathryn M. Brown, "The Education of the Woman Citizen, 1917–1918" (MA thesis, Bowling Green State University, 2010); Christopher Joseph Nicodemus Capozzola, *Uncle Sam Wants You: World War I and the Making of the Modern American Citizen* (Oxford: Oxford University Press, 2008), chap. 4; Eleanor Flexner, *Century of Struggle: The Woman's Rights Movement in the United States* (Cambridge, MA: Harvard University Press, 1959), 284; Graham, *Woman Suffrage and the New Democracy*, chaps. 5–7; Kimberly Jensen, *Mobilizing Minerva: American Women in the First World War* (Urbana: University of Illinois Press, 2008), preface; Julianne Unsel, "Woman's Hour: Suffrage and American Citizenship in War and Reconstruction, 1914–1924" (PhD diss., University of Wisconsin, 2005), chap. 1.

51 Jensen, *Mobilizing Minerva*, xi.

52 See Unsel, "Woman's Hour," chap. 1, 5, 28–29; William J. Breen, *Uncle Sam at Home: Civilian Mobilization, Wartime Federalism, and the Council of National Defense, 1917–1919* (Westport, CT: Greenwood Press, 1984), 115–36; Cott, *Grounding of Modern Feminism*, 59–61; Sara M. Evans, *Born for Liberty: A History of Women in America* (New York: Free Press, 1989), 172; Maurine Weiner Greenwald, *Women, War, and Work: The Impact of World War I on Women Workers in the United States* (Westport, CT: Greenwood, 1980); Rosalind Rosenberg, *Divided Lives: American Women in the Twentieth Century* (New York: Hill and Wang, 1992), 72–76; Sheila Rowbotham, *A Century of Women: The History of Women in Britain and the United States* (New York: Viking, 1997), 91–109; Barbara Steinson,

American Women's Activism in World War I (New York: Garland, 1982); Carolyn Vacca Summers, *A Reform against Nature: Woman Suffrage and the Rethinking of American Citizenship* (New York: Peter Lang, 2004), 120–23; Sandra F. VanBurkleo, *Belonging to the World: Women's Rights and American Constitutional Culture* (New York: Oxford University Press, 2001), 206, 226–29.

53 Ethel Puffer Howes, "The National College Equal Suffrage League," *Smith Alumnae Quarterly* 12, no. 1 (November 1920): 44.

54 Howes, "The National College Equal Suffrage League," 44.

55 Howes, "The National College Equal Suffrage League," 44.

56 Howes, "The National College Equal Suffrage League," 44.

57 Howes, "The National College Equal Suffrage League," 44.

58 Inez Haynes Irwin, "The Making of a Militant," in *These Modern Women: Autobiographical Essays from the Twenties*, ed. Elaine Showalter (New York: Feminist Press, City University of New York, 1989), 38–39.

59 Irwin, "The Making of a Militant," 38–39.

60 Irwin, "The Making of a Militant," 38–39.

61 Irwin, "The Making of a Militant," 38–39.

62 Irwin, "The Making of a Militant," 38–39.

63 Unsel, "Woman's Hour," 37.

64 "Urges Barton Memorial," *Washington Post*, October 24, 1916, 3.

65 "Sweets for Sammies," *Washington Times*, July 22, 1917, 7.

66 Lillian M. Landy, "CESL of Boston, 1918–1919, Report of the Secretary," reel 41, Subseries C. Suffrage and Women's Rights, Maud Wood Park Papers.

67 Lillian M. Landy, "Report of the Secretary College Equal Suffrage League of Boston 1917–1918," box 47, reel 32, Subject File, 1851–1953, NAWSA Records.

68 Edith Morgan, "Letter to the Editor," *Barnard Bulletin*, October 25, 1917, 2.

69 Morgan, "Letter to the Editor," 2.

70 Morgan, "Letter to the Editor," 2.

71 Margaret Perkins, "The Letter Box," *Radcliffe News*, October 4, 1918, 2.

72 Perkins, "The Letter Box," 2.

73 "Suffrage League Quits," *Washington Evening Star*, December 16, 1917, 4.

74 "College Suffrage League to Meet," *Trenton Evening Times*, November 7, 1915, 16; "Suffrage League Quits," 4.

75 "Nation's Suffragists to Meet in December," *Anaconda Standard*, November 9, 1915, 2.

76 "Suffrage League Quits," 4.

77 Chara Haeussler Bohan, *Go to the Sources: Lucy Maynard Salmon and the Teaching of History* (New York: Peter Lang, 2004), 39.

78 Bohan, *Go to the Sources*, 39.

79 Landy, "CESL of Boston, 1918–1919, Report of the Secretary."

80 Another possible explanation for the NCESL's demise in 1917 might have been the organization's expansiveness. By the late 1910s, suffragists were no longer just going to cities to create alumni leagues. The group had a network of college

chapters, and members were aspiring to create normal school branches. Trying to manage so many small sections throughout the country might have been difficult for NCESL leaders. The organization did not have the same staffing or resources as NAWSA.

81 "Suffrage Club," *Radcliffe News*, June 1920, 4.
82 "Revive Suffrage League," *Washington Post*, March 26, 1918, 8.
83 Landy, "Report of the Secretary College Equal Suffrage League of Boston 1917–1918"; Landy, "CESL of Boston, 1918–1919, Report of the Secretary."
84 Mrs. Charles Knoblauch, "Report of the College Section," in "Annual Report of the New York State Woman Suffrage Party and Proceedings of the Forty-Ninth Annual Convention," New York, November 20–22, 1917, box 12, folder 2, Sophia Smith Suffrage Collection.
85 "Time for Suffrage, Says College Head," *New Orleans Item*, October 30, 1918, 5.
86 "Suffrage Meeting," *Radcliffe News*, February 1916, 4.
87 Margaret Perks, Helen Nute, and Marion Syecenski, "The Letter Box," *Radcliffe News*, March 1919, 3.
88 Anne Wood, Helen E. Nute, and Margaret Perkins, "The Letter Box," *Radcliffe News*, March 1917, 2.
89 Throughout her study of female political activism in the South after 1920, Lorraine Gates Schuyler discusses extensively how woman suffrage threatened White supremacy. Lorraine Gates Schuyler, *The Weight of Their Votes: Southern Women and Political Leverage in the 1920s* (Chapel Hill: University of North Carolina Press, 2006).
90 Nikki L. M. Brown, *Private Politics and Public Voices: Black Women's Activism from World War I to the New Deal* (Bloomington: Indiana University Press, 2006), 2–3.
91 "Defeat of Woman Suffrage Due to Race Hate," *St. Louis Argus*, October 4, 1918, 4.
92 "Defeat of Woman Suffrage Due to Race Hate," 4.
93 "Defeat of Woman Suffrage Due to Race Hate," 4.
94 "Defeat of Woman Suffrage Due to Race Hate," 4.
95 "Defeat of Woman Suffrage Due to Race Hate," 4. For more information about the experiences of African Americans in the military during World War I, see Chad Louis Williams, *Torchbearers of Democracy: African American Soldiers in the World War I Era* (Chapel Hill: University of North Carolina Press, 2010).
96 "Suffrage Camouflaged," *St. Louis Argus*, March 1, 1918, 4.
97 "Jersey City, N.J.," *New York Age*, July 20, 1918, 5.
98 "Washington Letter," *New York Age*, January 31, 1920, 5.
99 "Protesting Women and the War," *New York Age*, September 21, 1918, 4.
100 Suffrage not only threatened the structure of race relations but also southern gender norms. Gilmore, *Gender and Jim Crow*, chap. 8; Schuyler, *The Weight of Their Votes*, chap. 1; Wheeler, *New Women of the New South*, chaps. 4–5.
101 Capozzola, *Uncle Sam Wants You*, 95.

102 Activists wrote many of the early suffrage histories themselves. NAWSA and NWP members battled over control of the legacy of and credit for the women's rights victory. Representatives from each group argued that their organization's methods were more central to success. See Carrie Chapman Catt and Marjorie Shuler, *Woman Suffrage and Politics: The Inner Story of the Suffrage Movement* (Seattle: University of Washington Press, 1921); Inez Haynes Irwin, *The Story of the Woman's Party* (New York: Harcourt, 1923), 319–34; Doris Stevens, *Jailed for Freedom* (New York: Boni and Liveright, 1920), 3–20. NAWSA's contributions to the women's rights campaign initially reigned supreme because of the four-volume publication *History of Woman Suffrage* (1881–1922), which shaped early scholarship on the equal-franchise movement, such as Eleanor Flexner's *Century of Struggle* (1959).

By the 1960s and 1970s, however, the new rise in women's rights activism attracted greater attention to the history of woman suffrage among feminist scholars. The studies that emerged were shaped by current events, the developing field of women's history, and popular methods of historical research at the time, like oral history, which led to fresh interviews with former suffragists like NWP cofounder Alice Paul. Scholars have commented that interest in interviewing Paul, in particular, helped to create a shift in historical focus to the NWP's role in the winning of woman suffrage. Unsel, "Woman's Hour," 13–14.

Recently, the growth of conservatism since the 1990s has led some scholars to reconsider the importance of the NAWSA's campaigns. Baumgartner, "Alice Paul, the National Woman's Party, and a Rhetoric of Mobilization"; Susan D. Becker, *The Origins of the Equal Rights Amendment: American Feminism between the Wars* (Westport, CT: Greenwood, 1981), 3–11; Linda Ford, "Alice Paul and the Politics of Nonviolent Protest," in *Votes for Women: The Struggle for Suffrage Revisited*, ed. Jean H. Baker (New York: Oxford University Press, 2002), 174–86; Christine Lunardini, *From Equal Suffrage to Equal Rights: Alice Paul and the National Woman's Party, 1910–1928* (New York: New York University Press, 1986).

103 The more comprehensive history of the NAWSA's campaigns remains Graham, *Woman Suffrage and the New Democracy*. An extensive body of scholarship documenting the arguments and tactics of the National Woman's Party has been published by both university and popular presses. For some of the most influential scholarly works, see Linda G. Ford, *Iron-Jawed Angels: The Suffrage Militancy of the NWP, 1912–1920* (Lanham, MD: University Press of America, 1991); Lunardini, *From Equal Suffrage to Equal Rights*; Belinda A. Stillion Southard, *Militant Citizenship: Rhetorical Strategies of the National Woman's Party, 1913–1920* (College Station: Texas A&M University Press, 2011).

104 Unsel, "Woman's Hour," 11.

105 Inez Haynes Gillmore, *The Story of the Woman's Party* (New York: Harcourt, Brace, 1921), 334.

106 Betty Gram, "Do Your Friends Subscribe for *The Suffragist?*" *The Suffragist* 6, no. 22 (1918): 12.

107 Baumgartner and other scholars have also noted that, at heart, Wilson was "a white southerner" who supported "almost exclusively" "states' rights." Baumgartner, "Alice Paul, the National Woman's Party, and a Rhetoric of Mobilization," 13; Nell Irvin Painter, *Standing at Armageddon: The United States, 1877–1919* (New York: Norton, 1987), 270; Southard, *Militant Citizenship*, 4–5, 135–36.

108 Carrie Chapman Catt and Nettie Rogers Shuler, *Woman Suffrage and Politics* (Seattle: University of Washington Press, 1921), 294–98, 316–42; Unsel, "Woman's Hour," 11.

109 Cott, *Grounding of Modern Feminism*, 59.

110 Southard, *Militant Citizenship*, 4, 22, 137–38.

111 Gillmore, *The Story of the Woman's Party*, 198; photograph, Suffrage Campaign, Pickets, "College Day," 1917, Washington, DC, February 3, 1917, National Woman's Party Photograph Collection, Sewall-Belmont House & Museum, Washington, DC.

112 According to scholars, during World War I, the government restricted "civil liberties" and made it a crime to speak out against the president. Scholar Janice Law Trecker calls the NWP pickets initially a "tourist attraction." Baumgartner, "Alice Paul, the National Woman's Party, and a Rhetoric of Mobilization," 10, 13, 15, 16–17; Southard, *Militant Citizenship*; Janice Law Trecker, "The Suffrage Prisoners," *American Scholar* 41 (Summer 1972): 415.

113 Baumgartner, "Alice Paul, the National Woman's Party, and a Rhetoric of Mobilization," 16.

114 Stevens, *Jailed for Freedom*, 356, 360, 362–65, 367–69.

115 Stevens, *Jailed for Freedom*, 354.

116 Elizabeth McShane Hilles, "Jail Notes," June 21, 1971, box 5, folder 23, Series II. Woman Suffrage–Vassar College, Vassar Woman Suffrage and Women's Rights Collection.

117 Stevens, *Jailed for Freedom*, 356.

118 Hilles, "Jail Notes," 4.

119 Hilles, "Jail Notes," 5.

120 Hilles, "Jail Notes," 5.

121 Hilles, "Jail Notes," 6.

122 Hilles, "Jail Notes," 9.

123 Katherine H. Adams and Michael L. Keene, *After the Vote Was Won: The Later Achievements of Fifteen Suffragists* (Jefferson, NC: McFarland, 2010), 30; Stevens, *Jailed for Freedom*, 361, 367, 371.

124 "The Watch Fire," *The Suffragist* 7, no. 51 (1919): 6.

125 "The Watch Fire," 6; Stevens, *Jailed for Freedom*, 354, 359, 363, 365, 368–69, 371.

126 Baumgartner, "Alice Paul, the National Woman's Party, and a Rhetoric of Mobilization," 14; Sara Hunter Graham, "Woodrow Wilson, Alice Paul, and the Woman Suffrage Movement," *Political Science Quarterly* 98 (Winter 1983–1984): 665–66.

127 For more information about President Wilson's transition to a position of support for equal franchise, see Beth Behn, "Woodrow Wilson's Conversion Experience: The President and the Federal Woman Suffrage Amendment" (PhD diss., University of Massachusetts–Amherst, 2012).

128 For the most recent looks at women's civic education work prior to 1920, see Brown, "The Education of the Woman Citizen"; Wendy B. Sharer, *Vote and Voice: Women's Organizations and Political Literacy, 1915–1930* (Carbondale: Southern Illinois University Press, 2007), chap. 1.

129 "Equal Suffrage Club Will Be Reorganized," *San Francisco Call*, December 12, 1911, 7.

130 "Noted Suffrage Worker Speaks at College," *Radcliffe News*, March 23, 1917, 1.

131 "Courses Offered in Woman Suffrage," *Columbia Spectator*, March 20, 1915, 4.

132 "College Equal Suffrage League Has Jollification," *Boston Globe*, May 22, 1920, 12; College Equal Suffrage League of Boston, *Manual for Massachusetts Voters* (Boston: College Equal Suffrage League of Boston, 1920); Florence H. Luscomb, Secretary, "Report on the Manual for Massachusetts Voters," 1920, reel 41, Subseries C. Suffrage and Women's Rights, Maud Wood Park Papers.

133 During World War I, women and men of all classes and races were encouraged to support the military crisis. Gilmore, *Gender and Jim Crow*, 195–99, 301.

134 "A Resolution," *The Crisis*, November 1917, 12.

135 Carrie Chapman Catt, "Votes for All: A Symposium," *The Crisis*, November 1917, 19–21.

136 Catt, "Votes for All," 19–21.

137 Untitled comments about suffrage, *New York Age*, March 13, 1913.

138 "Equal Suffrage League," *New York Age*, June 1, 1918, 8; "Manhattan and the Bronx," *New York Age*, May 25, 1918, 8; "Manhattan YWCA Notes," *New York Age*, March 1, 1918.

139 "Manhattan YWCA Notes"; untitled comments about suffrage.

140 Untitled comments about suffrage.

141 "Woman Suffrage," *The Crisis*, March 1920, 234.

142 "White Suffragettes Ask Colored Women to Help," *Baltimore Afro-American*, June 3, 1916, 1.

143 "Votes for Women," *The Crisis*, November 1917, 8.

144 "Votes for Women," 8.

145 "Votes for Women," 8.

146 "Compromises on the Suffrage Amendment," *New York Age*, March 1, 1919, 4.

147 "Compromises on the Suffrage Amendment," 4; Graham, *Woman Suffrage and the New Democracy*, 124.

148 Mark R. Schneider, *We Return Fighting: The Civil Rights Movement in the Jazz Age* (Boston: Northeastern University Press, 2002), 118.

149 Nannie Burroughs, "Divide Vote or Go to Socialists," *Baltimore Afro-American*, August 22, 1919, 4.

150 Burroughs, "Divide Vote or Go to Socialists," 4.

151 Kris Schumacher, "Black Women's Struggle for the Suffrage," *Womanspeak* 6, no. 4 (April 1985): 10.
152 Schumacher, "Black Women's Struggle for the Suffrage," 10.
153 "National Association of Colored Women's Clubs," in *U.S. Women's Interest Groups: Institutional Profiles*, ed. Sarah Slavin (Westport, CT: Greenwood, 1995), 298.
154 Schumacher, "Black Women's Struggle for the Suffrage," 10.
155 Jeanette Carter, "Women Celebrate in Honor of Vote Right," *New York Age*, September 4, 1920, 1.
156 Carter, "Women Celebrate in Honor of Vote Right," 1.
157 Ann D. Gordon and Bettye Collier-Thomas, *African American Women and the Vote: 1837–1965* (Amherst: University of Massachusetts Press, 1997), introduction. Also, see Gilmore, *Gender and Jim Crow*, chap. 8; Schuyler, *The Weight of Their Votes*, for more about African American disenfranchisement in the South.

CONCLUSION

1 Barbara J. Bank, *Gender and Higher Education* (Baltimore, MD: Johns Hopkins University Press, 2011), 160.
2 For the term "graying" used to explain this historiographical argument, see Myra Marx Ferree, review of *The Grounding of Modern Feminism*, by Nancy F. Cott, *Contemporary Sociology* 18, no. 1 (January 1989): 16–18.
3 Historically, scholars and popular culture have portrayed the LWV as a conservative organization with little effect on society. Most studies on the LWV, however, often overlook the group's influence on American education. Even scholarship that explicitly explores citizenship-education programs typically highlights their influence on other aspects of twentieth-century public life, such as consumerism, government, and politics, not academics. Jamie Mayhew Bufalino, "Reinventing the Body Politic: Women, Consumer Culture, and Civic Identity from Suffrage to the New Deal" (PhD diss., University of California–Riverside, 2009); Liette Patricia Gidlow, *The Big Vote: Gender, Consumer Culture, and the Politics of Exclusion, 1890s-1920s* (Baltimore, MD: Johns Hopkins University Press, 2007); Schuyler, *The Weight of Their Votes*; Louise Merwin Young and Ralph A. Young, *In the Public Interest: The League of Women Voters, 1920–1970* (New York: Greenwood, 1989).
   One exception is Wendy Sharer's recent text, which focuses on the LWV's influence in the political realm but also mentions some civic-literacy activism in relation to education. Sharer argues that LWV leaders held events on campuses because schools were open, familiar, and comfortable for women. In particular, she emphasizes the effect of the LWV's courses and classes on improving adult and continuing-education instruction at normal schools and junior colleges, institutions that "catered to female students." Wendy B. Sharer, *Vote and Voice: Women's Organizations and Political Literacy, 1915–1930* (Carbondale: Southern Illinois University Press, 2004), 135–37, 140.

4 Constance Roach to Mrs. Henry Randolph Brigham, May 24, 1934, box 16, folder 2: Organization—College Leagues, 1930–1947, League of Women Voters of Massachusetts Records, 1920–1975, Schlesinger Library, Radcliffe Institute, Harvard University, Cambridge, MA.

5 Gidlow discusses a change in how voting was publicly perceived after 1920. Over time, as the electorate expanded, it did not carry the same weight and have the same "social meaning" as in earlier periods. Before 1920, Americans connected "partisan identity" to ethnic and religious background, and it was a sign of particular "membership in the community." She also notes that during the twentieth century, the nature of political campaigns became more subdued; voting became more of a private rather than a public act; and people viewed voting less as an expression or form of "power" and more as a "duty," which deterred some electors. According to Gidlow, the major "nonvoters" during the 1920s were the "poor and working class, ethnic, African American, female, young and Southern" citizens. Liette Patricia Gidlow, "Getting out the Vote: Gender and Citizenship in an Age of Consumer Culture" (PhD diss., Cornell University, 1997), 27–30, 32, 50–51.

6 Donnette Smith Kesler, "Three Important Conventions," *Young Woman's Journal* 31, no. 5 (May 1920): 274; "Women Voters to Hold Institute of Government," *Idaho Statesman*, June 9, 1924, 3.

7 Gidlow, "Getting Out the Vote," 169.

8 The precise circumstances surrounding the Students' Council formation are unclear, and statements offer conflicting information. An article in the *Equal Rights* periodical notes that NWP members Elsie Hill, former DC CESL leader, and Florence Rogatz created the first chapter in 1922 at Yale University Law School. "Students' Council, National Woman's Party," *Equal Rights*, April 11, 1925, 66. A historical sketch by the editor of the National Woman's Party papers, however, situates the founding in 1923 and states that the Inez Milholland Memorial Fund Committee headed by NWP activist Lucy Branham organized the Students' Council. Branches then carried the title "Inez Milholland chapters." Thomas C. Pardo, ed., *Historical Sketch of the National Woman's Party, National Woman's Party Papers, 1913–1974*, Guide to the Microfilm Collection (Sanford, NC: Microfilming Corporation of America, 1979), 15. A third source, another article in *Equal Rights*, comments that NWP activists formed the Students' Council on January 4, 1924, at the private home of Bryn Mawr student Cornelia B. Rose in New York. "Students' Council of the Woman's Party," *Equal Rights*, August 16, 1924, 214–15. Sources on the NWP's activism sometimes also further reference another young adult group called the "Young Women's Council" in Washington, DC, during the 1920s. "Young Women's Council Organized," *Equal Rights*, April 13, 1929, 80.

9 "Students' Council, National Woman's Party," 66.

10 In youth campaigns, the NWP targeted various schools such as the State University of New York, New York University Law School, National University School of Law, Yale University Law School, Plattsburg Normal School, Columbia University, Sweet Briar College, Washington College of Law, University of Vermont,

University of Pennsylvania, Brooklyn Law School, Bryn Mawr College, George Washington University, Lenox Hill School, Park Henry High School, Essex High School, Vassar College, Smith College, Goucher College, Katharine Gibbs Business School, Low and Haywood School, Miss Wright's School, Miss Spence's School, and Mary Lyon's School. "Students' Council of the Woman's Party," 214–15; "The Students' Conference," *Equal Rights*, August 23, 1924, 223.

11 "Inez Milholland Memorial Organizes National University Law School," *Equal Rights*, February 23, 1924, 11; "Students Adopt Constitution," *Equal Rights*, March 26, 1932, 63; "Students' Council, National Woman's Party," 66.

12 "The Students' Conference"; "Students' Council, National Woman's Party," 66.

13 "Education Helps Equal Rights," *Equal Rights*, April 6, 1929, 71.

14 "Work of Woman's Party Discussed at Forum Luncheon," *Barnard Bulletin*, March 6, 1925, 1.

15 Margaret Robinson Maiten and Stella Turner, "First Meeting of Negro Girls," reel 16, frame 0001, Part I: Minutes of National Conventions, Publications, and President's Office Correspondence, NACWC Archives cont., Ella Phillips Stewart Administration cont., Records of the National Association of Colored Women's Clubs, 1895–1992, microfilm edition (Bethesda, MD: University Publications of America, 1993).

16 If they wanted, the NACG members could switch to the NACWC when age eighteen. Sallie W. Stewart, *Girls' Guide*, 1946, 10–11, box 14, folder 3: Nat. Assn. of Colored Women, Series I. National Organizations, United States, NAACP–National Council of Jewish Women, Miscellaneous Organizations Collection, Sophia Smith Collection, Smith College, Northampton, MA.

17 Michele Alishahi, "'For Peace and Civic Righteousness': Blanche Armwood and the Struggle for Freedom and Racial Equality in Tampa, Florida, 1890–1939" (MA thesis, University of South Florida, 2003), 14–15. For more information about the political style of Black clubwomen, see Evelyn Brooks Higginbotham, *Righteous Discontent: The Women's Movement in the Black Baptist Church, 1880–1920* (Cambridge, MA: Harvard University Press, 1996), 2; Stephanie Shaw, *What a Woman Ought to Be and to Do: Black Professional Women Workers during the Jim Crow Era* (Chicago: University of Chicago Press, 1996); Deborah Gray White, *Too Heavy a Load: Black Women in Defense of Themselves, 1894–1994* (New York: Norton, 1999).

18 Scholar V. P. Franklin writes that Black college students and graduates coming of age after the suffrage victory in 1920 saw themselves as "New Negroes" who could "use their collegiate training to advance their race." However, often, a "Victorian environment maintained on campus by white and black administrators" limited their activism. V. P. Franklin, "Introduction: African American Student Activism in the Twentieth Century," *Journal of African American History* 88, no. 2 (Spring 2003): 105–6.

Other scholars like Joel Rosenthal have argued conversely that in the 1920s, some social and political organizing on Black campuses took off. Black students protested for greater academic rights and challenged racial injustices, "confining moral codes," and Whites' control of African American higher education. Joel Rosenthal, "Southern Black Student Activism: Assimilation vs. Nationalism," *Journal of Negro Education* 44, no. 2 (Spring 1975): 115.

19 Scholars stress how cultivating "respectability" was important to upwardly mobile Black women. In the African American community, people often tied class to more than just economics and connected it to behavior and appearance as well, since Whites typically discriminated against Blacks in vocations. Alishahi, "'For Peace and Civic Righteousness,'" 14–15; Higginbotham, *Righteous Discontent*, 2, 14, 18, 204–5. Also, see Shaw, *What a Woman Ought to Be and to Do*; Anastatia Sims, *The Power of Femininity in the New South: Women's Organizations and Politics in North Carolina, 1880–1930* (Columbia: University of South Carolina Press, 1997); White, *Too Heavy a Load*.

20 Studies of student protest often overlook suffrage organizing when providing a trajectory for college activism. Most historians start their discussion of structured, large-scale campus campaigns for social and political causes in the 1930s and negate organizing in the early twentieth century. The rise of activism during the Depression is often tied to forces like pacifism, fascism, communism, and radicalism. See Philip G. Altbach and Patti Peterson, "Before Berkeley: Historical Perspectives on American Student Activism," *Annals of the American Academy of Political and Social Science* 395 (May 1971): 1–14; Ralph S. Brax, *The First Student Movement: Student Activism in the United States during the 1930s* (Port Washington, NY: Kennikat Press, 1981); Charles J. Holden, "'Patriotism Does Not Mean Stupidity': Student Antiwar Activism at UNC in the 1930s," *North Carolina Historical Review* 85, no. 1 (January 2008): 29–56; Rosenthal, "Southern Black Student Activism," 113–29.

INDEX

abolition: connections to women's movement, 17–20; in suffrage propaganda, 87, 100, 115–17

academic culture: against suffrage, 133–35, 151–52; for suffrage, 9–13, 96–98, 122–28, 206

African Americans: Black suffrage organizations, 49–51; churches, 50–51; clubwomen, 46–49, 89–92, 204–5; education of, 100–101, federal amendment, 184–87, 190–91, 195–99; Fifteenth Amendment, 20, 87–88; lynching of, 46, 50, 142–143; opposition on Black campuses, 132–34, 142–45, 157–59; suffrage activism on Black campuses, 115–18, 127

ageism, 9–10, 123

Alpha Kappa Alpha, 116

Alpha Suffrage Club, 50

American Equal Rights Association (AERA), 17–20

American Woman Suffrage Association (AWSA), 20

Americanization: citizenship education, civic education, and/or political literacy, 9–10, 49–50, 194–200, 206

Anderson, Naomi, 50

Anthony, Susan B.: death of, 24–25; establishment of Newcomb College, 102–3; illegal voting, 27–28; involvement in abolition, 17–20; public presentations, 108; retirement, 15; work with African American suffragists, 115–17

Antioch College, 100–101

antisuffrage movement, 129–64; agenda, 131; as big business, 142; concerns over motherhood and family, 104, 145–48, 150–53, 158–60; conservative womanhood, 13, 129–31, 156–63; junior leagues, 160–61; and liquor industry, 86, 142; arguments about intellectual inferiority of women, 30–31, 64, 134–35, 144–46

Ashley, Jessie, 40–45, 81. *See also* Collegiate Equal Suffrage League of New York

Associated Students of the University of California (ASUC), 122

Association of Collegiate Alumnae (ACA), 117–18, 168, 181

Barnard College: as site of activism, 11, 96–97, 109–12, 123–26; Barnard students and faculty, 40, 96–97, 105, 113, 180–81; history of, 102, opposition to suffrage, 129, 136–41, 148–49, 159–60

Barnard Suffrage Club, 105, 123, 125, 139–40. *See also* Barnard College

Belmont, Alva, 51

Bennet Bill, 88

Berkeley Equal Suffrage Study Club, 116, 194. *See also* University of California, Berkeley

Blackwell, Alice Stone, 20, 24, 28, 75–76

Blackwell, Elizabeth, 114

Blackwell, Henry, 20. *See also* American Woman Suffrage Association

ABOUT THE AUTHOR

KELLY L. MARINO is Lecturer of History at Sacred Heart University in Fairfield, Connecticut. She is also the Coordinator of the Women's, Gender, and Sexuality Studies program. Her research for this book was funded by grants from the Schlesinger Library, the Sophia Smith Collection, and the Newcomb Archives.